Diary of a Vet's Wife

Loving and Living with
Post Traumatic Stress Disorder

A Memoir

Published by BookLocker.com, Inc., Bradenton, FL.

Diary of a Vet's Wife is a true story. The characters, settings and events are taken from personal journals and written in narrative nonfiction to the best of the author's recollection. To protect the privacy of certain individuals, fictitious names are sometimes used.

Printed in the United States of America on acid-free paper.

BookLocker.com, Inc.
2012

First Edition

Cover designer – A special guy named Scott who lives in Australia and chose to remain anonymous.

Diary of a Vet's Wife

Loving and Living with
Post Traumatic Stress Disorder

A Memoir

Nancy MacMillan

This book is dedicated to

Tiffany, Scott and Michael,
My children, my strength and my joy,

Lorne, the love of my life,

And to God be the Glory.

ACKNOWLEDGMENTS

This memoir is in your hands because of an array of gracious people whom God sprinkled along my path on this journey into publishing my first book. To each I owe a debt of gratitude for their wisdom, encouragement and love.

To Joan Brandt—my mother-in-law, who shared much of this journey with me in love and support as we suffered in silence, unable to help the man we both loved.

To Karen Tuneberg—my sister and confidante, who was always there with just the right words when there was no one else. Her love and her love of God have been like a breath of fresh air.

To Pauline Sexton—an acquaintance, who invited me to attend a Writing/Publishing class in Santa Barbara in September 2009. I now cherish her like a sister. She also possessed the patience to shoot my author photo.

To Cork Millner—my teacher and my mentor. Cork was the first to read and critique my entire manuscript and call me "author." His encouraging words pushed me to do the impossible.

To Patricia Murdy—a fellow classmate and veteran's widow, who stepped up and volunteered to edit my manuscript during a summer break, her only request being that I would take her with me if I were ever asked to appear on Oprah

To Kay Thompson Lee—my free-lance editor, who groomed my work with a professional eye and patience, and yet left "my voice" in-tact. Her gentle approach and direction made this a wonderful experience.

To Tiffany and Scott—my daughter and son-in-law for their love and respect, and for designing this book's cover that gives life to my story.

To Evelyn Ceepo—my dear mother in Ohio, who sat quietly and listened as I read pages of my memoir over the phone. I thank her for her love and never-ending prayers.

To my Santa Barbara classmates—gifted and talented writers who accepted me into their fold with friendship and support. Their critiques were invaluable to my confidence as a new writer in their midst.

To all my sisters at The Bridge Bible Fellowship Church in Reseda, CA— there are too many to name, but they know who they are. Their love, encouragement and prayers have given me the courage to step forward and share my story with the world.

In memory of Carol Askey Moock, my beloved cousin, who loved God and knew the trauma of PTSD.

CONTENTS

Love is patient, love is kind.
It does not envy, it does not boast, it is not proud.
It is not self-seeking, it is not easily angered,
It keeps no record of wrongs.
Love does not delight in evil, but rejoices with the truth.
It always protects, always trusts, always hopes
And always preserves.

I Corinthians 13:4-7 NIV

PART ONE

Northridge, California

My nightmare

1

I felt like I was going mad

July 3, 1990 - Northridge, California

Fear followed me home like a big black dog.

At five-thirty in the afternoon the scorching sun still reigned, yet the neighborhood was deserted, void of another living soul. Propping the screen door open with my knee, I struggled to get my key in the lock, juggling totes of groceries and my briefcase. My hand shook as the door opened. I glanced over my shoulder and slipped inside; my heart pounded against my ribs. Sliding the brass dead bolt into place, I slumped against the solid wood barrier as the stifling heat invaded my lungs.

"Thank you, God," I whispered.

Wide eyed and barely breathing, I searched the unnerving quiet that saturated the room. The house was empty—no blaring television or Brad Bishop, my laid-back landlord, usually slouched in his eyesore of a chair, the remote control embedded in his palm like some benign growth. Then I remembered. He was driving up to Big Bear right after work. It was the Fourth of July weekend, and fishing with his buddies was the one thing that could pry him away from his new, big-screened TV.

I was alone.

Slipping off my shoes, I padded down the hall to my room, trying to ignore the helpless feeling of doom pursuing me. Fear was now my constant companion.

I stopped at the doorway. Across the room the agitated red light on my answering machine demanded attention. My throat tightened. I knew who called and I knew he was drunk. I wanted to turn and run, but the pulsating red eye dragged me in like a riptide, across the carpet and around the bed. I hesitated at the nightstand, then reached out and pushed the playback button.

"Nancy, this is Lorne." His voice was low, barely audible. "If you don't…if you don't really care if I live or die…why in the hell did you call 911 when I tried to commit suicide? I don't understand."

My heart stopped, I sank to the bed.

"Would you please come to my graveside…and tell me…goodbye?"

Tears spilled down my cheeks as his pain tore through me.

"Tell me that you…that you…tell me something! I need to talk to you…or you need to talk to me," he begged, his voice quivering. "I will die for you…if that's what you want…if that's the way I have to get," he paused, "right with you…then I will die for you. I will try tomorrow, July Fourth…to die on the Fourth of July for you. If you will just come to my graveside and tell me it's okay…tell me you love me…one…last…time. Just do that for me…"

"BEEP." The machine cut him off.

Lorne's desperate words exploded around me, ricocheting off the delicate green shamrocks in my wallpaper, crashing against my skull. He was my husband, the love of my life, but his drinking was killing him like it destroyed our marriage. He was teetering on the edge, and I was powerless to help him.

I buried my face in my hands, tears pooled in my palms. Monkey chatter swarmed the corridors of my mind. I pressed my fingertips into my temples, rotating them in a circular motion, trying to make the chatter go away. Some days I felt like I was going mad.

Three years earlier, Lorne had asked me to leave. He said I would be better off in a place of my own, admitting he could no longer handle the responsibility of living with another person.

I had no strength left to fight back.

When we separated he moved his belongings into our RV, but he would not leave me alone, calling at all hours of the night and showing up out of nowhere. Vivid images continued to consume me: Lorne wandering aimlessly, lost in his nightmare with alcohol, not knowing where to turn, except to me. I knew it wasn't my fault but I was drowning in guilt. How much more could I take? And, God forbid, would he really go through with it?

I fell to my knees beside the bed and made the sign of the cross. *"In the name of the Father and the Son, and the Holy Spirit,"* I begged into folded hands. *"Please, dear God, don't give him the courage. In Jesus' name I ask. Amen."*

I knew Lorne wanted me back but he couldn't stop drinking. Too many years and too many promises had come and gone. No matter how much I loved him I couldn't go down with him. Threats of suicide loomed in the shadows, but there was nothing left to do. God knows I tried. Lorne knew me too well, he knew how much I loved him and he knew what buttons to push. In the past I had always gone back, but this time was different. This time I had to resist. I had to be strong even though I longed to run to him, hold him in my arms and tell him everything would be all right.

But everything was not all right.

Just last week he showed up outside my bedroom window in the middle of the night. I knew he was drunk. His persistent knocking broke the glass. Terrified, I cowered in the shadows in disbelief. The ruckus awoke the neighbors, and eventually he was hauled off in handcuffs like a common criminal.

The police warned me, "Don't see him or talk to him until the trial."

But I knew it wasn't what it looked like; Lorne loved me and would never hurt me. He was just trying to get my attention…that's all.

But now it was time to leave the house; it was no longer safe to stay alone. Lorne's pattern had changed. I went to the closet, pulled a suitcase down from the top shelf, and tossed it onto the bed. Adrenaline surged through my veins. Yanking open dresser drawers, I grabbed enough clothes for a few days and flung them at the suitcase, then scooped up my hair dryer and a handful of bottles and jars from the bathroom counter, jamming them into side pockets.

In the kitchen, I rifled through the Yellow Pages, feeling like a hunted animal with nowhere to hide. I slammed the book shut. I had to get out of the Valley but I couldn't think of where to go. The monkeys were shrieking inside my head. I closed my eyes and rubbed my temples. Then I remembered a little motel tucked back off of the highway on my way to Point Dume.

The Malibu Hideaway...that's it.

I called information, then dialed the number they gave me.

"You're one lucky lady," the man remarked. "We're usually booked over a holiday weekend, but some guy just called with a cancellation."

"Great, I'll take it."

"And how many in your party?"

"Two," I replied impulsively.

Suddenly, the front door flung open.

"It's me," Brad hollered through the house. "I need my bait out of the refrigerator in the garage."

Visibly shaking, I went to tell him what had happened.

"Are you okay?" he asked, concern clouding his eyes. "Do you want me to go with you?"

"No, you made plans to go fishing," I hesitated. But I was grateful someone else knew what was going on. "I'll be fine as long as I'm far away from this house."

"No, I think it's better if you're not alone," he insisted. "Let me make a call, my duffel bags already in the car."

"Honest, I'll be all right," I reiterated

He may go looking for you, there's no need to take that risk," he stated. "Besides, there's safety in numbers."

The monkey chatter began to fade.

PART TWO

Houston, Texas

On my own again

2

Courage to leave

November 1972 - Houston, Texas

If you stop to think about it...life is an endless chain of choices from the beginning to the end. Most of us want to believe we have made the right choices for the right reason, but we never know until we get there.

After eleven years in a stale marriage, I finally gathered enough courage to leave. Separating the children from their father was painful, but clearly they were all Peter and I had in common.

I was twenty-one when Peter and I married after only a brief courtship. He was a decent man, a college graduate almost ten years my senior. Because I had grown up in a stunted dysfunctional family, I thought he had come to my rescue and would show me how good life could be. But that didn't happen. Basically he was a good father, but I ached for more of a man, a man with a passion for something other than eating and sleeping. I was too young to feel so old. After years of indecision, with only my faith and a spoonful of courage, I filed for divorce.

My next step was a better paying job. As secretary to the principal at Sugar Land Elementary School, my salary was slightly better than nothing. I located an agency close to the townhouse I rented with hope of securing a position nearby.

At the agency the following morning, I gave the receptionist my name and joined the others waiting to be called. A decent paying job was my main concern. After all, I had three children to feed and needed to keep a roof over our heads. The divorce decree awarded three hundred dollars a month in total child support which made me laugh. I had to laugh or else I'd cry. I hadn't held a real job in over ten years; Peter insisted I stay home with the children. The fact was: he was jealous. We wouldn't even have had a mailman come to the house if Peter had his way.

At three o'clock that afternoon, I sat in my car staring through a plate glass window. Bulging biceps and chiseled abs balanced on scaffolding high above the showroom floor. The first Porsche dealership in Houston was about to open and they needed a receptionist. My interview was at 3:30 p.m.

Surrounded by a plethora of exotic cars, my faded green station wagon with its ragged upholstery stood out like a nun at the beach. If only I could disappear. How could I land this job driving this ugly thing? It was my first interview since the children were born and now Scott was almost ten. Could I pull it off without making a fool of myself? What if they wanted someone young and sexy, someone without a lot of baggage?

*Stop...*I told myself. I had to do this. Not for me but for the children. Pivoting the rearview mirror I checked my makeup, then grabbed my purse and resume and stepped from the car. As I smoothed my skirt I took a deep breath and walked towards the entrance, my stomach in knots.

An hour later, I stepped into the parking lot; gentle rain tap danced at my feet. Halfway to the car I stopped, lifted my chin and let the warm raindrops bathe my face.

"Thank you, God," I whispered.

I did it...I got the job. The children and I were going to be okay.

3

Grant Taylor had a way

July 5, 1974

The bathroom was like a sauna, and I was running late as usual. Grant was due in thirty minutes, and no matter how hard I tried, the children invariably threw a monkey wrench in my timetable. Wiping the foggy mirror with my towel, I smiled...my mother always said I'd be late to my own funeral.

As I leaned over the sink I quickly swept mascara on my pale lashes, accentuating dark brown eyes and a creamy complexion. I tossed my head, pushing and pulling strands of pale blond hair into place and applied a final dab of lipstick before flicking off the light. In the closet, I stepped into a pair of white linen slacks and leather sandals. While pulling a sleeveless jersey over my head, I turned to catch my reflection in the full-length mirror. At five-feet-four inches tall, a subtle tan defined a strong lean body, my reward for years of boring exercise at the gym…my haven for sanity.

Grant Taylor was the only man I had dated in the eighteen months since my divorce. I met Grant while attending a Parent Teacher's Conference, literally colliding in the hall, sending my purse and its contents flying in every direction.

"I'm sorry," Grant had stammered, dropping to one knee. "Please let me help."

I couldn't help but smile as I watched him scramble for objects underfoot. When he stood up, he boasted at being the school's auditor, and to my surprise he asked me out for coffee.

Grant was a few years younger than I, and the complete opposite of Peter. He glowed with self confidence and witty conversation. His shock of unruly red hair gave him a look of surprise, and his Texas twang would raise any mother's eyebrow. He wasn't what I'd call handsome, but he made me feel young. I was lonely for a man who could give me what Peter lacked. And Grant Taylor had a way. He called me "Angel Face," and some evenings he would sit cross-legged on the floor strumming his guitar and singing to me. How could I resist?

But everything was not what I hoped for.

Grant had been married for a year but would never discuss it, only to say that there were no children. His father, a military man, raised Grant and his sister by the old adage, *children should be seen and not heard*, an attitude that grated on my nerves. I brought it up with no success, finally accepting the fact; Grant Taylor was not marriage material. Plus he failed the final exam…my children.

I jumped when the doorbell rang. It was 6:30 p.m. and Grant was on time as usual. Slinging my purse over my shoulder, I ran downstairs. Tonight we were driving into the city of Bellaire. It was Jackie White's birthday and she was throwing herself a party.

4

Our eyes locked

Jackie White and her ex-husband thrived on a love-hate relationship. Their marriage had been over for years. Stubborn as two five-year olds, they fought like Tyson and Holyfield under the same roof. Rumor had that he had been seen slipping out Jackie's back door under the light of a full moon like the neighborhood tomcat making his rounds.

Grant rang the doorbell. Moments later, Jackie flung open the screen door.

"I'm so thrilled y'all could make it," she said, hugging us tightly.

Jackie was in her early fifties, slim and attractive, with cropped platinum blond hair that framed huge Bette Davis eyes. Dressed in a simple sundress, she looked fresh as a new day.

"Happy Birthday," I said, kissing her cheek, "I hope you like these." I handed her a small gift containing a pair of sable paintbrushes.

"Happy Birthday," Grant echoed. Taking her wrist, he clicked his heels, bowed and kissed the back of her hand, then produced a bottle of red wine from behind his back.

"Grant, you are so gallant," Jackie giggled.

We followed her down a long narrow hallway to the back of the house. Oil paintings of subtle nudes and vivid flowers lined the dimly lit walls, casting the illusion of some archaic art gallery. The small three-bedroom house was old and unassuming, but the natural lighting in the den was an artist's dream.

Muffled voices drifted out into the hallway over the grumbling protests of an ancient air conditioner. Stepping into the den, Jackie introduced us to the small group already gathered, then hurried back to the kitchen for more appetizers.

I settled into a cozy blue chair opposite the doorway, setting my purse on the floor.

Grant tapped me on the shoulder, "Scotch?"

I nodded, "Please."

He strolled off to the kitchen and returned with a tall drink with lots of ice. He took a seat across the room at an old upright piano against the wall. Sitting tall, he closed his eyes, dissolving into his own rendition of *Lullaby of Bird Land*.

As I sipped my drink I looked around the room feeling lost and out of place. Stepping back into the world of singles was definitely a shock. So much had changed. Women were liberated, fighting for equal rights, a cause I supported but one in which I had little experience.

The doorbell rang. Jackie hurried down the hall to answer it. In the distance I heard the resounding echo of cowboy boots striking the hardwood floor. Jackie emerged in the doorway, her cheeks flushed. I peered over the rim of my glass, catching my first glimpse of the new arrival.

Standing in the shadows, a ruggedly handsome young man ran his fingers through his sandy blond hair, and from what I could see he was alone.

"I'd like y'all to meet Lorne MacMillan," Jackie announced, stepping aside.

My breath caught. Ahhh...Lorne MacMillan. He stood in the doorway rather awkwardly on display. His blue eyes caught me immediately. An open smile registered a roguish lift at one corner. Over six feet tall, he appeared to be in his late twenties. His body was lean and his complexion was honey-colored with high cheekbones and full lips. He wore Levi's and gray elephant-skin boots. Our eyes met briefly, but he looked away first. He had the same rugged good looks of the Marlboro Man, but Lorne MacMillan was shy.

"Come with me," Jackie interrupted, dragging him off to the kitchen, away from prying eyes.

"What'll you have?" I heard through the doorway.

"Glenlivet and water, please."

Compelled by some unknown force, I got up and followed them. Lorne was sitting at the kitchen table, talking with Jackie while she fixed his drink. He looked up and smiled. Hot blood rushed to my cheeks. I turned quickly, walked across the kitchen and proceeded to drop more ice cubes into my glass. My heart pounded in my ears. Marmalade, Jackie's yellow cat, tiptoed among the liquor bottles cluttering the counter, searching for something to eat.

Jackie handed Lorne his drink and sat down next to him. I wandered over to the table. Setting my glass down, I took a seat on the opposite side.

"Oh, Nancy," Jackie said, smiling shrewdly, "I'd like to introduce you to Lorne MacMillan. And Lorne, this is Nancy."

"Hi," I said shyly. My cheeks were on fire.

Lorne watched with amusement. "Hi," he replied warmly, "I saw you when I came in."

Our eyes locked, my insides squirmed. His hold on me was unyielding, I couldn't breathe. His eyes narrowed as he cast a curious glance at Jackie, who was deep in the clam dip. He rubbed his chin but said nothing to me, then went back to their discussion.

I sat spellbound by the sound of his voice; his slight drawl was alluring. He leaned in on his elbows, and slipped a ring from his finger, holding it up to the light. There was a slender body of a gold leopard crouched on a log, gracefully curved around a brown star sapphire, its shoulder blades protruding, a narrow tail encircling its muscular thighs.

"And while the wax was warm," he continued, "I elongated the neck and turned the head slightly to extend out over the stone, giving the piece character lacking in the original wax."

"May I hold it?" I interrupted, startled by my own boldness.

Reaching across the table, he watched me as he dropped the heavy ring into my palm. I held it between my fingers and gently stroked the delicate details of the leopard, seemingly crouched to drink. Bared teeth and flattened ears signaled danger nearby. I could feel Lorne's eyes on me. I knew he was intrigued but what was he thinking? I lingered, fondling the ring that connected us, if only for the moment, not wanting to break the spell.

"Your ring is beautiful," I said smiling. "I envy your talent."

At that moment, Grant stepped into the kitchen. "I wondered where you wandered off to," he said sarcastically.

It was after one in the morning when the party broke up. Grant was saying his goodbyes when Lorne stepped up behind me. Without a word, he pressed a note into the palm of my hand at my side, closing my fingers around it. My heart stopped. But when I turned he was gone. Grant was oblivious to what happened, but my mind was reeling. All I wanted was to be alone...alone to read the note hidden in my hand.

5

No mood for an argument

Raindrops shimmered beneath the streetlights like a canopy of silver threads against the dark night sky. Grant ducked his head and made a dash for the car. I pulled off my sandals and sprinted across the lawn after him, leaping over puddles, landing in others, mud squishing between my toes. The engine was running when I jumped in and slammed the door. Suddenly the car lunged forward, fishtailing on the wet pavement, barely missing a parked car across the street.

I bit my tongue, tossing an irritated glance Grant's way. Shaking my head I fumbled through my purse for a tissue. What was eating him? I knew he hadn't seen Lorne slip me the note, or he would have exploded on the spot. We seldom went out, and I did have fun, but I was in no mood for an argument.

Driving rain hammered the roof of the car; now and again stray headlights passed on the road. I stared into darkness. Lorne MacMillan had me puzzled; handsome, intelligent and shy, a rare combination. He joined my group early in the evening then never left. Was it intentional? I even toyed with the idea of flirting until I realized I had forgotten how…another thrill of motherhood. But we were never alone. So needless to say, I was stunned by the mysterious note hidden in my purse.

"What a fun party," I said aloud, instantly wishing I hadn't.

"What?" Grant barked.

"I only said what a fun party."

"Yeah," he huffed.

I turned. Grant's eyes were fixed on the road, his mouth set. White knuckles gripped the steering wheel. He was a man with an opinion; it was unlike him to say nothing. Trouble was brewing. I was sure he knew nothing of the note as he was too busy talking with Jackie to turn around. Maybe he saw us talking but that was all. Now I was doomed to the silent treatment.

Honestly, of all people, Grant Taylor had no right to be upset. He was the one with another woman in his life. Her name was Barbara. I'd known about her for some time, and to my surprise I didn't care. After all, Grant and I were only dating. We had no future, at least not in my eyes. My new-found independence outshined any insecurity I embraced from the past.

Heavy raindrops splattered the windshield like giant beetles. Grant pushed a button on the dash and the wipers picked up speed.

"Will you come in for a while?" I asked trying to ease the tension. "I've got chocolate ice cream in the freezer."

"What the hell were you doing back there?" he bellowed. His face was puffy and mottled in the dim street light fading in and out through the rain streaked windows.

"What are you talking about?" I snapped back.

"Since when do you go for cowboys?" Grant sneered. "I saw you hanging out with that guy in the cowboy boots like I wasn't even there."

I stiffened. "Grant...you knew I didn't know anyone at the party except Jackie. Yet you left me sitting by myself while you played *The Piano Man*." My voice trembled. "Now you're upset because I mingled. You don't make sense." The more I thought about it the madder I got.

"My only crime...I sat with people who liked to talk instead of watch you play the piano all night. Besides you had a big enough audience without me."

Grant's face turned to stone.

It was raining buckets by the time we pulled into the carport.

"Grant...I think we'd better call it a night," I said as I reached for the door handle. "Call me tomorrow when you've cooled down."

"Fine," he hissed.

I hesitated then leaned over and kissed him on the cheek. He didn't budge. Shrugging my shoulders, I opened the door and got out.

"Good night, Grant."

Teeming rain pounded the metal roof of the carport like a jackhammer.

I unlocked the backdoor, turning in time to see Grant's taillights fishtail through the parking lot and disappear in the downpour. I was relieved he was gone. He was acting like a jerk and I refused to waste another ounce of energy thinking about it. He'd cool down once he slept on it. Besides, Grant was the only man I had dated since my divorce, and he knew it. What did he want...blood?

"Goodnight, my angel," I whispered, picking up a one-eyed rabbit off the floor and setting it on my daughter's bed.

Tiffy was seven...my baby girl...my counterpart...another female. My boys came first, seventeen months apart. Happy rambunctious little guys; I adored them. But there were times when confronting a mountain of blue jeans and tee shirts that I longed for a little girl to dress in pink...a daughter of my own. *A son is a son until he takes a wife; a daughter's your daughter for the rest of your life.*

Her blanket covered her nose, though the room was hot and muggy. Tiffy wasn't happy sleeping alone while her brothers shared a room upstairs, but I couldn't afford to move. I bought her a puppy, a playmate to sleep at the foot of her bed. But he chewed up all her books and underwear and was banished from our family. I pulled back the blanket, kissed her cheek then slipped from the room, leaving a legion of stuffed animals to watch over her.

Harsh rain beat against the windows as I crossed the living room and headed upstairs. The door was open at the end of the hall. Soft light swept the boyish leg dangling from the top bunk. I stepped inside, tucking it back where it belonged. Scott was eleven, and growing like Jack's beanstalk…where had the years gone? I was young and naïve when Scott was born, enchanted with the fact that a girl could give birth to a boy.

Thinking back, I could still hear the thunder of wheels rumbling down the hall outside my hospital door, and feel the thrill. Hungry babies were coming. And once the nurses left, I would uncover my baby undo his diaper and marvel at my creation.

My precious first born was now the man of the family. His self-appointed duty was to watch over and protect us. What a heavy burden for a young boy.

Curled up in a ball on the bottom bunk, Cory, my nine-year-old, slept peacefully entwined in his sheets. Carefully I untangled him and grinned. His tousled blond hair and rosy cheeks gave him the looks of a Valentine cherub. From the day Cory was born I sensed his soul. In the dark before dawn, I cradled him in my arms, rocking as he nursed, his tiny hands kneading my breast like a newborn kitten. His blue eyes watched me unblinking, penetrating my thoughts like he had something to say.

He stirred, his sleepy eyes opened. "I love you, Mom," he whispered, drifting back to sleep.

"I love you too, baby. Sweet dreams." I pushed his damp hair aside and kissed his forehead.

My children were my world. I was young when Peter and I were married; I grew up with my babies. When nothing else made sense, my children stabilized my life. Things were so different now, so unsure.

6

I withdrew the note

Life in essence is a mingling of ordinary days, slipping away unnoticed like faces in a crowd. Then one day comes along that will change your life forever.

Slipping into a nightgown, I prolonged the sweet anticipation surging through my veins. Nothing this exciting had ever happened to me. It was like something from a movie. I leaned over the bathroom sink, splashed warm water on my face, and my thoughts drifted back to the party.

It was an ordinary party. The kind where broad smiling strangers stand fondling their drinks, laughing at nothing and talking about anything. Deep down I wasn't much of a party girl. I preferred more intimate gatherings sparked with thought provoking conversation, something I never had with Peter. Meeting Lorne was an unexpected surprise. Intelligent and shy, he had a presence without the least bit of arrogance. This intrigued me. All in all, it was a perfect evening. At least it was up until Grant had his temper tantrum. But that was trivial. Something extraordinary happened tonight, something I could not explain.

Patting my face dry, I remembered slipping the note into my purse when Grant wasn't looking. It must be downstairs. I hurried down to the kitchen, found it on the counter and raced upstairs. Pulling back the covers, I plopped cross-legged on the bed. I stared at the small purse in my hand, then twisted the clasp and it opened...I withdrew the note.

It was a small piece of paper with a torn edge, folded in quarters. I touched it to my bottom lip. What prompted a note? After all, we had only talked casually, and he knew I was there with Grant. But then again, I felt compelled. Had he sensed it also? I held the note a moment longer, and then slowly unfolded the corners. There written in blue ballpoint pen...*Call me anytime 996-2734.*

Interesting…I stared at his handwriting, but it was not what I expected. Who was I kidding? Only myself. Being a hopeless romantic was truly the pits. The man was gorgeous and could have any good-looking female he wanted by snapping his fingers. Where did I fit in, me and my three children?

As I gazed at the note, an insane notion popped into my head. *Why not call him? After all, he gave you his number.* The battle began. First of all, I wasn't the type of woman who would call a man I didn't know. *But then again, you did sit at the kitchen table and covet his ring, did you not?* But that was different! Anyway, even if I could gather the courage to make the call, what would I say to him?

I set the note on the nightstand and turned off the light. I closed my eyes and tried to sleep, but my mind refused. His eyes, his hands, the gold leopard…all drifted aimlessly through the darkness, his voice echoing in my ears. I tossed and turned, but I could not escape the haunting feeling in my soul.

The next day, Sunday, around ten in the morning, I went upstairs to make my bed while the children played outside. I noticed the note on the night stand, and slipped it into the pocket of my jeans, then made my way down the hall to the boys' room. Opening their closet door, I faced a mountain of laundry overflowing its basket. With a sigh, I picked up a stray pair of jeans, only to spot a hole in the knee. I made a mental note to buy iron-on patches. New jeans cost money, and extra money was something I did not have.

Downstairs, I loaded the washer and closed the lid. When I looked up I spotted the phone hanging on the wall. My finger slipped into my pocket to touch the note.

Cradling a stack of warm towels, I shut the laundry room door and walked over to the phone. Setting the towels down, I withdrew the note. My monkey chatter switched into high gear. *What will you say after "Hello…Duh?"* Talking about the children was definitely out, I didn't remember if I mentioned the children. And the weather was lame. I leaned back against the counter. Maybe his ring? *That's it!* I could tell him how I enjoyed his discussion, even though the technical stuff sailed over my head. *Good idea!*

I was visibly shaking when I picked up the receiver. Why was I doing this? Normally I was the responsible, level-headed mother of three. But this was different, something was driving me, I knew I must make the call right now, or I never would. I dialed the number then paced the kitchen floor.

"Brrringgg,"…pause.

"Brrringgg,"…pause.

"Brrringgg,"…click.

"Hello?" said a sleepy female voice.

Stunned, I slammed down the receiver and stood staring at the phone. Reality slapped me across the face. I felt like a fool. Of course, he had a girlfriend; any man that gorgeous had to have a girlfriend.

7

Prove him wrong

August 1974

There were days when I longed to be a simple ordinary housewife again; the lady of the house in control of her boring little life. Total responsibility for the children and paying the bills were wearing me down. But the nagging memory of Peter's parting words still made my blood boil, filling me with a strength and determination I never knew I had.

"You'll be back," he had said smugly. "You don't know how to do anything!"

Don't know how to do anything! How could I when he kept me confined like a prisoner in my own home and refused to let me work? Yes, it was my decision to leave. I would pay the price and I would prove him wrong…even if it took my last dying breath.

After a grueling day at the dealership, the boys started arguing the minute I opened the back door. *"Lord, give me patience,"* I prayed.

Once I put an end to the squabbling, I turned on the broiler, pulled thawed chicken and salad fixings from the refrigerator and a can of corn from the pantry. Soon the children were eating quietly, sprawled in front of the TV.

I sank into the couch, put my tired feet on the coffee table, and set my plate in my lap. My hands fell limp. Too weary to eat, I looked down on my children absorbed in "I Love Lucy." My heart ached. I knew they were going through struggles of their own because of me. I knew this was why the boys constantly quarreled. The sadness in my daughter's eyes revealed her pain. I knew she missed her father. If only there had been another way.

After dinner I stood in the kitchen washing dishes by hand, inasmuch as my dishwasher went down the drain with my marriage.

"Mom," Cory squealed from the living room. "Scott pinched my arm."

"But Mom," Scott protested, "he took my best comic without asking."

I took a deep breath and counted to ten. "Okay you two, knock it off!" I yelled from the kitchen, trying to sound in control. After all, I was the grownup, even though there were times when all I wanted to do was sit in a corner and cry.

"Cory, you're not to take your brother's things without permission. You know this," I hollered. "And Scott, you're not to pinch your brother. Do you both understand?" I hated myself for yelling at them. "Besides, you're both supposed to be doing your homework."

"Yesss, Mommm," I heard in unison from the other room

Whoever wrote *"A woman's work is never done"* hit the nail on the head, I thought as I climbed the stairs. Dirty laundry multiplied faster than rabbits, and the boys still needed clean underwear for school in the morning.

8

Of all days to have an attitude

August 15, 1974

Grant Taylor was the only man I had dated since my divorce…but not by choice. Masquerading as super mom left me barely enough energy to look beyond the end of my nose for a better prospect.

When the phone rang on Saturday morning, I assumed it was Grant.

"Hello?" I said dryly.

"Hi there," a male voice lulled in my ear.

An instant shyness swept over me, hot blood swept my cheeks. It was the same familiar accent lingering in the darkness of my room each night, leaving me to toss and turn for hours.

"I thought I might hear from you," he stated with concern.

"Oh…Hi," I stammered. "I thought you were someone else"…*of all days to have an attitude.* "I'm really happy you called." *The words slipped out before I could stop them. Now he was certain to think I'm needy.*

"When I didn't hear from you, I thought I'd call to see if you were all right," he said openly. "I got your number from Jackie, I hope you don't mind?"

"No, that's okay. It was nice of you. Honestly, I'm fine." I paused. "Honestly!" I took a deep breath. "The truth is I don't call strangers who hand me their phone numbers on little pieces of paper. I hope you understand."

"That's refreshing," he chuckled. "Most women these days don't share your values. I admire your conviction."

I felt like two cents for lying to him. And lying was no way to start a relationship, or whatever it was, even though I was the only one who knew.

He hesitated, "Can you talk a while?"

"I guess so," I said.

I stretched the phone cord into the dining room, pulled out a chair and sat down. I heard the flick of his lighter and could picture him stretched out in an overstuffed chair, with his long legs crossed at the ankles, wearing gray elephant skin boots.

Lorne was easy to talk to. I began to relax and lower my guard, letting this handsome stranger step into my life, convinced he would take off running the moment he learned I had three children. Rather than drag my feet, I mentioned them casually, sharing that they spent most of the summer with their father in Chicago. But Lorne wasn't surprised. It seemed Jackie had revealed the fact when he called to ask for my number.

We talked for over an hour, when my offspring burst through the door in search of food like hungry puppies.

"Its lunchtime," I interrupted, standing up. "I need to feed my children before they pull everything out of the refrigerator."

"That's fine. Can I call you again?" Lorne asked.

"Yes, I'd like that."

I hung up the phone still in a daze. It happened. Lorne MacMillan actually called me.

And better yet, he didn't seem to mind that I had three children.

9

It was a mystery

To my surprise, Lorne called every night after the children were in bed for the next two weeks. We talked sometimes for hours, each intimate detail drawing us closer. Little by little he opened up, sharing pieces of his life **and** his dreams, slowly peeling away the delicate layers of his existence.

"...and my grandfather came from Scotland," Lorne went on. "He left home when he was fourteen. Years later, he married my grandmother, who is half-French and half-Iroquois Indian. Guess that makes me one-eighth Iroquois…"

"Things were different then," I replied. "My paternal grandfather left Helsinki to come to America when he was about fourteen. I could never picture my boys leaving home at that age."

It was a mystery…society says handsome young men fall for attractive young women, not an older woman with three children. What was happening? Not that it really mattered. I was flattered. But I was afraid to believe it was anything more than an infatuation. And I didn't want to be left hurt and bleeding.

Lorne was twenty seven, even though he seemed older. He was born in British Columbia, in the city of Prince George. His parents separated when he was two and he moved to Texas with his mother. The divorce became final when Lorne was five. He never met his biological father, which weighed heavily on his mind. After years of searching, Lorne finally located the town where his father lived, only to learn he had passed away several years earlier.

His father had worked in the coal mines as a medic. Some say a mine collapsed, some say his father committed suicide. Lorne's mother's side of the family came from Ukraine, accounting for his blondness.

His phone calls became the highlight of my day. His intelligence bordered on the serious side, but his laugh was warm and hearty, luring me like a crackling fire.

"Tomorrow's Saturday night," he said softly. "I'd like to take you to my favorite restaurant, that is, if you don't have a prior commit?"

I hesitated in surprise. "No, I don't have any plans," I said. "And yes, I'd love to have dinner with you."

He finally made a move. We have a date tomorrow night. Reeling thoughts flooded my mind and nudged me off balance. What if he was disappointed when he saw me again? And meeting the children face to face, what kind of impression would that make? And the age difference?

Nervous and excited, I could barely think straight. Was he really as handsome as I remembered? Suddenly Grant's face popped into the picture.

He'd be furious when he got wind of my date with the cowboy. Then again he dated someone else. What was I worried about?

I felt like I had just been asked to the prom. Our date was tomorrow night and Lorne was picking me up at eight. What in the world was I going to wear?

10

Wise beyond his years

August 24, 1974

"Hey guys, we need to talk," I said meekly at breakfast the next morning.

Who would have thought it would be so hard to explain my date with Lorne to the children? Wasn't I the grown up? Yet I stammered like a teenager, enduring an awkwardness reserved for my parents. Grant was the only man the children had seen me with. How could I tell them what I needed? How I dreamed of falling in love, a feeling I only read about in books. How I longed for someone who would love me and my children yet had plans and dreams of his own. Most of the men in my life had been dull as door-knobs.

"I have something to tell you," I blurted out. My head throbbed like a migraine was about to attack. "Tonight I'm going to dinner with someone you've never met before. He's going to be here at eight and I'll introduce you."

"What's his name?" Scott asked between mouthfuls of Cheerios.

"Lorne," I said aloud for the first time. "He's a new friend of mine. Marilyn will stop by, but if you need anything her number is by the phone."

And that's all that was said. Why was I so unnerved?

I surveyed the living room, fluffing pillows and rearranging magazines for the umpteenth time. I wanted everything perfect. Hours earlier, I had ransacked my closet looking for just the right outfit. Rejects were tossed onto a heap on my bed. Finally I settled on a simple black dress and my grandmother's pearls...conservative, yet classic.

The doorbell rang sending a jolt of adrenaline through my body. I nervously glanced in the hall mirror, licked my lips, took a deep breath and opened the door. Lorne stood on the porch, grinning from ear to ear. He wore a well-tailored gray suit with a light blue shirt, accentuating the color of his eyes. He looked nothing like the cowboy I remembered. He was breathtaking. A hot flush crept up my neck.

"Hi," I said shyly, stepping aside. "Please come in."

After an awkward introduction to the children, who were more at ease than I was, we were ready to leave. Scott was to babysit. Protesting that he was too old for a sitter, he promised not to boss his siblings. Marilyn, a close friend from work, lived in the same complex and had agreed to pop in unannounced just to be sure they weren't killing each other. Snacks were on the counter, and emergency numbers were taped on the wall by the phone. I kissed them goodbye, leaving them sprawled on the living room floor, glued to the television.

The gentle scent of summer hung in the warm night air. Lorne had made 8:30 dinner reservations at Ari's, a quaint French restaurant I never knew existed, not that I ate out on my budget. And Grant was a penny pincher.

Lorne held the restaurant door as I stepped inside.

The maitre d' bowed, "Mr. MacMillan, please follow me."

A handful of guests were seated in smaller dining rooms, plush with highly polished wood and antique wallpaper, off the dimly lit hallway. The maitre d' ushered us to a secluded table and pulled out my chair. The room was bathed in candlelight. A single red rose graced the white linen tablecloth. Seductive French music lingered like fragrant orange blossoms.

"Ari's has the best escargot and frozen margaritas in town," Lorne said, surveying the menu. "How does that sound for starters?"

"Perfect," I said, "I love them both."

Lorne was the type of man you saw posed on the cover of Esquire magazine, young and virile with that sultry faraway look. Tonight he was a soft-spoken gentleman, unlike the cowboy who first appeared in Jackie's doorway. And, as I began to learn, wise beyond his years, stimulating my mind and challenging my thoughts. He displayed an insatiable curiosity. He questioned everything including life itself. I was captivated. Every time I looked up he was watching me. It felt like I was falling in love, but this was beyond my control.

After dinner, Lorne suggested we stop at *The Big Mouth Frog,* a trendy restaurant with live music in the lounge. He had a friend who played there he wanted me to meet. When we walked through the door, I felt like I had stepped into a ski lodge high in the Alps: knotty pine walls with lush plants suspended from the huge half-circle balcony that jutted out over the first floor. Crackling wood fed the flames in a massive stone fireplace that was large enough to stand in. The only things missing were the skiers sipping mugs of hot toddies.

Lorne followed me up the wide carpeted stairs to the lounge. We were seated at a front row table; a reserved sign caught my eye. Up on stage, a man and his guitar were perched on a tall wooden stool, bathed in a single beam of light. Narrow, two-story windows black with night loomed like monoliths behind him. He waved, Lorne waved back. Drinks were ordered and the house lights dimmed. Lorne reached for my hand across the table as gentle, haunting music filled the room.

It was after one in the morning when we pulled into the carport. Lorne quietly walked me to the door. His head down, hands buried in his pockets. I felt his eyes watch me turn the key in the lock.

"Would you like to come in for coffee or a drink?" I asked.

"Not tonight…it's late, but I'll take a rain check," he said from behind me.

The door opened, I stepped into the dark hallway and turned. Lorne stood in the doorway, a towering silhouette against the soft yellow porch light. He moved towards me. I felt his hands on my shoulders; he bent down and kissed me. Lost in the moment, I leaned against him. Suddenly he stopped. Stepping back, he turned and was out the door into the night.

"I'll call you tomorrow," he whispered over his shoulder.

"Okay," I said, trying to regain my composure, "and thank you for a wonderful evening."

Standing in the doorway I watched him walk to the car. He turned and waved before he got in. Then he was gone. The only thing he left behind was the scent of his aftershave lingering in the dark hallway. Never in my life had I met anyone like him. Would I wake up to find it was only a dream? But if it was real, what did I have to offer him? I had no answers.

11

Saturday and sunshine

September 7, 1974

My life had taken on a new, yet undefined, shape which I feared would vanish as quickly as it appeared. Lorne called every night after the children were in bed. He made me smile, but it was his mind that held me captive. Ever since I could remember, I was enthralled by men who dwelled on the unordinary, who thought on a different plane, who marched to a different drummer; men whom I could learn from. My father was one of those men. Albert Einstein and Carl Sagan were at the top of my list. Yet something bothered me. Something I could not put my finger on. It may have been a few words or a sentence out of context, something dark or painful Lorne had not shared. Even though I wondered, I pushed it aside. At this moment I was happy and I wanted to savor this feeling as long as I could.

In the distance, the hollow roar of a motorcycle echoed through the still morning air. The children raced up and down the sidewalk, their faces flush with excitement. Saturday and sunshine, the ideal elements for a bike ride in the country. I grew up as a tomboy in Ohio, and could climb a tree or scale the hollow shell of a new house to the roof as fast as any boy in the neighborhood...but I never rode a motorcycle. My heart stirred with a thrill I hadn't felt since I was a kid.

Lorne pulled into the driveway settled on a huge black motorcycle that glistened in the sunlight, its hot pipes sputtering as he rolled to a stop in front of us. The children stared in awe. A black helmet completely covered Lorne's face giving him that Darth Vader look. He lowered the kickstand, pulled back on the handlebars, and forced the bike to rest in its cradle. Unfastening the chinstrap, he pulled off his helmet and tucked it under his arm. Damp curls clung to his forehead; our eyes met.

"Good morning," he beamed. "Are you ready to go for a ride? We picked a beautiful day."

I could only smile and nod. I couldn't find my voice. He sure looked good on that bike. Faded Levi's and cowboy boots accentuated his long firm legs, straddling the gas tank like a tripod. *My, Oh My...* His broad shoulders and strong lean arms were visible beneath his lightweight cotton shirt. I wanted to pinch myself.

Lorne dismounted and the children rushed to him like a once-a-year sale at Toys R Us. Leaning down, he picked up Scott and placed him on the seat.

"Brrumm, Brrumm," Scott mimicked, sprawled over the gas tank, twisting the hand grips back and forth.

"Me too, me too," Cory and Tiffy chimed in.

Once each child had had a turn, Lorne passed me a helmet from the back of his seat. I pulled it on, stuffing my hair in around the edges. Then I leaned down and kissed my brood goodbye. Lorne tromped the kick-start, and the bike roared to life. Placing one foot on a peg, I swung around behind him like I'd seen in the movies, wrapping my arms around his waist.

Lorne turned. "Remember, lean with me no matter what," he shouted over the noise.

I nodded and the bike leaped forward. Looking over my shoulder, I waved briefly then held on tight as we took off. The children bounced up and down, their arms flailing, waving in the morning sun. Marilyn was strolling down the sidewalk towards them. Lorne changed gears, the tires dug into the asphalt and we picked up speed. The euphoric rush was unlike anything I had ever known.

Toxic fumes burned the inside of my nose as we merged onto Highway 10, heading out into the country away from the snarl of city traffic. Soon Lorne turned onto a two-lane road and opened her up. I hung on tight. The narrow strip of asphalt dipped and twisted without warning, snaking through the rolling fields while a broken white line blurred beneath us. Chilling wind beat against my arms, tugging at my hair, pulling strands free to whip my face. The air smelled fresh and clean.

I clung to Lorne, my body pressed into his, feeling his warmth penetrating my tee shirt. He felt good in my arms like he belonged there. I held on tight, leaning with him on every curve, my eyes squeezed shut. Brown and white patterned cows that munched on meadow grass lifted their heads to watch the bike roar by. Intoxicated with a feeling of freedom, I rode the back of the wind aimed at some unknown planet.

12

My imagination ran wild

I was standing in the shower reflecting on my afternoon with Lorne when suddenly the bathroom coiled around me. I grabbed the wall. Engulfed in steam, I inhaled deeply...and again. Still wobbly, I switched to cold water and icy pellets peppered my skin. Pure torture...I grabbed a towel and got out. *What was that all about?*

Two hours earlier, Lorne sat on his bike getting ready to leave.

"Nancy, how about dinner tonight?" he asked to my surprise.

"Oh…I'm a mess," I stammered, pushing hair from my face, "and I don't have anyone to watch the children."

"Maybe you could give Marilyn a call and see if she would pop in on them? It would be something simple, nothing fancy."

I wavered; his eyes pleaded.

"Okay, I'll call Marilyn," I said, "but I need time to shower and fix the children dinner. Call me when you get home. I should know by then."

Marilyn was home and agreed to the favor. I had only time to feed the children, take a shower and get ready before Lorne arrived at seven.

I was drying my hair when it hit me. I was falling for Lorne much too fast and I was terrified. An older woman and a younger man, a scenario I had only read about but never considered until now. My imagination ran wild, finger pointing at all the reasons why the relationship would never work. After all, who did I think I was? And what did I have to offer him? I was simply a woman, the mother of three, yearning for an impossible dream.

The children devoured their favorite dinner of macaroni and cheese mixed with slices of hot dog like I never fed them, then they went up to put on their PJs. Marilyn would check them throughout the evening, but Scott was in charge. They were good kids. They had ground rules and I trusted them not to burn the house down.

The traffic on Highway 10 was at a standstill. An early evening thunderstorm left the streets a mirror of red and white lights blending into reality. This made it difficult to know where one stopped and the other began. Angry drivers irritated by the delay jockeyed for positions. Lightening cracked sharply across the night sky and thunder rumbled in the distance. I sat up straight, double checking my seat belt, and peered out the rain-spattered window as I toyed with the sweater in my lap.

"I'm really a good driver," Lorne said.

"I'm sure you are," I said embarrassed, "It's the other drivers I'm worried about."

"I promise to take good care of you," he said, "cross my heart." His index finger drew an imaginary cross over his heart.

Taking a deep breath, I folded my hands in my lap and tried to relax. I had no idea where we were going. When I asked, his answer only left more questions.

"It's a surprise," he said, "but if you don't like it we can go somewhere else."

Twenty minutes later, Lorne put on his turn signal and pulled into a long narrow driveway lined with large white-washed boulders. The car's high beams swept a spacious green lawn, capturing a complex of buildings, hidden in the trees like a herd of wide-eyed deer. A sign, standing like a sentry, appeared on the well-manicured knoll, "*Singles only...One and Two Bedroom Apartments.*"

Now I knew...we were going to his apartment. Panic set in, hoisting a red flag. Lorne maneuvered through the narrow maze of two-story buildings like a homing pigeon. Peering into brightly lit apartments, I saw levels of ordinary people living their lives, totally unaware they were being observed. I felt like a voyeur. Within minutes I would be entering Lorne's world. I nervously chewed the inside of my cheek.

"We're here," he said, pulling into his parking spot. "I hope you're hungry."

Lorne got out and walked around the car, pointing up at the second floor balcony. I sat rigid looking up at the dark patio windows overhead. He opened my door.

"Is this okay?" he asked, leaning down into the car.

I followed him up the damp concrete stairs, unsure of what I was doing, or why. Delicious aromas wafted through the air from other apartments. Lorne unlocked the sliding glass door and stepped aside, ushering me into darkness dipped in moonlight. I felt him move behind me. My stomach clenched. I heard the metallic click of his lighter, then gentle candlelight unveiled the room and a side of this man I had not seen.

The unexpected aroma of warm baked potatoes caught me by surprise. I had to smile. A masculine brown couch and loveseat, trimmed with wide leather straps, overpowered one wall. In the corner was a matching chair and ottoman. This was probably where Lorne sat every night when we talked on the phone.

"Make yourself at home," he called from across the room. He was squatting next to a pricey-looking stereo sitting on the floor, which clearly came from the nearby cartons.

An exquisite driftwood coffee table sat in front of the couch, its natural surface bent and twisted by the hands of time. Three fat candles flickered in the center of the thick plate glass top. The tapestry of a crouched tiger hung over the couch; its piercing yellow eyes stared back at me. It reminded me of the ring Lorne wore.

Candlelight drenched the room casting long shadows up the wall. I was still standing in the middle of the room, holding my sweater, contemplating whether I should ask Lorne to take me home...when he stood up.

"Well, what do you think?" he asked walking towards me, his hands deep in his pockets.

"Your place," I stammered, "I like it...and I love your coffee table. It's really unusual. Where did you get it?"

I knew I was babbling like a magpie but I couldn't help it. I had no idea what to say or do. I liked him a lot but I didn't want to get hurt. This was my greatest fear.

He stopped in front of me. His eyes searched mine. Before I could speak he took my shoulders and leaned down and kissed me. His mouth was soft, but his kiss grew hard; crushing my lips, he pulled me close. Instinctively my arms slipped around his back. My knees weakened and I dissolved into him. He held me a moment, then stepped back, holding me at arm's length. My head was whirling like a carnival ride.

Lorne only smiled.

"I've been waiting to do that all day," he said. "Now how about some dinner?"

He slid open the screen door and stepped out on the balcony. The rain had stopped. He lit the grill and waited for the flames to die down then came back inside. I followed him into the kitchen. The aroma of baked potatoes filled the room along with the warmth of the oven.

"Can I help with anything?" I asked, leaning against the counter.

"Maybe fix a salad," he said, twisting a corkscrew into a bottle of dark red Merlot. "Everything's in the refrigerator."

Soon we were sitting on the floor at the driftwood coffee table, enjoying steak, baked potatoes and a salad…a romantic dinner for two. *"Sgt. Pepper's Lonely Hearts Club Band"* played in the background. Fluttering candlelight tossed playful images across the ceiling.

Lorne poured more wine and raised his glass to make a toast. "Destiny," he said looking across the table at me. Our glasses clinked.

"I'd like to show you my workshop," Lorne announced after dinner. Reaching for his glass, he stood up, took my hand, and led me down the hall.

An old wooden desk sat opposite the doorway stacked with papers and magazines, its pigeon holes stuffed to overflowing. Under a long narrow window shaded with drawn mini blinds, a wooden work-bench was strewn with the clutter of dusty bottles and strange tools. In one corner, there appeared to be the project of some mad scientist. The bottom half of an old 55-gallon oil drum was half-filled with concrete, and a stainless steel arm of some sort protruded from the center. When I questioned him, Lorne explained it was a centrifuge, and then went on to describe how it spun liquid gold, casting it into jewelry.

He reached out and dropped a ring into my hand. I turned it in my fingers, examining the intricate details under his jeweler's light. And as I did I felt him watching me.

Perched on a stool at the workbench, Lorne took me gently by the arm. I felt the heat of his hand. He drew me closer. I stood between his legs facing him, his firm thighs resting lightly against the outside of my legs. For a moment, we searched each other's eyes.

That night was like no other. For the first time in my life, I felt truly alive. And for some unknown reason, I now knew my destiny, and Lorne was to be part of it.

13

All the pieces fit

November 1974

Transformed like a butterfly freed from a cocoon, I was a new creature never to return to who I was before. For the first time in my life all the pieces fit, everything made sense. The puzzle to my existence was over. With Lorne I was complete.

Yet, there was something unsettling deep within my belly. It haunted my happiness. How could I be sure he was the one? We never talked about us…I had no idea what was going on in his head. And I was afraid to push it. Crushing doubts tumbled through my mind, but I refused to listen. I would back off. Give the relationship room to grow; if it was meant to be it would happen.

So life went on. A few nights a week, Lorne would have dinner with me and the children, listening patiently to their endless barrage of questions. The children seemed to like him. And once I had them tucked into bed, Lorne and I would curl up on the couch with a glass of wine where he would tell me tales of the universe. I had never known another man like him. With all his wisdom, he awakened in me a ravenous curiosity I never knew I had. I glowed with contentment.

One Saturday night, we dropped in at *The Big Mouth Frog* for a drink. It was packed. Tom spotted us from his perch up on stage and waved openly. He then immediately switched to *Blackbird,* a favorite piece of mine. Lorne appeared to be in a good mood the entire evening, but later at his apartment he grew intensely quiet.

I leaned against the doorway in the kitchen watching him. Lorne was more of a thinker than a talker but he hadn't uttered a word since we left the restaurant. That worried me. I was afraid to ask questions, afraid of his answer.

He led me to the living room. Setting his glass on the coffee table, he lit a candle and sank to the edge of the couch. When he looked up, I saw sadness in his eyes. He reached for my hand and drew me close. When I stepped between his legs, he wrapped his arms around my hips, burying his face against my body. I reached down, running my hands through his hair, feeling his silky curls wrap around my fingers.

"Lorne, what's wrong?" I asked, my throat gripped in fear.

In the stillness of the room he clung to me; our shadows stretched up the wall. When he finally looked up, tears glistened in his eyes. Afraid to say anything I stroked his cheek like a child's, trying to ease his pain.

Soon I was in his arms again.

Cradled in candlelight, I was unable to contain the restless words trapped behind my lips. "I love you," I whispered.

Suffocating silence filled the room; the walls pressed in on me. My heart hammered like jungle drums I feared he would hear.

"It's time to go," he said abruptly.

Gentle rain fell on the city. It was late and only a few cars had passed us on the road. Lorne drove in silence. I stared out through my reflection in the window, not knowing what to say. If only I could take a walk, get a breath of fresh air. What have I done?

The rain stopped by the time we pulled into the carport. Lorne walked me to the door trailing a few steps behind. I could not look at him. I was embarrassed and hurt. I was at a loss for words and had no idea what I had done wrong.

When I unlocked the door, Lorne followed me into the dark hallway. He pulled me into his arms. Then cradling me gently he kissed my lips, my nose and my eyelids. I began to weep. For a moment he held me close, resting his cheek against my hair. Then he stepped away, his hands dropped to his side, the dim porch light captured his sadness.

"Nancy, I never say I love you," he said. Without another word, he turned and walked out the door, closing it behind him.

I was paralyzed with confusion, tears rolling down my cheeks. My life had stopped.

All night I tossed and turned, unable to sleep. I was exhausted when the phone rang the next morning. It was Lorne. My heart leaped at the sound of his voice.

"Nancy, I'm sorry about last night," he said. His tone was different...distant. "I really like you a lot, you know that," he went on, "but I'm not ready to get married, not for at least another five years. And I can't expect you to wait that long."

I was stunned.

He rattled on, his words well chosen. "Nancy, I can't say the words you want to hear. I can't say them until I'm ready to marry again, that's just the way I am. Can you try to understand?"

I leaned against the doorway to keep from sliding to the floor, unable to speak. I felt like I had been punched in the stomach.

"I think we should start seeing other people," he said. "That way you'll have a chance to meet someone...someone who is ready to get married."

I stared at the kitchen wall, unblinking. I could not think.

"Please say something," he said, "I need to know you'll be all right."

Straightening my shoulders, I lifted my chin, "I'm not ready to get married either," I said through silent tears. "But do you really think we should start seeing other people?"

"Yes," he said, "I think it would be best for both of us."

An annoying buzz filled my head like a hive of angry wasps. I hung up the phone.

Was this the end?

My life was on hold. I was still a mother, and I must go to work, grocery shop, clean the house and do laundry. Physically I went through the motions, but inside I was dead, a walking zombie. My only joy was my children. Lorne called a few times to check on me but words were difficult for both of us. A new awkwardness had developed between us. I feared I would lose him completely.

Through all this, Grant continued to pursue me like a door-to-door salesman without success. Finally, I decided it was time to get out of the house. I was tired of sitting around feeling sorry for myself. Grant called to invite me to Thanksgiving dinner and he was shocked when I accepted. Peter was coming in from Chicago to be with the children, and I didn't want to be alone.

Grant was an inspired cook. He whipped up a feast fit for royalty. I tried to enjoy myself for his sake and all his hard work, but my thoughts were with Lorne. Agonizing questions plagued me. Where was he today? Who was he having dinner with? My broken heart ached like never before.

14

Tapping at the window

December 8, 1974

"Tap...tap, tap...tap..."
Silence
"Tap, tap...tap, tap, tap..."
Silence

It was the middle of the night. Groggy with sleep layered in darkness, I tried to comprehend what I heard. My mind raced. It sounded like someone was tapping on the window but my bedroom was on the second floor.

"Tap…tap…tap, tap…"

There it was again. Pushing back the covers, I got to my knees and pulled myself up to the window over my bed. I peeked out between the overlapping drapes. My heart stopped. There under my window, standing in the bright security lights was Lorne. And as I watched he leaned down, gathered a handful of gravel from the walkway, and with his other hand he pitched a few stones at my window.

"Ping…ping," they hit the glass sharply. I jumped out of bed, grabbed my robe and ran downstairs to let him in.

When I flung open the back door I caught him red-handed. He quickly slipped his hands behind his back grinning from ear to ear.

"I missed you," he slurred, eyeing his boot tops. "I just wanted to drive by your house, but my car went off the road into a ditch!" Lorne pointed over his shoulder, his eyes wide with disbelief.

He was drunk. Smashed! I had never seen him like this.

"Are you all right?" I asked, stepping closer.

"Yes." He sounded bewildered.

"Come inside and I'll make you some coffee." He dropped the gravel and took my hand. I led him into the house.

"Nancy, I've gotta get my car out of that ditch," he said. "Shit…it's my company car, and I've got a sales meeting first thing in the morning." He plopped on the couch. Leaning back he seemed to melt in slow motion until his head rested on the back cushion.

"I'll be right back with some coffee," I said, patting him on the leg.

I put a mug of water into the microwave, and pushed the button. Then I called a private towing service used by my dealership. The owner was a friend, and after a brief conversation, he grumbled under his breath and swore he'd have the car out of the ditch by 6:00 a.m.

When I returned with the good news and the coffee, Lorne was out like a light. After fetching linens from the upstairs closet, I wrestled off his boots and lifted his legs onto the couch. I then slipped a pillow under his head and covered him with a blanket. I kissed him on the lips, turned off the light and tiptoed up to bed.

But I couldn't fall back to sleep. My mind was alive with questions. And why was he so drunk? I had never seen him like this. It was probably nothing to worry about; men do stupid things sometimes. I closed my eyes but his words continued to echo in the darkness.

"I missed you and just wanted to drive by your house."

Lorne cared…and that was all that mattered.

We never discussed that night. The one time I tried, he changed the subject. I was afraid to corner him. Having some of Lorne was better than having no Lorne at all; so I let it go.

His evening phone calls resumed, and we went back to dating, but he still urged me to see other men. Did he really want me to find someone else, or was this just an excuse to date other women? The whole idea turned me off…but what choice did I have?

15

"A penny for your thoughts"

December 14, 1974

It was eleven days before Christmas and we were off to buy a tree. The children chased each other down the sidewalk before piling into the back of Lorne's car, each clamoring for a seat by the window. Their carefree giggles warmed the chilly afternoon air. On the surface we looked like any ordinary family…too bad it wasn't true.

What a difference two years make.

It had been almost Christmas when the children and I had moved out on our own. I had overspent my budget on their presents, and had absolutely nothing left to buy a tree. But they never complained. It hurt my heart.

I'll never forget that Christmas Eve if I lived to be a thousand…how I waited until they were asleep so I could slip out of the house. The streets were dark and lonely, except for a sprinkling of Christmas lights waiting for Santa to arrive. It was late when I finally spotted a vacant tree lot.

Mustering up the courage of a mother lion, I turned off my lights, rolled into the driveway and pulled around back. I was alone. I got out of the car and walked up to the fence. There on the other side, under the light of the moon, sat a stubby, white flocked tree…all alone like me. My hands were shaking when I grabbed hold of the cold chain link and hoisted myself up. Fear ran through my veins like salt water as I fought to climb the wall of wire.

The next morning was Christmas and I was horrified to think I actually stole a tree. But the look on my children's faces was worth any penance I would someday have to pay.

Lorne struggled to free another tree from the huge compressed pile at his feet. Then one broke loose; he vigorously pounded the trunk on the ground, releasing the branches.

"Okay kids," he called across the lot, surveying the tree up close. "Run back, and tell me if the trunk's straight."

Cory ran over to me, his pale hair flying, his cheeks flush. "Mom, Mom, come look," he said, tugging me by the hand. "Can we get this one? It's a real good tree."

His innocent wonder was like food for my soul.

Later that evening, Lorne sat quietly watching the children rummage through the dusty old boxes I had dragged down from the attic. Each year they helped me trim the tree; it was our tradition. They would hunt for treasured ornaments stored in boxes wrapped in tissue paper, calico stars and hand painted angels they had made in kindergarten; stained glass ornaments embellished with their names, made by their Aunt Karen, my sweet sister.

With the last ornament hung on the tree and baby Jesus was safe in the manger, I turned off the lights, signaling Scott to plug in the tree. It sprang to life, fat and robust, dancing in lights. Draped in gold garlands and layered with shiny red balls, tiny gold flutes and red velvet bows, the tree resembled a Norman Rockwell painting.

"Okay kids, its way past your bedtime," I announced standing up. "It will still be here in the morning."

I left Lorne staring into the twinkling tree lights while I put Tiffy to bed.

"Mommy, when is Santa coming?" she asked, crawling under her covers.

"In eleven days," I replied, tucking in her blankets. I leaned down, tweaked her nose and gave her a kiss. "He will be here before you know it."

I knew the boys no longer believed but I hoped to hide it from her as long as possible. When the boys brought up the subject trying to corner me, I simply said, "Santa doesn't bring presents to children who don't believe in him." And for the time being, that worked.

Once the boys settled down, I kissed them goodnight and headed downstairs. Glancing over the banister, I noticed Lorne was still fixated on the tree.

"A penny for your thoughts," I said, sitting next to him.

Lorne turned, then reached out and took my hand. A strange look covered his face. He hesitated a moment. "Nancy, I love you," he said, knocking me off guard. "I'm still not ready to get married, but I want you to know how much I love you."

A choking knot filled my throat as I fought back the tears.

"I've never known anyone like you," he said, "and if I was ready, I'd ask you to be my wife in a minute."

He pulled me into his arms, softly kissing my lips, my eyelids and my forehead, over and over again, holding me close in the shadows of the twinkling tree. Time stood still as I wept.

The holidays were a blur. Christmas was a project in penny pinching, and I still had to mail token gifts to my family in Ohio, in time to avoid a ransom in postage. By Christmas morning I was exhausted. But the children's delight in Santa's presents, while buried amid piles of colorful wrapping paper, was my gift.

Late that afternoon, Peter picked them up, taking a piece of my heart with him.

16

A twinge of nerves

January 4, 1975

Saturday afternoon at Denny's was bedlam. Weekend shoppers were forced to tolerate crowded tables of teens, sated with ill-mannered hormones, all vying for attention. I spotted Lorne from the doorway the minute I walked in. He sat in a booth by the window and there was no mistaking that Tommy was his son, his platinum hair held my eye as I made my way through the crowd. The four-year old bundle of energy scrambled back and forth on the seats, Lorne reached across the table trying to get him to sit still. He had described Tommy to a tee.

A twinge of nerves was no surprise when Lorne spotted me and waved. Six months earlier a shy handsome cowboy stood in the doorway at Jackie's party. Today I was meeting his child.

"Hi there" I said, rather timidly. "Hope I didn't keep you waiting."

Tommy knelt in the booth with his elbows on the table. He looked up at me, then to his dad. "Is that her?" he asked with the frankness of a four-year old.

Lorne winked at me; he smiled at Tommy and nodded. Tommy scrambled out of the booth and crawled up next to his dad. I took a deep breath and slid across the seat Tommy vacated. A pretty little girl with bashful brown eyes and long brown hair sat on the other side of Lorne; she looked to be a few years older than Tommy.

"Hello...and what's your name?" I asked, leaning in closer.

She peered out from under long dark lashes, blinked once, then scooted closer to Lorne, leaning against him, her small hand tightened on his arm.

Tommy was born in December, a month before Lorne left for Vietnam. All I knew about Shirley, his first wife, was that she sang in a nightclub. They had dated on and off for about a year. Later I learned that she became pregnant when Lorne enlisted. But Lorne knew none of this until basic training in El Paso. Wanting to do the right thing he asked for permission and they were married there. Shirley went back to Houston. After El Paso, Lorne had special rifle training in Fort Polk, Louisiana. He was then sent to Fort Bliss, Washington, where he shipped out to Vietnam. Shirley was older than Lorne and had a daughter named Becky by a previous marriage. Tommy was just one year old when Lorne was discharged. He said their marriage was rocky from the start. He worked full time as a milkman and went to college at night. It was during these times that Shirley grew restless. They lived together less than a year before the divorce.

Three pairs of eyes watched my every move from across the table; I felt like a lab rat. Back on his knees, elbows on the table, Tommy propped his chin on his knuckles and studied me. The rough and tumble little guy was in dire need of a haircut.

I was defenseless. I had no idea what Lorne had told them about me. But from his smug grin it was obvious. His lady was in the hot seat and he was enjoying every minute of it.

"What's your name?" Tommy asked.

"Nancy."

"Do ya' have any kids?"

"I have three," I said smiling, eyeing Lorne to rescue me.

"What's their names?"

"Scott, Cory and Tiffy."

"You have some boys," Tommy stated, planning his next assault.

The waitress came to my rescue and we ordered lunch. Lorne and I tried to talk, but with little success. Tommy continued to hammer me with questions. Becky remained silent during the entire meal.

17

Weak as a newborn puppy

January 23, 1975

Still weak as a newborn puppy, I finally gathered enough strength to drag myself out of bed. It was three in the afternoon. The flu had hit me like a runaway freight train. For three days I lay moaning and groaning, the children hovering close by. Moms weren't supposed to get sick. Afraid my brood would catch whatever I had, I shooed them from the room. I was heaving green bile into a stainless steel pot on the floor next to the bed. Eventually the children sneaked back upstairs and placed soda crackers and a glass of ginger ale on the night stand while I slept. That's what I gave them when they were sick. Marilyn brought homemade chicken soup which ended up in the pot on the floor. But enough was enough. Determined to get up and join the living, I pulled on a pair of jeans and a tee shirt; my stomach gripped with another wave of nausea.

Gazing into the bathroom mirror, I blended into the pale wall behind me like a lingering ghost. I ran hot water over a washcloth, squeezed it out and held it to my face, pulling some blood back into my cheeks. I brushed my teeth, savoring the minty flavor on my tongue, before I spit it into the sink. Then I ran a comb through my hair to work out the snarls. Feeling somewhat better, I went back to make my bed. I hated getting into an unmade bed.

I was bent over smoothing out the sheets when I heard footsteps vaulting up the stairs, two at a time. I assumed it was Scott. When I glanced up I was surprised to see Lorne standing in the doorway, a devilish grin crinkling the corners of his eyes. Mortified by my appearance, I turned away and went back to my task.

"Hi there," I said, wrestling a tangled blanket. "You can see I wasn't expecting you."

Lorne stepped into the room; a solemn look replaced his grin. He came toward the bed with his hands in his pockets.

"Lorne, don't get too close," I said, stepping back. "I might still be contagious."

He stood over me. Reaching out, he took me in his arms and kissed me on the mouth...hard. Caught up in his embrace, I closed my eyes, dissolving against his familiar body.

Suddenly I came to my senses. "Lorne, what are you doing?" I asked pushing him away. "Are you crazy? You're going to get sick!" Stepping back, I banged into the nightstand. "Besides," my voice lowered with my eyes, "I look like something the dog dug up."

"Sit down," he said, pointing to the bed.

Startled by his command, I dropped to the bed. Wide eyed, I stared up at him. Lorne pushed a pillow aside and sat down beside me. He turned and studied my face before he reached for my hands. My insides were trembling. His eyes were clear but something was different. Fear rose in me like the evening high tide.

"Nancy," he said, then paused..."will you marry me?"

My reaction was shock, disbelief. A wild hallucination brought on by the flu. I tilted my head to one side; quizzically I looked at him. Then I reached up and touched his cheek. He was real, his skin was warm.

"Well, Baby...will you marry me?" he asked again.

My eyes flooded with tears. "Lorne, don't tease me," I sobbed, too weak to hold them back. "I've been sick and I don't understand what you're doing."

"Nancy, I'm not teasing," he said, lost in my tears. He squeezed my hands. "I love you and I want you to be my wife. I want to spend the rest of my life with you."

"Are you sure, Lorne?" I sniffled, not believing my own ears. "I thought you planned to wait five years before even considering marriage again. It's only been six months."

"I know. But if I wait five years...I'll lose you and I couldn't bear the thought," he said, staring at the wall in front of him. Then he turned, his eyes were tender. "I want you to be mine and only mine."

My head was throbbing; monkeys chattered in my ears, questions without answers whirled through my mind. "What about the children?" I said, feeling queasy and unsure. "I have three children to think about."

"I know, Nancy, and I've thought about them too," he said. "I realize I can never be their father because they already have one. And I know they love Peter. They're good kids Nancy; you've raised them well, and I really like them," he said. "Right now, I feel we've become friends and I think we'll grow from there."

The children were my world and Lorne knew it.

"But I'm older than you." I said, still in disbelief. "What will people say?"

"First of all," he chuckled, shaking his head, "who cares what people say? The only opinions that matter belong to us. We're talking six years, so big deal. Personally, I'm unaware of any difference between us." He stopped, his eyes narrowed. "Or are you saying I'm immature? Is that it?"

I had to smile at the look on his face.

"Oh, Lorne...No, you're not immature. I love you so much sometimes it hurts. And I do want to be your wife more than anything." I reached for a tissue from the box on the nightstand. Twisting it in my hands, I lowered my head. "But I'm scared."

"What are you afraid of?"

"I don't know," I said, unable to look at him, "Maybe it's the unknown."

"Is that all?" Lorne said with relief. "I thought maybe there was another man."

I smiled, tears spilling down my cheeks. "Lorne, there is no one else. You're the only man I love, or ever will."

"Then it's settled," he said boldly. "We're getting married!"

Reality hit me like a brick. Lorne reached out; he crushed me in his arms and swallowed me with kisses. Choking sobs shook my body as we tumbled backward on the bed. This time I didn't stop him. Lying on the crumpled bedspread, I gazed up into his handsome face, still trying to grasp what had happened. Propped up on one elbow, he took a corner of the sheet and wiped away my tears.

"Now that that's settled," I said, finally convinced, "when do you want to get married?"

"Next Friday," he said, with a twinkle in his eye.

18

How do I love thee?

I was much too excited to sleep; it all seemed like a crazy dream. Lorne had asked me to be his wife and I had said yes. Now for the first time in my life I knew the soul-surrendering love I had only read about. The kind of love Elizabeth Barrett Browning knew when she penned the words, *"How do I love thee: Let me count the ways...to the depth and breadth and height my soul can reach."* The kind of love I would die for.

Thinking back on my marriage to Peter, I knew I had never been "in love" with him. Actually, my love for him was more a feeling of respect.

After high school, all I wanted to do was get married and have babies like my girlfriends did, to escape the hurt of my Mommy Dearest. I felt like Cinderella growing up, wearing my friend's hand-me-downs. Even though there was enough money for my mother to make three house payments each month, there was never enough for new clothes for me. I could never meet my mother's standards. And being the oldest of three I was always in trouble. When my siblings misbehaved, it was my fault; I must have shown them how. Isolated and unhappy, I sometimes turned to my father, which escalated my mother's anger. I felt like she hated me but I never knew why. The more I thought about it, the more I was sure marriage would solve my problems. Peter was on the chase. So when he asked me to marry him I said yes.

All too soon I learned the difference between intercourse and passion. Intercourse was for reproduction, whereas passion was the mortar that held a marriage together. Passion of any kind was better than nothing. Thinking back I could not remember one time when Peter's kisses left me breathless.

"Mom, are we going to have a new name?" Cory asked the next evening. His young hands gripped the couch cushion as he rocked from side to side.

"No, Honey, your names will stay the same," I said. "My last name will change but I'll still be your mom just like I am right now."

"Does Lorne have any girls?" Tiffy asked.

Growing up I vowed never to treat my children the way I had been treated. The children were the joy of my life. They were my backbone, giving me the strength and courage to go on. They were a part of me, the most important part. And now, after all of the pain I had caused, we were going be a family again.

With a grin, Cory poked Scott in the arm, "Hey, we get to cut school to go to Mom's wedding," he announced, darting out of Scott's reach.

"Yeah," Scott rebounded after him. "How many kids get to do that?"

I left the boys tousling on the living room floor and headed for the kitchen to make dinner. Tiffy latched onto my pant leg.

"We're going to be a family again," I said pulling her close. "I promise." I leaned down, and kissed the top of her head.

After dinner I knew I must bite the bullet and call my family. There was no time to procrastinate. In one week I would be Mrs. Lorne MacMillan.

"Hi, Mom," I said, feeling like I was twelve years old again.

"Nancy...I'm surprised to hear from you," my mother replied coolly.

I took a deep breath. "Mom, I've met a wonderful guy and he's asked me to marry him." Rushing through the details of our courtship, I pictured my mother's stern look, grateful we were not face to face.

"That's nice, dear," my mother said casually. "I'll let your brother and sister know." Polite indifference, what had I expected? I was the black sheep of the family; the stray who left the flock. Peter's job transfer to California allowed me to break the matriarchal chains I grew up with. Good manners dictated congratulations...nothing more and nothing less.

The next day I went to see my father who lived in the next county. He and his second wife lived in a sprawling ranch-style house. He was a quiet, self-contained man and I loved him dearly. My father was my first mentor, stretching my mind with visions of black holes existing throughout the universe.

That afternoon he sat in his recliner, dressed in a one-piece gray jumpsuit, puffing on his pipe. A strained smile revealed his disapproval.

"Lorne is special...and brilliant...and I'm in love with him," I continued, trying to gain his blessing. "The children and I...well, we're going to be a family again."

However, my father had always liked Peter. Actually, Peter got along better with my father than he did with me.

My Dad stood, walked over, leaned down and kissed me on the cheek.

"I'm happy for you, Nancy," he said kindly. "But you do know this is short notice?" He walked back to his chair, held a lighter over his pipe and puffed. Smoke seeped from the corners of his mouth. "I'm afraid Elsie and I won't be able to make your wedding. We planned a trip to Dallas with Ladye and Pat over a month ago; our reservations are in and paid for."

I noticed how uncomfortable he looked waiting for my reply.

"Of course, I understand," I said politely, "and it is short notice." I bit the inside of my cheek to keep from crying. Tears waited behind my lashes as I kissed him goodbye.

Hurt and disappointed, I drove through the long circular driveway, refusing to let anyone spoil my wedding. My children would be there to share my happiness. Who else did I really need?

19

Uncommon shade of blue

January 25, 1975

The old brick building sat in the core of downtown Houston, the home of the homeless. Menacing black iron gates stretched across the windows and door. Standing in the archway, Lorne pressed the button on the wall and waited. A revolting stench like urine rose from the concrete.

"Buzzzzzzzzzz," the secured door echoed.

We stepped inside and the heavy metal door slammed shut with a clank behind us. My eyes swept the small room with curiosity. It was nearly empty, quiet as a funeral parlor. A young couple leaned over a glass showcase filled with trays of dazzling diamonds; deep in discussion, their whispers floated in the air like feathers. Coming toward us, a stocky middle-aged man adjusted his watch; an expensive suit draped his body. His thinning black hair was slicked back like a movie gangster; massive gold rings covered his stubby fingers.

"Good afternoon," he replied, his Middle Eastern accent heavy as the cologne he wore.

"MacMillan," Lorne stated, "I have an appointment."

"My name is Arimon, come this way," he said, turning on his heels.

As I trailed behind him I felt awkwardly out of place. I always wondered who bought jewelry from places like this. Nobody I knew. And even if I could afford it, I doubted I would spend my money so frivolously.

At the end of the aisle, Arimon stepped behind a counter. Bending over, he unlocked a drawer and took out a black leather box which he placed in front of us. He opened the lid and withdrew a small white envelope. I was fascinated. Inside the envelope was a smaller packet; Arimon unfolded its corners. Nestled in the crevices were three stones exquisitely cut and shimmering in an uncommon shade of blue.

"These rare stones are from Tanzania, Africa," the jeweler boasted. "At this time, there is only one mine producing the Tanzanite and only a handful of these precious gems have reached the United States."

Lorne pulled me close. "Baby," he said, "I picked this stone because I wanted your ring to be special…like no one else's."

His finger toyed with them.

"And every time you look at it you'll know how much I love you. And always will." Then he hesitated, "Of course if you don't like it, you can pick something else."

"Oh no, Lorne," I said, misty eyed. "I love it."

Too much to do and too little time.

My stomach coiled like a boa constrictor the minute we left the jewelers. Our next stop: Lorne's parents' house. I was about to meet them for the first time and I was a basket case.

Staring out the window, I tried to think about something else, but I couldn't. What if they didn't like me? After all, I was older than Lorne and I had three children. Cradle snatcher! I hated the terminology. But then again, how would I feel if it were Scott? I knew the answer and I knew I would try to talk him out of it. Was this about to happen to Lorne? Would his mother try to stop the wedding? Could she?

We were driving through Bellaire, an older part of Houston, when Lorne pulled up to the curb in front of a well-kept, one-story house on a quiet tree-lined street. Colorful flowerbeds edged the well-manicured lawns; stately oaks cast welcome shade from the bright afternoon sun. This was the house where Lorne grew up.

Petrified, I looked at him with pleading eyes.

He only grinned and winked. "Everything's going to be fine," he said gently, "I promise." He leaned over, kissed me, then opened the door and got out.

I took a deep breath and waited, rigid as an ironing board.

"Remember I love you," he whispered in my ear as he helped me from the car.

He cupped my hand in his and we started up the driveway. Suddenly, the front door flung open and I came face to face with Lorne's mother.

"Mom, this is Nancy," Lorne said, drawing me close.

"Come in, Nancy," she said, smiling graciously. "I'm happy to finally meet you. We've heard so much about you."

She was beautiful, radiating the same quiet elegance as Princess Grace of Monaco whom she resembled. Her sky-blue eyes and strong cheekbones were definitely those of her son.

"Thank you," I said timidly, stepping past her into the house.

I stood in wonder. It was the middle of winter, yet the room teemed with fresh flowers, filling the air with the sweetness of spring.

Lorne's stepfather was a calm obliging man with an easy smile. That afternoon he made me laugh, sharing tales of Guatemala, where he had been a geophysical engineer exploring for oil in his younger years. We all talked openly, sipping gourmet coffee and nibbling on homemade pastries. And I felt at home.

My worries had been in vain, and Lorne was right. The children and I were welcomed with open arms. Lorne's loving parents blessed our marriage.

20

Sea of empty pews

January 31, 1975

The alarm buzzed like an angry mosquito in my ear. I rolled over and hit the snooze. The clock read 6:00 a.m. I buried my face in the pillow and closed my eyes. Then it hit me...today was my wedding day. Tossing back the covers I leaped out of bed.

"Everybody up," I hollered down the hall, tying my robe at the waist.

I bounded down the stairs like a teenager. Early morning before the children were up was my favorite time of day, when everything was quiet and new.

"Time for breakfast, Sleepyhead," I announced cheerfully, poking my head into Tiffy's room.

I stood at the kitchen counter mixing frozen orange juice in a Tupperware pitcher, trying to think of anything I might have forgotten. I had laid out the children's best clothes the night before while they were taking their baths. Then I wrote them each a note to get back into school explaining their tardiness. All I had left to do was shower and throw a few things in an overnight bag for my honeymoon. Honeymoon...what a nice word. Lorne and I only had the weekend free, but that was better than no honeymoon at all.

Lina, my best friend at work, insisted on watching the children and wouldn't take "no" for an answer. When Lorne heard the news he booked the honeymoon suite at the *Flagship* hotel in Galveston. Even now I felt like I was living in a dream.

It was the perfect day for a wedding. The morning air smelled clean from last night's rain. Overhead, puffy white clouds hung suspended like apples in a tree waiting to be plucked. Flocks of tiny birds zigzagged through the sky oblivious to the busy world below.

"Good morning, beautiful," Lorne said, leaning across the front seat to kiss me. He smiled lovingly and then started the car. "Are you ready for our big day?"

A strange calm enveloped me as we backed down the driveway. It felt like God had tapped me on the shoulder. Theoretically I should have been a nervous wreck. Maybe I was in shock. After all, everything had happened so fast.

Turning around I smiled adoringly at my children.

My normally rambunctious offspring sat quietly in the back seat; their faces shined like new pennies. Their hands rested in their laps, totally out of character for them. And now that I noticed, the boys looked a little ashen.

"Are you guys okay?"

Scott and Cory slowly nodded.

"Mom, how can you be a bride without a veil?" Tiffy piped up.

Suddenly, I realized this was their wedding, too. From this day forward Lorne would be a big part of their lives and the boys knew it. My life was finally coming together. I felt blessed to have three healthy children I adore. Plus I was head-over-heels in love with the man who would be my husband in a matter of hours. And at that moment, we would all be a family "till death do us part."

Lorne's parents were waiting in the church parking lot. We hugged and chatted briefly; the children raced ahead across the lawn. A flagstone walk led the way to the church; the smell of freshly cut grass filled the air. I looked up. A plain, golden cross shimmered boldly on the steeple of the modest Presbyterian Church where Lorne went to Sunday school as a boy and learned about God.

I converted from Lutheran to Catholic right out of high school. At the time I was engaged to my high school sweetheart who was Catholic, but it hadn't worked out. And it just so happened that Peter was Catholic as well. My parents paid for a big Catholic wedding and later, each of the children was baptized Catholic.

In the eyes of the Catholic Church my marriage to Lorne would be null and void, even though Peter and I were legally divorced. This saddened me but I refused to let it hinder my choice. This did not make me a bad person. There were certain ideals of the Catholic Church I questioned and this happened to be one of them.

Our guest list was small. The children and Lorne's parents sat in the front row swallowed up by a sea of empty pews. I glanced around, secretly hoping my father would show up to surprise me. But no such luck. *Stop it, I* thought. Wishful thinking only causes pain, and today was for happiness. Lorne and I were getting married in front of God and the children. Nothing else mattered.

Standing at the front of the church my knees felt like marshmallows. I took a deep breath and looked over at Lorne. He was standing by his parents, tall and handsome in his good gray suit. He winked and the love in his eyes reassured me I had made the right decision. Walking over to me, he reached for my hand and together we stepped up to the altar.

The minister stepped forward, clutching a small black book to his chest. Lorne squeezed my hand. I could feel the children's eyes on my back; if only I could see their faces. What were they thinking? A new chapter in my life was about to begin, one I had only dreamed of.

The minister began to speak. I watched his lips move but was distracted by the warmth of Lorne's hand. Glancing to my right I found him watching me. His gentle smile eased my tension, while he traced a tiny circle in the palm of my hand with his finger. I blushed as I turned back to the minister. I tried to concentrate, but one thought persisted...when I finally turn around I will be Mrs. Lorne MacMillan.

"I now pronounce you man and wife," said the minister, closing the book. "You may kiss your bride."

Lorne turned to me. His eyes were filled with emotion. On my finger the Tanzanite shimmered in subtle shades of the sunset, surrounded by star-like diamonds. And I knew how much Lorne loved me. He gently took my shoulders, leaned down and kissed me. At that moment, lost in his embrace, I was the happiest woman alive. Lorne was my husband...and would be forever.

PART THREE

Houston Texas

The love of my life

21

Everything was perfect

I had to pinch myself. Sometimes I found it hard to believe that Lorne was my husband. He was a handsome, virile specimen women turned to gaze at and he was mine. I was head over heels in love. I had finally found the man who filled the emptiness in my soul, my other half. And he loved me. The children seemed to adjust to their new extended family behaving like nothing much had changed. What more could a woman ask for?

Everything was perfect. Well…for the first seven months.

August 26, 1975

A muffled scream nudged me from a deep sleep. I turned over, pulling the sheet with me. There it was again. Slowly I opened my eyes; the room was dark in shadow. Without warning, a blood curdling cry sliced the stillness, shattering my nerves. *My God it was Lorne!* I bolted upright in bed. Terrified, I reached for him.

"Lorne, wake up!" I yelled, grabbing his arm. His muscles were rigid; his skin bathed in a cold sweat.

The second I touched him, he lunged at me, savagely tossing me aside. I hit the mattress hard. Stunned, I didn't move. Then a sound even more frightening reached my ears, a soft pitiful whimpering like a dog hit by a car. Panic choked me.

Dear God, what's happening? Heavy metal doors in my head slammed shut one at a time…CLANG…CLANG…CLANG!

Carefully I made my way to the edge of the bed. Groping the nightstand in darkness, I found the lamp and flicked the switch. A haven of soft light permeated the room.

Then I turned. There beside me huddled a man I did not recognize, his arms wrapped tightly around his legs, his chin on his knees, his face a twisted mask of terror. I was shocked. His naked body glistened in perspiration. Then I realized his eyes were closed; he was still asleep.

"Lorne, wake up," I pleaded, boldly inching closer. "Lorne, it's me, Nancy. Please wake up, you're scaring me."

I reached out to touch him, prepared for the worse. This time he scurried backwards like a frightened creature cowering shamelessly against the headboard, animal-like noises seeping from his lips. Suddenly his eyes snapped open. Startled, I jerked backwards. His blank stare was chilling.

"Lorne, it's me," I demanded. "Wake up."

The whimpering stopped and the room grew quiet. Lorne blinked, his eyes cleared. Soon he recognized me and reached out, his face distorted, his eyes wide with terror. I pulled him close to me. Deep, wrenching sobs shook his body. I cradled him in my arms, sitting in the middle of our king-sized bed, rocking him like a baby, running my fingers through his damp curls, trying to calm his nightmare.

"It's all right; it was just a "bad dream," I cooed softly, holding him close.

What just happened? Was I dreaming?

I rocked him for what seemed like an hour; stroking his hair, letting the warmth of my body soothe him until he drifted off to sleep.

The next morning was Saturday. I stood at the stove, cracking eggs into a frying pan, lost in thought. I reached for my coffee and lifted the steaming liquid to my lips. I could hear water running through the pipes between the walls telling me Lorne was up and in the shower.

I still had no idea what happened. What nightmare had crept into his sleep, terrifying him to such a degree? He really scared me. It was totally out of character. Lorne was a Texan, a man's man, afraid of nothing.

He strolled into the kitchen draped in his blue terrycloth robe, damp ringlets dripping down his forehead. Coming up behind me, his arms encircled my waist; bending down, he planted a wet kiss on the back of my neck.

"Morning, Baby," he whispered, nibbling on my ear. He patted me on the butt and took a seat at the table.

"Good Morning," I replied meekly.

I poured coffee into a mug and placed it on the table in front of him.

"How do you feel this morning?" I asked, as I dished up the omelets. I set our plates down and sat next to him.

"Great," he replied, spreading raspberry jam on his toast.

"I thought you might be tired," I said cautiously. "You had such a rough night."

This got his attention.

"What do you mean?" he said as his eyes narrowed.

I proceeded to go into detail. When I finished, Lorne swore up and down he had no idea what I was talking about and laughed the whole thing off.

"You, my love, must have had the nightmare, not me," he said sarcastically, taking a bite of his toast.

But my female instinct told me something was wrong, terribly wrong...I just didn't know what.

22

The love we shared

September 1975

"Hey, let's take a ride, it's a beautiful day," Lorne announced one morning as he strolled into the kitchen.

The Sunday paper with headlines dominated by war and violence lay scattered on the living room couch. In the garage, Lorne's black 850 Norton backfired loudly before bursting to life. He waited patiently while I locked the back door, anxious to get on the highway, leaving civilization behind.

The sting of the wind banished any doubts lingering like cobwebs from the other night. Away from the city, fresh clean air filled our lungs and renewed my hope. With Lorne in my arms I was complete. The heat of his body soothed me like a warm bath and I knew the love we shared would make everything all right.

Half an hour later, Lorne pulled off the road onto a shoulder of red Texas clay. We had stopped in the middle of nowhere. He lowered the kickstand and got off. Removing his helmet, which he tucked under his arm, he strolled over to the fence, pulling a cigarette from his shirt pocket.

"What's up?" I asked, climbing down off the bike.

The smell of fresh mown hay encircled us. Two curious horses meandered over to the fence poking their sleek velvet noses through the barbed wire. I pulled off my helmet and wandered over to pet them.

"Well, I think it's time you learned to ride alone," Lorne said, flashing a grin. "Today's your first lesson."

I whirled around in amazement, "Really?"

I knew Lorne got a kick out of the fact that his wife was still a tomboy, but the bike was his baby...his pride and joy. And I knew I'd be in big trouble if I put a scratch on it, let alone dump it...but this was his idea.

"First lesson...how to start it," he said, flicking his cigarette butt onto the road.

He grabbed hold of the handlebars, and nimble as a ballet dancer, flung his long leg over the gas tank. I watched intently. He tilted the bike and released the kickstand, then stomped the chrome kick start. Once the engine roared to life Lorne looked at me and nodded. Then he shut off the engine and got off the bike.

Now it was my turn. Lorne held the bike while I climbed on. The gas tank felt as broad as the back of a horse between my legs. Standing on my tiptoes, I struggled to balance the heavy machine.

"Let me know when you're ready," he said, holding the handlebars and the back of my seat like I was five years old.

"Okay, let go," I replied in a thin voice.

Lorne stepped back, slowly releasing the full weight of the bike. The muscles in my shoulders, thighs and calves screamed. It felt like the bike weighed a thousand pounds but I knew I couldn't weaken or my lesson would be over. Once steady I cautiously leaned the bike, set my foot on the kick start and stomped. It didn't budge. I tried again...nothing. Out of the corner of my eye, Lorne stood watching, his arms folded across his chest.

I had an idea. I lowered the kickstand and got off. I then grabbed the handlebars, put my right foot on the kick start and pulled myself up until both of my feet rested side by side. Balanced precariously like a tight-rope walker, I jumped hard. The engine ignited. Startled, I swayed somewhat before gaining control.

Lorne laughed openly shaking his head back and forth. I loved to see him laugh. It happened so rarely.

I threw my leg over the gas tank, raised the kickstand and steadied the bike on my tiptoes. Lorne walked over and gave me a crash course on how to work the gears. Then he patted me on the butt and sent me on my way.

"Go ahead," he hollered over the noise, "take her for a ride and enjoy yourself. I'll wait for you here." He stepped back and took out another cigarette.

Still balancing on my tiptoes, I shifted into first gear. The bike lunged forward, throwing me back like a bucking bronco trying to toss me to the ground. But I hung on, weaving from side to side down the road, my feet searching blindly for the foot pegs. Once in control, I glanced in the rearview mirror. Lorne stood at the side of the road, his hands on his hips, shaking his head. But he was smiling.

Cloaked in a gush of wind, I was conscious of the thundering power between my legs, the feeling was intoxicating. Alive and in love; it was perfect.

The road was deserted when I decided to make a U-turn and head back. The cumbersome bike did not maneuver like a car; it had a mind of its own. Suddenly I was up over the curb plowing through a muddy field like an army tank.

When I finally returned, Lorne was sitting on his helmet by the side of the road. Long tufts of wild grass embedded in thick mud caked the rims of his tires and cried for attention. I knew I had some explaining to do.

That afternoon we made love on a red plaid blanket in a field of lemon yellow buttercups, concealed in their foliage. Curled in each other's arms, drowsy and warm, we watched flocks of tiny birds form patterns against the rich blue Texas sky, safely hidden from the rest of the world.

23

He longed for a refuge

September 27, 1975

Lorne shouted back at me over the roar of the engine; the index finger of his left hand pointed at a dark wedge of trees off in the distance. His tossed words swept past me. I had no idea what he said.

Without warning he veered off the road coming to an abrupt halt on the narrow shoulder. I lunged forward, lifting off the seat.

"Hey you," I fussed, "what's going on?"

He balanced the bike between his legs and unbuckled his helmet, his gaze fixed in the distance. He pulled out a cigarette.

Every man dreams of owning a home someday. This is normal, status quo. But with Lorne it was an obsession like some mysterious force driving him with a vengeance. He longed for a *refuge*. This was the exact word he used. He talked about it constantly, a place where we could shut out the rest of the world. I found the word a bit odd. One day I looked it up in the dictionary, adding another piece to the puzzle. As published in Webster's New World Dictionary, the word refuge means *"shelter or protection from danger, difficulty, etc."*

"Look over there in those trees," Lorne pointed, squinting into the sun. "I can't believe I never saw it before. We've been down this road a hundred times."

Dead air dense with moisture covered our skin like a wet shower curtain. Releasing my chin strap, I hooded my eyes with my hand to focus on the cluster of trees deep in shadow. I could vaguely make out the skeleton of a house under construction. When I looked closer I saw more than one.

We sat in the middle of nowhere, probably fifteen miles east of Houston; Lorne was lost in thought. I looked around. Across the highway a tractor sputtered and spat, trampling cornstalks as it went. Dense woods reached the edge of the shoulder beside us. I peered into the brush, surprised to see what looked like a first-rate golf course, with sprinklers quenching the greens. Up the road a sign read: "*Bear Creek Park.*"

"Let's go take a look," Lorne said as he pulled on his helmet.

Hidden behind the tall trees were rows of midsized homes lining the sun-baked streets. An identical stick of a tree stood in each yard. Bald mounds of red clay announced the newest neighbors on the block. But nobody was in sight.

We cruised up and down the empty streets; toys and bikes were left scattered where they were dropped. The day was hot enough to fry bacon on the sidewalk. But I liked it here. The children could make new friends; we would have neighbors to talk to and be a real family. But could we afford to buy a brand new house?

We spotted a white sign standing in deep green sod like a small tree…*Sales Office.* The model home's exterior looked like the cover of Better Homes and Gardens; the landscaping was to die for. Lorne rolled into the driveway and turned off the key. With the bike on its kickstand he stood and watched me, as I attempted to resurrect my hair flattened by the helmet.

He leaned over and planted a wet kiss on my lips and took me by the hand. "Are you ready, beautiful?"

Hand in hand, we headed up the driveway to the converted garage, which was now the sales office. I silently prayed that my husband's dreams would not be crushed. We'd been looking for months and he wanted this so much. The overweight realtor had a difficult time maneuvering his bulky body out of a folding lawn chair.

"Howdy, y'all," he said, his drawl thick as peanut butter. A bloated hand reached out to greet us. "I'm Norman King."

Norman gave us the tour. The living room and kitchen were open and airy. Sunshine flooded across the carpet where I pictured the children sprawled on the floor playing games. In the big back yard the boys could play ball, we could have a dog again and I could finally have my garden. And Lorne...he would have his *refuge.*

"Ya know," Norman said, mopping his dripping forehead with a crumpled handkerchief, "y'all will find this to be the next best thing to drawing up your own plans. See that heap of catalogs on the table in the corner?" He motioned. "Well, you get to choose everything and I do mean everything...down to the very last detail."

Norman proceeded to go over our finances, income and obligations; his short fat fingers poked away on a black plastic calculator. He scribbled numbers on a pad of paper. Lorne and I answered his questions anxious to hear the verdict.

"Being a Vietnam vet you're entitled to a VA loan. In short...no down payment," he said, punching numbers on the calculator. "If you have a little something to put down, that's good. If not, that's okay too."

I took a deep breath and closed my eyes. *Please God,* I prayed silently.

Norman looked up. "From my calculations I see no reason why your loan should not be approved."

Lorne smiled and shook his head, then reached over to squeeze my hand.

"You can afford this house as long as you both continue to work."

Our search was over. This house would finally give our family roots.

"And think of this," Norman continued, blotting the sweat from his face. "You even get to pick the street you want to live on."

Norman slid the contract across the desk to Lorne and offered him a pen. Leaning forward, Lorne turned and smiled at me, then signed on the dotted line. I saw calmness on his face I'd never seen before. Then he handed the pen to me.

"It's your turn, Mrs. MacMillan," he said, grinning from ear to ear, reminding me of how he looked standing on the porch the night of our first date.

24

Nightmares returned

But things began to change.

During the next few weeks Lorne's nightmares returned. And once again he had no recollection and refused to discuss it. Maybe the honeymoon was over. After all, ours was a whirlwind romance...and marriage happened suddenly. One does not expect the unbridled passion of wedded bliss to last forever. Yet our bond grew stronger day by day, each needing the other almost in desperation. I had never felt like this before. We still made love almost every night, that is, when Lorne came home at a decent hour. But more and more he wandered in late, sometimes very late and never bothered to call. I would hurry home from work and fix dinner. Then feed the children by 6:30, if he wasn't home. Once they were in bed, I'd sit and wait and wait and wait, while countless dinners dried out on the stove. And if I questioned him, he'd turn on his heels and stomp off to bed. I had no idea what was wrong or what to do...and I had no one to turn to.

On the evenings Lorne did come home, he'd sit staring at the television after dinner, smoking one cigarette after the other, lost in thought someplace far away. It was like I wasn't even there. So I'd read. But his distant grim moods were short lived. Sooner or later he'd wander back to reality and his eyes would clear. Then he'd scoot closer to touch me, to please me, eager to make peace. Later as we lay in the dark, he'd gently caress me, reassuring me of his love.

"Baby, I'm sorry. I don't know why I act like that," he'd whisper, stroking my face with his fingers. "Something just comes over me. I can't explain."

And neither could I. I loved him so much. All I wanted was for our marriage to be solid and the children to be happy.

One night, the sound of a key in the lock startled me; I must have dozed off. I glanced at the clock over the TV. It was after 2:00 a.m. The front door opened. Lorne stepped into the dark foyer; he turned to lock the door fumbling with the deadbolt. Jamming his hands in his pockets, he made his way to the living room purposely placing one foot in front of the other, flaunting a sheepish grin. It was obvious he was plastered.

"Lorne, you're drunk," I accused, getting to my feet.

"Baby, somebody had a birthday," he slurred, "and drinks were on the house."

"You shouldn't be driving in that condition," I said, walking towards him. "You could have had an accident or worse yet killed someone."

"Don't be mad. I was just up the street. I didn't have to drive far," he pleaded; his blue eyes at half mast. "Gee, you look beautiful."

And just like that he changed the subject. It did no good to yell at him. He wrapped me in his arms and planted kisses all over my face. I loved him so much. It was hard to stay angry even when I tried.

"I think it's time to put you to bed," I said firmly, smiling to myself, "while you can still make it up the stairs." He was like a big kid. I took his hand leading him up to bed. His free hand reached out to touch me. He was out like a light the minute his head hit the pillow, leaving me to wrestle off his boots and undress him.

Lorne was seldom drunk but deep down his drinking concerned me. Alcoholism was a topic of which I had little experience. During my first marriage, Peter and I had pool parties at the house. There had been times I definitely had too much to drink. But the next day I wanted to die. The splitting headache and vomiting were unbearable.

Funny thing, Lorne never had a hangover.

25

The seed was planted

I saw a young mother at the market pushing her little one in a grocery cart, chattering as only a mother and child can do. I noted with envy the child's innocence and wonder, its dimpled knuckles, its pouting lips, each a masterpiece in God's creation. Now they were in front of me in the checkout line. As the mother unloaded her cart, she turned and noticed me smiling at her child.

"Hug and kiss your baby every chance you have," I said, " because one day you'll turn around twice and he'll be all grown up."

Scott, my meticulous take-charge son, who had always carried a grin in his pocket, had suddenly turned sullen, challenging my authority every time I turned my back. I tried to talk with him, but like with Lorne it was useless. I spent sleepless nights searching for an answer. It could be anything. My sudden marriage to Lorne or raging hormones taking over his young body like killer bees; or maybe the simple fact that he missed his dad.

But it went on for months. Scott was building a wall that I could not penetrate. To make matters worse, he and Lorne often engaged in shouting matches. Maybe in his young mind he was jealous of his stepfather, and was behaving like a jilted lover hurt and angry. But whatever the reason, I was losing. Scott was slipping through my fingers like water from a stream and it broke my heart.

One evening I was down on my hands and knees scrubbing heel marks off the white linoleum floor in the kitchen. My day at work had been rough. Scott appeared at the kitchen doorway, marched past me to the counter and lifted the lid off the cookie jar.

"No cookies," I called over my shoulder. "Dinner's almost ready."

A short time later I walked back into the kitchen, surprised to find Scott sneaking cookies.

"Put the cookies back and go up to your room until dinner is on the table," I said crossly.

At dinner, Scott moped through the meal, barely touching his food.

Finally I had enough. "Maybe, if you're so unhappy here," I said standing up, starting to clear the table, "you should go live with your father."

If looks could kill I'd be dead. Shoving his chair back from the table, Scott dashed upstairs. "I hate you," he yelled over the banister, slamming the door to his room.

No one said a word. I never meant what I said, the words just slipped out. But it was too late to take them back. I would never forget the hurt I saw in my son's eyes. The seed was planted and like a speeding car headed for a cliff there was nothing I could do to stop it.

December 1975

I apologized. I told Scott over and over how sorry I was; but by now his father had his foot in the door and was bringing out the heavy artillery.

Scott and I sat side by side on the bottom bunk bed talking quietly.

"Dad says he's lonely," Scott said, staring down at his tattered tennis shoes. "He said you kept all the kids and he doesn't have any."

Scott was by nature a sensitive, caring young man. Peter knew this and was lacing his mind with guilt. Day by day I watched my son struggle, wrestling with his decision. A week later the other shoe dropped and the stakes got higher. I learned Peter had offered to buy Scott a sailboat if he moved to Chicago. That was a crushing blow. I knew I had lost the battle.

Scott's decision was painful. Cory and Tiffy didn't say much; they seemed to be in a fog. I knew my son and I knew he was suffering in silence, afraid to tell anyone his true feelings. I knew what I had to do. No matter how much it hurt I had to find a way to help him make the transition. But I also knew the day would come when the novelty of moving to Chicago and owning expensive toys would wear off. That day he would know the pain of loneliness. And I knew that pain could be unbearable.

Numb with grief, I gathered the necessary paperwork Scott needed to start school in Chicago. I withdrew his birth certificate from the small box in the closet and ran my fingers over the paper. I remembered the day like it was yesterday. Printed in bold black letters was his name, date of birth, weight, and parents. My first born was leaving home.

I drove to school to pick up his records before Christmas break. Then I called my doctor and had Scott's medical records mailed to my office where I could sign for them.

The dread of Scott's departure hung in the air like someone awaiting an execution. Cory and Tiffy were withdrawn and barely talking. Lorne stayed out of the way, giving us room to handle our grief.

During the last few weeks I talked with Scott every chance I had. I knew he was stubborn and would never change his mind, even if he wanted to stay.

"Scott," I said one evening during a quiet talk, "I want you to remember how much I love you"…tears filled my eyes…"and know I'm going to miss you a lot."

I could not let him leave burdened with guilt. I could not do that to my son.

"I want you to know that I'm not angry because you chose to live with your dad. It was a hard decision to make," I said bravely. "A sailboat will offer you great opportunities and is something I could never afford to give you. And to tell the truth," I said honestly, "if I were in your shoes I'd probably make the same choice."

Christmas was quiet. Scott's belongings were boxed and sent to Chicago by UPS. Peter was flying into Houston to accompany him back on the plane. I packed his suitcase, tucking a sealed envelope between his tee shirts. The letter inside was meant to reassure him of my love and the special place he held in my heart that only he could fill.

I closed with…*You can always come home if you ever change your mind. All my love forever, Mom.*

December 30, 1975

Scott was only twelve when he moved to Chicago to live with his father.

26

Giving in too easily

Spring 1976

The torrential winter rains with their raging rivers of mud had all but dried up, leaving a path of destruction in their wake. But the newness of spring brought proof that life goes on. Our new house was finally under construction but far behind schedule.

"Feel like riding out to see the house?" Lorne asked, standing in the kitchen, his hands deep in his pockets. "It's a gorgeous day. I think it would do us both good."

He had strolled in long after midnight and knew he was in the doghouse.

"Sure...I guess," I said, staring out the window as I rinsed the breakfast dishes. "Give me a couple of minutes to change and situate the children."

The Sunday morning traffic was light. The brittle wind engulfed us on the bike, stinging my cheeks and numbing my fingers. I perched behind Lorne and clung to him. The warmth of his familiar body melted my anger and soothed my soul. For a while I felt safe and secure.

The naked wood frame of the house looked lonely against the clear blue sky, like a barren tree in winter. Lorne got off the bike and turned to face me. Putting his hands on his knees, he leaned down to look squarely into my face, smiling warily.

I always gave in too easily. I turned my head, but he took my hand and pulled me towards him and off the bike.

"I got the message," Lorne admitted. "You're still mad about last night."

"I'm able to get off by myself you know," I said, resisting his pull like a dog going to the vet.

Lorne ignored my stubbornness and led me into the house. Stepping over a maze of wall braces protruding from the floor, we surveyed the layout. Lorne ducked under a crossbeam and headed over to check out the plumbing. I stroked the fresh new wood, trying to imagine living here. As I looked around, I could only hope our new home would be the answer to Lorne's problems. Only time would tell.

Construction was finally moving forward and it should be time to celebrate, but the joy and laughter were missing. I worried about Lorne. Just the other day he told me he was having problems at work. And this was not the first time.

Lorne was a brilliant man. He had the mental capacity to calculate complex mathematical formulas in his head at the snap of a finger. Yet, feelings of insecurity gnawed at his self-esteem like terminal cancer, leaving him suspicious and vulnerable. He complained that the people at work were out to get him, purposely conspiring to make his life hell. He told me not to worry. He was dealing with it. But I did worry. Lorne had already changed jobs once since we were married, for similar reasons.

Then there was that speeding ticket I only recently learned about. To make matters worse he was driving his company car. Most of the time Lorne kept problems to himself. Even though I begged he chose not to involve me. Entangled in his silence I searched for a reason. At the same time I wrestled with my own feelings of loneliness and despair.

May 1, 1976

The day had finally arrived. Excited, the children and I stood behind Lorne on the porch, while he inserted the key into the lock, officially unlocking the door to our new home. It swung open and Lorne stepped in first, leading the procession. The strong smell of paint swept past us like a fleeing ghost.

"Wow," Cory exclaimed squeezing past us, Tiffy at his heels. They dashed down the hall to check out their new rooms. Lorne and I stood in the middle of the living room, drinking in our new home like a fine glass of wine.

"Well Baby, we finally did it," Lorne said, stepping up behind me. He wrapped his arms around my waist and pulled me to him, hugging me tightly. "I've waited a long time for this," he whispered in my ear. "A home."

Then he kissed me on the cheek and headed out the front door to help his brother and stepfather unload the U-Haul.

I stood motionless trying to absorb everything around me, imprinting the moment to memory. I grew calm as I pictured a crackling fire in the fireplace, lush plants and huge pillows on the hearth, Lorne in a leather chair, his feet propped on an ottoman. His tranquility softened by the burning embers. Maybe our new home would be the answer to my prayers and Lorne would finally find the peace he had been searching for.

While Lorne and his brother began to bring in the furniture, I wandered into the kitchen. Spacious glass windows covered one wall overlooking the backyard. I noticed the huge clods of red Texas clay piled in mounds behind the house and wondered what Lorne knew about growing grass because I hadn't a clue.

"Nancy, I need your help," he called from another room in the house.

"I'll be right there," I hollered back.

I walked through the living room greeted by the sounds of laughing children and barking dogs floating in through the open door. I smiled. This will be a fine place to raise my children. The divorce had been hard on them, uprooting their lives. But here they would have stability and a place to call home.

27

"No one understands"

May 28, 1976

For days, the children hovered three feet off the floor on a cloud of excitement. They were flying to Chicago to see Scott for the first time since he left and were staying the entire summer. Our home hummed with happiness as they crammed last minute "must haves" into their already bulging suitcases. I knew they missed their brother. Even though they didn't talk about it, I could see it in their eyes.

Cory's suitcase lay open on the bed. Cory was my game boy. If he had his way, he would take every game he had, leaving no room for clothes. I had to dig through two layers of games to double check to be sure he packed socks and underwear.

I was curled up on the couch reading when I heard Lorne unlock the front door. I looked at the clock; it was after midnight. It was another typical weekend, Lorne out until all hours and never bothering to call despite my protests and concerns. After a while I simply gave up.

I had rushed home from work to cook a special dinner just for the two of us. I even picked up fresh strawberries and shortcake, Lorne's favorite. With the children in Chicago, we had the whole house to ourselves but he never showed up.

"Where were you?" I confronted him, hurt and angry.

"I worked late and stopped for a few drinks," he said defensively, his words thick with alcohol. "After all, it's Friday night."

"You could have called so I wouldn't waste my time making dinner."

"Get off my back," he snapped. "I have enough problems without listening to you bitch." He walked over to the liquor cabinet and took out a bottle of Scotch.

Here we go again. I knew we were in for a long night.

"Lorne, you don't need another drink," I said gently.

"It's my house and if I want a drink, I'll have a drink," he stated sarcastically from the kitchen. He poured Scotch into a glass, opened the freezer and dropped ice cubes into the caramel-colored liquid.

I picked up my book, lowered my eyes and pretended to read. What in the hell was wrong? It's the same old question. I knew Lorne loved me. That wasn't the problem and our love life was great. He couldn't be jealous because he always knew where I was. My routine was simple, go to work and come home. Three days a week I went to the gym to work off tension. We seldom went out and never had anyone over. What kind of life was that? I couldn't get angry or out the door he'd fly into the night. So I bit my tongue and kept my mouth shut.

Lorne walked back into the living room and clicked on the TV. Sitting on the couch he set his drink down, pulled off his boots and put his feet on the coffee table. He lit a cigarette then proceeded to watch the *Tomorrow Show* like I wasn't even there.

There sat my husband, the love of my life behaving like a total stranger, isolated in his own private world. I set my book aside and turned to him. His eyes were distant, his thoughts elsewhere.

"Honey, what's wrong?" I asked, leaning on the arm of the couch. "Please tell me what's bothering you, maybe I can help?"

He slowly turned and looked at me. His face was slack; his eyes shadowed in the same sadness I'd seen before.

"Lorne, please talk to me," I begged.

Canned laughter filled the room from the nearby television.

He studied my eyes. "You wouldn't understand," he said grimly turning away. "No one understands."

"Lorne, I'm your wife. I love you. Please don't shut me out." I leaned closer and reached out to touch his leg. "Please let me try to understand."

I got up, walked around the coffee table, sat down next to him, and put my hand back on his leg. He watched my every move; his eyes brimmed with tears.

Invisible demons oozed from the pits of hell, taunting their helpless prey.

Lorne hesitated for a moment then spoke. "Baby...I can't get away from 'Nam. I'm still a prisoner and it won't let me go. It's always in my head hiding just below the surface. Daytime...nighttime...always. Horrible memories play over and over and over," his voice choked, tears slipping down his cheeks. "I can't get them to stop!"

He paused, staring past me into the kitchen, his eyes unblinking. Then he continued, "My platoon was first on the ground. Our mission was to search and destroy. It was our job to clear a way through the jungle for the rest of the troops. A Huey chopper flew us in, literally dropping us in a landing zone, out in the open...totally exposed. Then tail up, it took off...leaving us behind." He went on, "As we hit the ground we made a mad dash for the jungle, not knowing if a sniper's bullet would tear through our guts. Or worse yet, were there gooks in there waiting for us? The smell of death and shit saturated the air. You wanted to puke." His eyes were glazed. "The jungle's thick and hot. There's no air to breathe. Breaking trail meant chopping through dense bamboo, sometimes advancing only twenty five yards in an hour. It was a bitch and this went on from morning until night, twelve to fourteen hours a day." His hands trembled as he pulled another cigarette from the pack and lit it. "Point had to break trail. I always walked point." He took a drag and exhaled slowly. "You learn fast that the point usually survives. It was the guys behind you that die."

I was stunned by the reality of what Lorne was saying. He was sharing a past I would never experience and a terror I would never know except through his pain. At 23 years old, he endured something so horrible it haunted him day and night.

"I met a man over there who was my platoon leader," he went on. "We got to be close buddies. His name was Proctor, a military man in for the duration. We talked a lot. He showed me pictures of his wife and kids. Proctor respected me. He would sit and listen to what I had to say. We even shared some ideas." Lorne leaned forward, resting his elbows on his knees; he twisted the gold leopard ring on his finger. "It got to be that I looked up to him like a father, the father I never had," he said through quiet tears. "You know, if I could've handpicked a dad, it would've been this man."

He lowered his head, rubbing his face with both hands. Then he went on. "Our platoon landed in Da Nang. We're humping rucksacks down this trail in the jungle—the brush dense and overgrown, the hot sticky air teeming with mosquitoes. I was walking point...and scared...you're always scared. Your hearing gets razor sharp. You listen to the jungle like an animal. Then I heard it. Up ahead, off to the left, the snap of a single twig. I hit the ground and rolled off the side of the road, laying flat. I started firing. So did the guy behind me...Proctor was third." Lorne paused. "He didn't hit the ground in time...they got him. The lousy bastards got him," he sobbed, his voice seething with pain. "Nancy, they killed him." Turning, he looked at me, tears dripping from his chin. "They blew him away like he was nothing and it was my fault. He got the bullet that was meant for me." His eyes never left mine. "We got the sons-of-bitches that attacked us...every last one of them. Then we went back. I picked up Proctor and held him in my arms. The shot was fatal. I never hurt so badly. Just like my dad, he was dead."

I could feel my husband's pain; my heart ached for him.

Lorne sobbed shamelessly. "Where was God?" His swollen eyes searched my face. "Where was He? How can God be here and not there?" His face contorted. "It's not fair. It should have been me who died...not him...it should have been me." His head dropped into my lap, heavy sobs shaking his body. I wept with him as I ran my fingers through his hair, trying to ease his suffering, trying to make it go away, but knowing I never could.

After a while I stood up, leaned over and turned off the light. Taking him by the hand, I led him down the hallway to our bedroom. He sobbed softly as I gently undressed him. I helped him into bed then took off my clothes and crawled in next to him. Pulling him close I held him in my arms until he fell asleep, a deep restless sleep. In the wee hours of morning, I lay staring into the darkness reliving Lorne's nightmare over and over in my mind.

A few nights later, we were watching TV after dinner when I mentioned Vietnam. Without saying a word Lorne crushed his cigarette in the ashtray, picked up his car keys and stalked out of the house. As I sat alone I heard the car pull out of the driveway and then peal down the street. Why did he always get so angry with me?

I was still awake when the car pulled into the driveway. I looked at the clock. It was very late. I heard a key in the door and knew Lorne was home safe. Life went on as usual. We continued to have our ups and downs, but neither that night nor Proctor were ever mentioned again.

28

What now?

January 20, 1977

It had been another rough day at the dealership. Too many customers, too many unresolved problems. I looked forward to a quiet evening, curling up with a new book I picked up at Borders on my lunch hour. I set the mail and my keys on top of the TV and hurried down the hall to change. All I wanted to do was get out of my pantyhose which by now had me feeling like a stuffed sausage. No sooner had I pulled on a pair of jeans than I heard Lorne charge through the front door.

"Nancy," he bellowed from the other room.

"I'm back here," I called out, buttoning the fly on my jeans.

The sound of Lorne's cowboy boots stomping down the hall told me he was upset about something. *What now?* Every day was a new adventure living with Lorne. Some were good, some were bad, and I never knew what lurked in the attic of his mind. But one thing I did know; he was my husband and I was in love with him and that alone made up for a lot.

Lorne barged into the bedroom and plopped on the edge of the bed opposite the dresser; a look of agitation etched his face.

"You'll never guess who called me today at work," he said sarcastically, watching me finish dressing in the mirror. He stretched out his right leg, slid his hand into the pocket of his Levis and pulled out his Zippo, lighting the cigarette resting between his lips. "Shirley!" he fumed, the smell of lighter fluid saturating the air. "She called me at work…after I've specifically told her not to!"

He minced few words in his disapproval of his ex-wife and the way she was raising their son, Tommy. The child had absolutely no ground rules.

"Is everything all right?" I asked, clipping my slacks on a hanger.

"No, everything's not all right, damn it!" Lorne seethed. "It seems Tommy has been acting up in school again. Shirley says she can't take it anymore. My God, Nancy, he's only in kindergarten!" Lorne was furious. "She wants me to pick him up on Saturday. He's moving in with us…permanently!"

I was stunned. Reality hit with a G-force. *I was about to have another child.* I stared across the bed at the back of Lorne's head. My mind scrambled to escape but was jerked back like a yoyo. *God help us.* Lorne's mental state was hanging by a thread; I worried that this added pressure could send him over the edge.

Tommy was only six and all boy. I knew Shirley loved him, but she lacked basic parenting skills, a fact that was evident the first time Tommy spent the night.

It was the crack of dawn; everyone was still asleep when I heard an unusual noise coming from the kitchen. I got up and tiptoed into the living room. Through the kitchen doorway, I saw Tommy standing on a chair at the stove, a carton of eggs on the counter, a frying pan on the burner.

"Tommy, what are you doing?" I inquired, trying to stay calm.

"Cookin' breakfast, I'm hungry," he replied innocently.

It seemed his mother let him cook whatever he wanted as long as he was quiet. We could have burned to death in our sleep!

Maybe I could help Tommy. He would see what a real family was like and I could tutor him with his lessons while I made dinner. Besides I loved children. I gradually talked myself into the idea. After all, Lorne had accepted my three without a word. So what's one more?

"Doesn't look like we have much of a choice," I said, trying to sound positive. "What did he do that was so bad that she wants to get rid of him?"

"All I know is what she said…he stands on his chair in class and shouts across the room, disrupting the other children. It seems he's done this before and she was told to correct his behavior," his face flushed with anger. "He's flunking kindergarten! Can you believe that? And it's all her fault. She lets him stay up until all hours watching TV."

I walked around the bed. Lorne continued to watch me in the mirror. I sat down next to him and kissed him on the cheek.

"Honey, we'll do what we have to. Besides, what's one more child?" I was startled by my own words. I only prayed Lorne could handle it. "What time are you supposed to pick up Tommy on Saturday?"

"She said to come by about one." Lorne stared at the floor, his shoulders stooped.

"Well, now that we know what we're doing Saturday," I said, sounding a bit too cheerful, "why don't you go fix a drink and watch some TV, while I make dinner." I stood up and put my hand on his shoulder. "Give yourself some time to get used to the idea."

"Baby, I love my son," Lorne said, sounding defeated. He looked up at me. "I hate the way Shirley's raising him, but I can't get custody because she's his mother. A child always goes to the mother."

I took Lorne's face in my hands and leaned down to kiss him on the lips.

"Everything will work out fine, you wait and see," I said, trying to believe it myself.

"I love you, Nancy. You'll never know how much." He stood up, squeezed my hands and left the room, looking like he was carrying the weight of the world on his shoulders.

Tommy's kindergarten lasted only half a day, which meant I had to act fast and find a sitter for him. This would not be easy. I had no real friends. I was embarrassed by Lorne's erratic behavior, so I preferred to keep to myself.

Fortunately, luck was with me. I found a sweet little woman who lived down the street who was more than happy to watch Tommy after school, plus she was affordable. I could pick him up after work and take a few extra minutes to chat with a neighbor like a normal person.

The atmosphere around the house was strained with the addition of a new child. Cory and Tiffy tried to tolerate Tommy, but I could see that they resented the intrusion on their privacy when Tommy barged into their rooms with his insatiable curiosity. Sparks would fly at the drop of a hat.

There were some wordy battles while our family adjusted to the change, but eventually things got better. Lorne's company required him to travel a few nights a week, which gave us all a little relief from his surly moods. I took on the extra work and responsibility, and I had to correct Tommy, not Lorne.

On weeknights I insisted Tommy sit at the table and do his homework while I cooked dinner. He struggled with his alphabet, writing the letters over and over. He was not a happy boy. I watched pencils sail across the kitchen in frustration, which I insisted he pick up. Tommy's job was to sweep under the table after dinner while Cory and Tiffy did the dishes. His six-year-old mind resisted, and he often slammed the broom and dustpan to the floor and stomped out of the room.

"I don't want to go to bed," Tommy complained at bedtime. "My mom lets me stay up as long as I want."

"Well, this is your home now, and there are rules," I said firmly. "Cory and Tiffy follow the rules and so will you. Rules are important lessons in handling life," I said, walking him into the bedroom.

Maybe that was hard for a six year old to comprehend, but I made my point. I leaned over the trundle bed, tucked him in and kissed him goodnight. "I love you," I whispered in his ear.

Gradually Tommy became part of the family. His grades improved rapidly, and to everyone's surprise he made B's on school papers. I guessed all along he was smart, and I was delighted to watch him blossom into a happy, well adjusted little boy with an infectious laugh...and a twinkle in his eye like his dad's.

29

Falling into place

May 31, 1977

Traffic was at a standstill on Interstate 10 as Memorial Day weekend was underway. Inching my way home from work, I felt like I was caught in a cattle drive going nowhere. Cars crammed with folding chairs, coolers of Budweiser, camping gear and cranky children encircled me as we crawled out of the city, each longing to escape the pressures of everyday life. I reached down and turned off the air conditioner to keep the car from overheating, then rolled down the window. The old cowboy in the truck next to me had been picking his nose for the last half of a mile.

Thoughts of the children crossed my mind. I grinned while remembering their happy voices at breakfast, contrary to the usual squabbling. Tiffy had even crawled under Tommy's bed to rescue his missing tennis shoe and then showed him how to tie his own shoelaces, making the laces into long bunny rabbit ears. If only there were more days like this.

Life seemed to be falling into place. Tommy's angry streaks had passed; there were no more temper tantrums when he didn't get his way, and house rules were no longer an issue as he carved his niche into our family. Also, Lorne's parenting role had done a complete turnaround. Having Tommy live with us gave him something of his own to focus on, offering him the stability he lacked and making him seem less distant.

That evening, at 7:45 p.m., the doorbell rang. Shirley was late as usual to pick up Tommy for the weekend. Lorne answered the door and showed her into the living room. Supposedly she had planned a short trip out of town but Lorne didn't recall the details.

Tommy scampered back to his room to fetch something he forgot.

I remember my shock the first time I saw Shirley. She was nothing like I had imagined. Lorne never talked about her except to say they met while she was singing at a nightclub. He liked her style. He did mention she was slim with long red hair. I tried not to dwell on it; still his words haunted me with a vision of my enemy, wife number one. But meeting her face to face was an eye opener. Shirley was now overweight and short, or maybe the extra pounds made her appear short and much older than she really was. Makeup was nonexistent, and short mousy brown hair edged a round face. I knew her appearance embarrassed Lorne…and the fact that she was once his wife.

"I'll have Tommy back by seven on Monday." Shirley flashed a Cheshire cat grin as she headed out the door with Tommy in tow lugging his little brown suitcase. "I promise," she yelled back over her shoulder.

"Fine," Lorne snipped, watching Tommy scramble into her car.

That weekend Tiffy had her first dance recital. When the curtain went up she saw her family and grandparents in the front row. I knew she had butterflies, but she forced a smile and focused on me, ignoring the sea of strange eyes watching. The show was a hit and Tiffy beamed as she took her final bow with the chorus line. I clapped until my palms turned red.

On Monday, we went to Astroworld, Houston's biggest amusement park. Family outings were a rare treat because of Lorne's mood swings, but the day was perfect. We indulged in junk food and rode all the rides at least once. Exhausted, we arrived home in time for a light supper before Tommy was due to return to the fold.

Seven o'clock came and went but no Tommy appeared. Maybe Shirley was trapped in traffic with everyone heading home at the same time. Lord willing, they were safe. Besides, Shirley was a bit of a flake at times, and maybe she just lost track of time.

I cleaned up the kitchen while the children took their baths. Lorne settled in front of the TV awaiting Tommy's return. At nine o'clock, Lorne called Shirley's apartment but there was no answer. I worried about an accident but said nothing; Lorne was upset enough, pacing the floor like a caged bear. Finally he picked up his keys.

"I'm going to her apartment," he announced, heading towards the door. "Maybe they'll stop there first, and I can bring Tommy home rather than wait here any longer."

The children were asleep when I heard Lorne's car pull into the driveway. The clock read 10:45. I rushed to the front door, arriving just as it opened. Lorne stood there alone, his face ashen, his eyes blank.

"Lorne, what's wrong? Where's Tommy?" I said, grabbing his arm. "Did you go to her apartment?"

He stood looking at me for a moment. "Yes, I went to her apartment." One brow arched and a cynical grin crossed his face. "The bitch is moving." Then he laughed.

I was confused. "What do you mean, she's moving?"

"The scheming bitch planned this all along," he announced, storming past me to the liquor cabinet. "Seven o'clock, my ass."

I'd never seen him this angry.

He pulled out a bottle of Scotch and went to the kitchen. "This weekend she picked up and moved to a bigger apartment. Says she has room for Tommy now that he's better. He gets good grades and behaves in class so she took him back," he said sarcastically, mocking her words. He put the glass to his lips, took a drink and then turned to me.

"She kidnapped him! The bitch! Plain and simple and there isn't a damn thing I can do about it. Our terrific court system is slanted towards the mother even though it may not be in the child's best interest. And you know as well as I do Tommy should not be living with her. It's not fair."

Hurt and defeated, Lorne gave up. But from that day forward he hated Shirley with a passion for taking away his only son. And from that day forward, our lives began to crumble from the backlash.

30

A walking time bomb

Time is predictable. It lingers for no one as it travels forward through the days and the years of one's life. We can neither stop it where we might like to linger, nor go back to a better time, or begin again. Lorne and I stumbled down the rocky road we traveled. Yet I held firm to the belief that our love would defeat his demons from the past.

Many newspaper articles discussed Vietnam vets and the problems they encountered trying to cope with life after combat. Our nation was confused about its involvement in Southeast Asia and the people grew numb. No one was prepared to hear the truth; it was too bizarre. These men and women were simply told to get on with their lives, bury whatever they had seen and done. After all, they were home—and they were alive. Dreams of happiness evaporated like spit on a hot sidewalk, when the pieces no longer fit and there were no answers.

I devoured every article on Vietnam I could find: stories of men who were barely old enough to shave; stories of how they lived and died for their country in a God-forsaken jungle on the other side of the world. Vivid accounts of death and how it smelled; and the paralyzing fear that flowed through their veins. These stories only scratched the surface of the torment the troops were forced to endure. Lorne was not alone. There were thousands like him...each with his own nightmare. And I wept for them all.

Lorne seemed to have no control over his moods, pivoting from lucid happiness to furious pits of hell. At times he was a walking land mine ready to explode on impact. I thought, if only he would confide in me, maybe I could come up with something that would help. When I suggested counseling, he blew up.

"That's for crazy people," he bellowed, "and I'm not crazy."

Anything would have been better than the silent wars we fought. It was like tiptoeing through a minefield. I was afraid to say anything that might set him off so I remained silent. If only I had someone to talk to...but there was no one.

After the kidnapping, as Lorne referred to it, he didn't seem to care about anything anymore. He defiantly stayed out late, coming home drunk whenever he pleased. If challenged, he became hostile and stormed back out into the night, or he'd simply pass out on the couch. I wasn't afraid; Lorne never struck me. But every once in a while I'd get too close in the heat of an argument and he'd push me, launching me across the room like a volley ball. Incredibly he always seemed to aim for a soft landing.

Most evenings I turned off the television with its programs slanted towards murder and violence, preferring to sit in the stillness reading as I waited for my husband. Peace and quiet is a luxury of the lonely.

One evening, that peace and quiet was shattered when Lorne pulled into the driveway. It was still daylight, but I knew he was drunk the moment he stepped through the door. I was glad the children were in Chicago with their father for the summer, and didn't have to see what was about to happen. I could tell that Lorne was already in a foul mood for some reason and looking for an argument. With rage in his eyes he started towards me.

And for the first time I tasted fear.

"Lorne, stop," I yelled, inching backwards.

His face looked strange and unfamiliar, almost crimson, as he crossed the living room. I bumped against the raised hearth of the fireplace...I was trapped.

"Lorne, calm down," I begged tearfully, groping behind my back. "Let's sit down and talk, please?" My fingers touched the hard cold metal of the fireplace tools. Taking a firm grip, I wiggled one free and yanked it around in front of me...the brass shovel.

"Don't come any closer," I threatened, tears distorting my vision.

With glazed eyes he advanced.

He was not going to push me again. Grabbing the handle with both hands, I lifted the shovel and swung in an arch from right to left. The edge of the shovel sliced across his outstretched palm, instantly producing a gash of red blood.

Stunned, Lorne stopped in his tracks. "You've cut me," he said in disbelief, staring at his hand. His face softened.

"I warned you but you didn't listen," I cried hysterically, "and don't you ever push me again...ever!" Angry tears streamed down my face. I stood my ground, holding the shovel in front of me like a saber. "I didn't do anything wrong!" I screamed at him. "And I don't deserve to be treated like this."

Lorne looked crushed. "Baby, I'm sorry," he said, unable to look me in the eye. "I don't know why this happens. You know I'd never hurt you." Cradling his bloody hand he turned and slowly walked towards the couch. Sitting down, he covered his face with both hands as blood tickled down his arm. His sobs broke my heart. The room darkened into the shadows of evening.

After that night I knew I had to talk to someone to save my own sanity. Gathering all my courage, I let go of my pride and called Lorne's mother. Joan never had a daughter and was grateful I called. And for the first time, she learned of her son's haunting dreams and our troubled marriage. At last, the two women in Lorne's life who loved him the most united, but neither had an answer.

31

I knew better than to ask

August 1978

I was surprised to see Lorne walk in the door before dinner. This made four nights in a row. Why the sudden transformation? I knew better than to ask. One thing was sure—it couldn't last any more than I could sing opera. Usually Lorne prowled bars like an alley cat after dark, talking with people who knew only what he wanted them to know, while I tossed and turned trying to sleep but imagining the worst.

"Hi there," I called from the kitchen, taking another plate from the cupboard. "How was your day?"

Lorne mumbled something as he sulked past the kitchen door. He looked tired, drawn.

"Got any wine?" he asked dryly, already absorbed in the evening news on TV.

I tried to discourage his drinking but learned long ago not to make it obvious, or he'd walk out the door and find someone else to drink with. I opened a bottle of wine.

Every evening was the same with no hope of conversation, and this particular evening was no different. After dinner, I picked up my book, *My Mother, Myself*, from the coffee table and settled into the corner of the loveseat. Lorne sat on the couch glued to the TV, a cigarette cradled in his fingers. He had barely spoken a word all evening. If only I could read his mind.

Life had been calm all week, with no quarrels or sudden outbursts and I wasn't about to push it. I was grateful for quiet days when my insides weren't tied up in knots. I actually felt almost peaceful, an indulgence I wasn't used to.

After an hour of individual solitude, Lorne got up and headed down the hall towards the bedroom. I watched him over the top of my book. Then something nudged me to get up and follow him. I had no idea why. He was most likely going to the bathroom.

When I stepped into the hallway I noticed that our bedroom door was shut. That was odd. With the children in Chicago we enjoyed the freedom of parading around half dressed, never closing off the rooms. Upon reaching the door I opened it. Total darkness sucked me in; something was wrong. My heart pounded loudly in my ears, my eyes searched for Lorne. The master bathroom was dark and deserted. Then I noticed a sliver of light outlining the door to our walk-in closet. Monkey chatter screamed in my head. I rounded the bed to the closet, put my hand on the knob, turned it and pulled the door open.

Shards of light struck my eyes like mace. Then I saw Lorne. The man I loved more than life itself. He stood motionless, his eyes unblinking, his back against the clothes on my side of the closet. In his hands he held the Viet Cong rifle he'd smuggled back into the states, a souvenir hidden in his duffle bag, a token of terror. The lethal gray weapon leaned vertically against his body. Against his Levi's, against the light blue shirt that brought out the color of his eyes, paused like a snake ready to strike. His lips were sealed around the end of the cold metal barrel, his thumb taut on the trigger.

Without thinking, my right hand shot out like a bolt of lightning, grabbing the barrel and yanking it down towards the floor. At that split second Lorne pulled the trigger. "BAMMM." The explosion was deafening as the deadly stench of gunpowder permeated our nostrils.

Suicide was the intent. But instead the force of the blast ripped away the carpet, sending concrete shrapnel ricocheting throughout the closet, whirling in all directions, slashing jagged holes in the door and nearby clothing. By a miracle from God we escaped without a scratch. Unfortunately, the human mind is more fragile.

Sudden shock has an ingenious way of numbing the senses, blocking the horrific pain of reality. Time stopped. Confusion circled my awareness like an airplane trying to land. After a moment I took a deep breath and my eyes focused on Lorne slumped against the clothing, his head down, his eyes closed. I reached over and gently extracted the dangling rifle from his fingers. I backed out of the closet and slipped the gun under the bed. Lorne never moved; his pale face was blank of expression. I grasped his hand and lifted it to my mouth, kissing his palm; I held it to my cheek. Tilting my head naively, I looked up into his empty eyes.

"Lorne, I love you so much," I whispered in a tiny voice I did not recognize. "Please don't leave me. I don't want to live without you."

Then I took his hand and led him from the closet, guiding him back to the living room. He shuffled down the hall behind me, dazed and disoriented. I settled him on the couch, turned off all the lights and sat down, drawing him to me until his head rested on my lap.

I looked down at my husband and stroked his cheek with the back of my hand. Lorne sobbed. His body shook with hard, racking jolts.

"Easy now," I cooed in the flickering light of the television. Running my fingers through his hair, curls encircled them like tentacles. "It's all over. Don't worry. Everything's going to be all right."

I stared off into nothingness. The quiet numbing was like a powerful drug that allowed me to breathe deeply without feeling anything. No anger...no sadness...no pity...no tears. My body was a vacuum, empty and hollow with an ebony black hole in my soul...my dreams had just died.

No one can prepare to handle a suicide attempt. Instructions are not printed in a First Aid manual or listed in the front pages of the telephone book. Shame and fear are tightly inter-woven, causing the suffocating sensation of helplessness and isolation, being cut off from the human race, totally alone. Isolated on an island in the middle of nowhere, one shattered human being trying to comfort another.

32

My dark secret

The clock continued to tick; minutes and hours swirled by unnoticed. Days blurred into weeks. I went to work every day like normal; we needed the money. I could not afford the luxury of a nervous breakdown. But my reality was far from normal. I went through the motions of mindless routine while my insides crawled with the haunting echoes and images of what I had seen. No one knew or suspected my dark secret. And Lorne was in denial.

When I did mention that night, he stormed out in a silent rage, returning long after I was asleep, reeking of wine and cigarette smoke.

Embarrassment kept me from telling anyone. What would I say? The truth would only frighten and shock people, especially my down-to-earth Midwest family. The truth was something you read about in the newspaper or see on the news, something that happens to someone else, not to your own flesh and blood. I knew they would fear for the children and me. I didn't want to worry them. Ohio was so far away. Besides, there was nothing anyone could do. I had to deal with this myself, even though I had no clue where to start. At times it all seemed like a bad dream...until I opened the closet door. Gaping holes and shredded clothes still on their hangers removed any doubt. I searched for the strength to focus on what to do next. It was all up to me.

Three weeks passed before I gathered enough courage to make the phone call I knew I had to make.

Saturday sunshine spilled boldly across the white chenille bedspread where I sat cradling the phone in my lap. Feeling the warmth of the sun on my skin, I sat up straight, took a deep breath and dialed the number I had copied from the phone book the day after the incident... the incident, what a strange name to call it.

"VA Hospital," a strong male voice answered.

"I...I need to talk to someone about an attempted suicide," I said softly. This was the first time I had said the words out loud. I felt like I was going to vomit.

"Just a moment, please."

Silence on the other end of the line magnified my thoughts. Lorne would be furious if he knew I was making this call. Maybe I should hang up before it goes any further.

"This is Dave, how can I help you?" said a soft spoken voice interrupting my choice.

"I hope...I didn't know who else to call," I stammered. My leg was crossed; my right foot was jiggling like crazy. "My husband is a Vietnam vet. About three weeks ago he tried to kill himself."

"I'm glad you called," Dave said, without hesitating. "First of all," he paused, "I want you to know I'm your friend and I'm here to help you." I heard genuine compassion in his voice, while he coaxed me to trust him. "I've dealt with many situations like yours. And I can help, that is, if you'll let me."

"Thank you," I said meekly, suddenly self-conscious. I hoped he wouldn't ask my name. I wanted to remain anonymous. Lorne would be livid if he knew I had told anyone, especially a stranger. After all, this was a family matter, not something you broadcast to the rest of the world.

Can you tell me what happened?" Dave continued.

I began reliving that night. Vivid pictures flashed across my mind. Images I wanted to forget, yet knowing I never would.

"We hadn't been arguing or anything," I remembered saying.

It felt like my words were running together. But once I started I couldn't stop. I had to get it all out. The relief of telling someone else felt like metal shackles slipping from my ankles. I felt like I was part of the human race again, alive and breathing, no longer a silent shadow walking among the living.

"I want you to remember one thing," Dave said. "I'm on your side, okay?"

"Okay," I said, almost giddy with relief. I sat up straight anticipating the solution to the problem, the answer to my prayers.

"Now...my recommendation is that your husband needs to come in for an evaluation."

"And how do we do that?" I asked naively.

"You ask him to set up an appointment..."

"Well, I know he won't," I interrupted.

"It only takes one signature to have him committed and only then can he get the help he needs."

This was not the answer I wanted to hear. I wanted something easy.

"Isn't there any other way?" I pleaded, more frightened than ever.

"This is the only way to start the program. We have to get him in here to help him. If he won't come in on his own...with your signature we can come and pick him up."

I sat petrified, my eyes wide with fear. "I can't do that," I said.

Pure panic crept over me. Now I was scared. "My husband always says he fought for his country in Vietnam and no one is going to take away his freedom. This is his right as an American citizen, freedom and the pursuit of happiness. If I signed those papers I would be the one taking away his freedom...Me!" I took a deep breath. "Besides he has a gun. And there's no way he'd go without a fight."

"We're primed for situations like that," Dave said calmly.

"Well I'm not primed for a situation like that!" I said boldly. I stood up, carrying the phone with me as I walked around the bed, stretching the cord as far as it would reach. By now all I wanted to do was hang up and find a cigarette. I never should have called.

"You could pick him up, take him in, and hold him for an evaluation. But it wouldn't last." My voice grew higher. "He's a good salesman. Before you know it, he'd convince you that he's better and you'd release him. Then he'd come looking for me!" I was scaring myself more by the minute. "I would be the one who had him committed. I would be the one who had him locked up. I know he loves me but no one is going to take away his freedom and put him away...*not even me.*"

Without a second thought I hung up the receiver.

33

Jaw muscles twitched

It was all like a bad dream and I couldn't wake up. I remember reading a book written by Robert A. Heinlein, *A Stranger in a Strange Land*. The title seemed to mirror my life and I knew I was destined to make the journey alone. I was walking on a tightrope. I must proceed with caution. One thing was sure…Lorne must never know I made that phone call. I buried the phone number under a turquoise pendent in my jewelry box. He would never think to look there but I could still reach it in an emergency.

I lay awake unable to sleep, feeling abandoned and miserable. I finally gave up and groped for my cigarettes on the nightstand. I struck a match and inhaled deeply, allowing the nicotine to rush through my bloodstream, numbing the edginess. Exhaling, I watched the lazy white cloud expand and then dissipate in the dim blue light of my hanging lamp. If only I could disappear so easily. Lorne's drinking had accelerated since the night of "the incident." Most nights I went to bed alone.

The monkey chatter would not cease, pitching painful questions I could not answer. Answers I didn't want to know. Was Lorne really taking solace with his buddies or was he in the arms of another woman, a warm body to ease his pain, someone who did not know his secret? The thought terrified me as much as his suicide attempt. In either case I could lose him.

Some nights I was still up when he wandered in. Barely saying a word, he'd plop on the couch, turn on the TV and stare at the screen until he dozed off. Then in the wee hours of morning, he'd get up and come to bed, leaving his clothes in a heap on the floor. Sometimes he'd reach for me in the dark and we'd make love. Other times he'd roll over and face the wall. But I was drawn to him like a moth to a flame. Sliding across the sheets I'd fit my body against his, longing for anything from him if only his warmth. My sin…I loved him too much.

I turned in my sleep, automatically reaching for my husband. But my hand touched cold empty sheets. I opened one eye and glanced at the clock. It was 4:00 a.m. An alarm went off in my head; the bars close at two. Unable to fall back to sleep I slipped out of bed, wandered out into the hall and turned on the light. Shivering in a thin nightgown, I made my way to the living room. There in the shadows Lorne slept on the couch, fully clothed, curled in a fetal position. Still half asleep, I shuffled barefoot across the carpet; my only thought was to coax my husband to bed where he would be more comfortable.

"Lorne," I whispered, leaning over him, gently laying my hand on his shoulder.

Suddenly, his eyes snapped open. He leapt from the couch, landing in a tight crouching position. His jaw muscles twitched in the dim light, his fists clenched at his chest, ready to strike. He scared me to death.

"LORNE!" I shouted, backing away, "IT'S ME, NANCY!"

Hearing my voice, his eyes came into focus and his facial expression softened. He was groggy and shaken, but he realized where he was and straightened up, letting his hands drop to his side.

"God damn it, Nancy," he reprimanded me, "don't ever do that again. I could have hurt you bad. And God knows I don't ever want to do that." Shaking his head, he ran his fingers through his hair. "Nancy, you just don't understand. You have no idea what I'm capable of doing. Promise me you'll never do that again."

"I promise," I said timidly, sinking into the couch. I reached up and turned on the lamp.

Lorne sat down next to me, his brow creased, confusion obscuring his face. He lit a cigarette, leaned forward, rested his elbows on his knees, and stared out into the dark kitchen.

"Baby, I've seen and done things I can't tell you about. Terrible things," he said, not looking at me. "The jungle in Nam was hell. And the nights were worse. Black as pitch, you couldn't see your hand in front of your face; I never saw anything like it. You sleep with one eye open. You never knew when one of those gooks in their black pajamas would reach out and stick a knife in your gut. Couldn't see the little bastards but you knew they were there. You couldn't hear 'em but you could smell 'em. Never knew who would get it next. Which sorry bastard would get his throat slit?"

I cringed at the thought of what he was saying.

"One thing I knew," he continued, "I wasn't going down without one hell of a fight."

34

Pulsating blue strobe light

July 1979

I watched Lorne weave his way through the crowd and around the dance floor, sidestepping heated bodies writhing to the pounding beat of *Maneater*. He gingerly guarded the two drinks he held high over his head. The pulsating blue strobe light gave the illusion of make-believe; the shifting mass of skin and color moved like animated robots.

The Rainbow Room was a favorite hangout on the weekends when Lorne felt like having me along. A crowded, smoky hole-in-the-wall, it was a place where couples could shelve the pressures of everyday life and for a few short hours feel young and invincible. These were the weekends I lived for...a time when Lorne wanted me by his side.

But this is what hurt. Lorne seemed happiest when he was out with other people, instead of at home with me. After several drinks his serious facade melted like an ice cube in summer and he'd loosen up, talk to other people...and pay attention to me. Attention I craved...the more unstable my life, the greater my need. On those weekends I dressed to please him. My goal was to turn him on and bring him home where he belonged, one day for good.

Lorne approached the table, his eyes fixated on me. I glowed with contentment. Setting the drinks down, he reached for my hand and guided me to the dance floor. Alcohol released his inhibitions; he no longer cared what people thought. He found a small opening in the crowd, squeezed in, and pulled me with him. Soon the music changed to a slow dance. Reaching up, I wrapped my arms around his neck, laying my head against his chest. He held me close and kissed the top of my head, gently rocking to the music. No matter how much torment he put me through, I knew I could never leave him.

The music stopped at 2 a.m. and the house lights came up, revealing a dense cloud of smoke hovering above the dance floor. Couples began to leave. Lorne helped me slip into my jacket. Then, putting his arm around my waist, he guided me through the crowd towards the exit.

"Hey you two, how about stopping by the house for a night cap?" came a voice from behind us.

"Gee, thanks for asking," I replied without thinking, "but we're really tired. Can we take a rain check?"

"Sure, no problem, see you guys soon," the man called out, heading into the parking lot.

Without warning, Lorne dropped his arm from around my waist and took off towards our car. Hiking up my long skirt, I ran after him, but my heels made it impossible to match his stride. When I reached the car, he had unlocked my door and was getting in on his side. The door slammed and I realized I had spoken out of turn. Lorne was angry. The tires squealed loudly as he barreled out into the empty street. Opening the window, he lit a cigarette and inhaled deeply.

"Can I have one, please?" I asked softly.

He shook one from the pack, handed it to me and pressed the lighter on the dash; his eyes never left the road.

Cool night air swirled in through the open window. Overhead, the star laden sky was endless and clear, a welcome change from the stuffy nightclub. I sat quietly looking out the window, hoping the storm would pass. I didn't want to fight. We seldom went out and I was looking forward to going home and making love like we used to.

"Honey, I'm sorry I didn't ask you first," I finally said, gently placing my hand on his leg.

"Forget it," Lorne snapped.

"I'm just tired and wanted to go home," I continued. "Besides if I had one more drink, I'd probably throw up."

"I said forget it," Lorne ordered, bearing down on the gas pedal.

I pulled back my hand, put it in my lap and turned towards the window.

A huge Texas moon hung high over our solitary car, but darkness surrounded the deserted country road in the middle of nowhere.

"Are you going to be mad at me the rest of the night?"

Lorne slammed on the brakes, thrusting our bodies hard against the seat belts. He shoved the gearshift into park, and got out, leaving the car and me in the middle of the road with the door wide open. He walked to the front of the car with his hands in his pockets, crossed in front of the headlights, and took off up the shoulder of the road.

I sat stunned. Unbuckling my seat belt, I hiked up my skirt and crawled over the console into the driver's seat. I pulled his door shut, put the car into drive and followed him up the road.

"Lorne, I'm sorry," I called out the open window. "Please get back in the car."

"Get out of here and leave me alone," he yelled over his shoulder, squinting into the headlights.

"Please, Lorne," I begged. "It's late and its pitch black out here." By now my head was throbbing. "I won't say another word, I promise. Just please get back in the car and let me take you home."

"GET THE FUCK AWAY FROM ME!" he bellowed across the open field.

"Lorne, please," I appealed, tears streaming down my cheeks. "I can't just leave you here."

Lorne stopped and turned to face me. Enveloped in the headlights, I watched him lean down and struggle fiercely to dislodge a boulder from the hard Texas clay. The muscles on his back and shoulders strained against his shirt. And as I watched, he lifted the massive rock high above his head and heaved it at the car.

"CRASHHH"... the huge rock bounced off the passenger side of the windshield and the hood before it hit the ground.

Shock dulled my thoughts. I stared at the giant web of cracked glass. Nausea rose in my throat but I swallowed, refusing to throw up in my own car.

DAMN IT, DAMN IT ANYWAY...my eyes blurred with tears...Dr. Jekyll and Mr. Hyde. His moods were wearing me down. Why in the hell was he so angry? I was too exhausted to think.

Meanwhile, Lorne had turned on his heels and headed off into the night.

FINE! If that's what he wants! My hands were shaking when I pulled the car sharply onto the road. I tromped the gas pedal, spraying gravel in every direction, leaving Lorne behind in the dark.

I heard his key in the door shortly after 4 a.m. Thank God he was home safe. Curled up on my side of the bed, I pretended to be asleep when he crawled in under the covers. I was still furious over his stupid stunt, another needless expense we couldn't afford, plus he mutilated the car I drove to work. What was I going to tell everyone when they asked what happened?

"Can you believe," Lorne grumbled under his breath, "I had to walk home? No one would give me a ride. I fought in Vietnam for this country and not one son-of-a-bitch would give me a ride."

35

Begging my forgiveness

Tension filled the air like London fog. I pretended everything was all right but I knew there was little I could do to change the collision course we were on. My future rested in the hands of a Vietnam vet, an alcoholic and only God knew the final chapter.

Lorne was having a hard time coping with family life and it was magnified by the burdens of a new home. I would hear him out in the garage cussing and swearing, followed by the clamor of tools being hurled across the concrete floor. Sometimes he'd simply vanish for a day or so, leaving me to pace the floor feeling used and stupid for loving a man who treated me so thoughtlessly. Then he'd call begging my forgiveness, or show up on the doorstep with an armful of roses and a shy boyish grin. I always caved in.

What was I to do? I knew I should leave him. No woman in her right mind would live like this but I was in love with Lorne. My husband was sick with an illness caused by a war on the other side of the world. And you don't abandon someone you love when they're sick…you stay and take care of them. Only now I knew I was sick as well. Trapped on Lorne's merry-go-round of highs and lows, I was miserable. This secret life I lived was now eating me alive on the inside.

I often wondered how many other women out there were suffering in silence like I was. Women who never set foot in Vietnam were fighting that war daily, alongside the men they loved. I desperately needed someone to talk to but there was no one. I scoured the phone book only to come up empty handed.

Veterans' wives, where did we belong? Who could we talk to, to know we weren't alone? Counseling was out of the question at a staggering rate of seventy dollars an hour. The war and alcohol controlled our lives. Lorne had to stop drinking; there was no other way to get his life together. But how to stop was the question.

September 1980

The alarm clamored, announcing another Monday morning, the beginning of a new week. I rolled over and slapped the snooze. It was then I realized Lorne wasn't there. I pulled on my robe and went to the living room. The couch was empty. Lorne had not come home. He was making me crazy. Monkey chatter kicked in, mute hysterics began to build. What in the hell was he doing? Why was he torturing me? Lurid pictures flooded my head. Maybe there was an accident and he was lying mangled in a hospital. *But someone would have called.* Maybe he was dead and they didn't know who to call. Or…maybe he was with another woman.

I was a mess. One would think by now I would be used to this, but try as I might there was no way I could pull myself together and go to work.

Finally, I crushed my cigarette in the ashtray and dialed the number to my office.

"Stacey, this is Nancy. Can I please talk to John?" I said, perched on the edge of the bed.

"Yeah, Nancy?" John asked, always direct and to the point.

I took a deep breath. "I won't be in today," I said, forcing each word. "Lorne never came home last night and I'm worried sick. I'll be in as soon as I know something."

His sigh was audible. "I'm not happy with your decision," he said. "I need you here today but do what you have to." Then he hung up.

I sat a while holding the receiver to my ear, the dial tone continued.

For three agonizing days I waited, never changing out of my robe. I told the children I had the flu. After they left for school I wandered from room to room or sat in front of the TV staring off into space, smoking one cigarette after another. How could he do this to me? I felt so stupid but I couldn't help myself. Lorne was my husband, the love of my life, my addiction.

When he finally walked in the door, I crumbled like a cracker.

"Lorne, where in the hell have you been?" I blubbered, getting to my feet. A new onslaught of tears broke loose. "I've been worried out of my mind. I had no way of finding you. I don't know any of your friends or their phone numbers." I paced the floor like a caged animal, wiping my nose on the sleeve of my robe. "For all I knew you were dead."

Lorne stood meekly at the edge of the foyer, his head down, his hands behind his back, not saying a word.

"Why in the hell didn't you call me?" I whimpered. "You could have called to say you weren't coming home."

"Baby, I'm sorry," his voice was calm. "Honestly, I didn't mean to worry you. I wasn't thinking." Walking up to me, he wrapped my trembling body in his arms. "Everything was closing in on me; I just had to get away for a while." He held me close, stroking my hair. He let me cry. "I bunked at Kyle's for a few days to clear my head."

I knew Kyle vaguely. He and Lorne were friends before we were married. Lorne and I had stopped at his house a couple of times when we were out riding. I knew Kyle's wife, Julie. It all seemed innocent enough, but Lorne's behavior was unacceptable. Not only did he worry me but his stunt was costly.

When I showed up for work the next day, I was fired on the spot.

36

Pangs of guilt

November 1980

I stepped off the escalator on the third floor of J.C. Penney's, turned the corner and came face to face with a towering display of gyrating Santa Claus dolls. Dressed in red fuzzy suits and dark sunglasses, they wiggled their butts to the tune of *Jingle Bells*. The scene struck me like an abscessed tooth. I turned on my heels, rushing off in the opposite direction

The first signs of Christmas sent pangs of guilt gnawing like ravenous termites at my last morsel of sanity. Where was I going to get the money to buy presents for the children? Lorne was out of control. His bar bills were shocking. Last month alone his American Express charges totaled over three hundred dollars. Indeed, some were business expenses, but Lorne was also months behind in turning in his expense reports. What was I going to do? I knew better than to say anything. But I ached for the children. With all my problems they seemed not to notice. Or were they pretending? Somehow I would find a way.

Hot steam fogged the wall of windows over the kitchen sink. I was draining cappellini into a colander when Lorne sneaked up behind me and grabbed me around the waist.

"Ohhh," I said, startled, "where did you come from?"

He maintained his hold, playfully nuzzling up under my hair, planting wet kisses on the back of my neck, and sending delicious shivers down my spine.

"Mmm," I purred, my shoulders scrunched up under my ears. I set the pot in the sink to keep from dropping it on the floor. Lorne's mustache brushed the delicate skin under my hair; a surge of heat rippled through my body.

"My, you're in a good mood," I said, my voice soft and silky, "What's the occasion?"

For a moment I let my guard down while indulging in the sensation of his touch. But all too soon the subtle scent of red wine drifted past me, mingling with the aroma of spicy sauce simmering on the stove. I turned to face him.

Then he leaned down and kissed me completely. When he finally straightened up he looked at me and smiled.

And for an instant I caught a glimpse of the man I fell in love with.

"You'll never guess," he said, patting me on the butt. He headed for the refrigerator. "The company actually wants me to move to Corpus Christi. Can you believe it? After all that driving back and forth for the past year they finally came to their senses." He grabbed an icy can of Coke, tilted his head back and drank deeply, then sat down at the kitchen table.

Pale as dawn, I turned to face the steam-curtained window; heavy winter rain beat against the glass. Frantic thoughts shouted in my head as shock gripped my vocal cords. I steeled myself, then turned to Lorne, clutching the counter for support.

"Lorne, how can we do this?" I said, fighting to stay calm. "When do they want you to be there?" A myriad of questions battled to be answered. What about my job? The children? And school? The whole idea of moving right now was a bad one. Our marriage was too frail.

I anxiously watched him tap a cigarette from the pack and light it. For a moment a veil of smoke concealed his face. Then he settled back, stretching his legs into the middle of the kitchen, crossing them at the ankles.

"Well, Baby," he hesitated, "I've decided to go alone. Then, eyeing his boot tops to avoid eye contact he added, "I think the separation will do us both good."

I felt like I'd been hit in the face with a two-by-four. I was tumbling over the edge with nothing to grab on to. Lorne had already thought it through...he was moving out. Leaving me here alone with the children...and there was nothing I could do to stop him.

With my last ounce of self respect I steadied myself. "Lorne, I have one question."

He looked up.

"Does this mean you'll be asking for a divorce next?" A lump the size of a cantaloupe lodged in my throat. I could scarcely breathe.

"No, Baby," he chuckled. "I don't want a divorce...honest. I just think living apart for a while will do us good. Besides, I'll probably be coming home every other weekend. And you can drive down anytime you want. I'll send money out of every paycheck," he promised, "as much as I can afford."

Hot tears stung my eyes as painful thoughts ripped at my heart. Lorne had everything all worked out. For himself that is. There was no way I could pretend to be pleased with this arrangement. Sure Lorne got to leave. Escaping into an exciting new world, leaving me stuck in Houston with a broken heart and a pile of unpaid bills.

That night we made love like it was for the last time. Lorne gently caressed me, reassuring me in sweet desperation. The haunting notes of a saxophone wept softly in the darkness.

37

Covered whispers

December 21, 1980

Four days before Christmas Lorne maneuvered a black and orange U-Haul up the driveway like a pro. He walked around back to unlock and lower the tailgate while Tommy scrambled out the other door, raced across the lawn into the house and flashed me a smile as we passed in the doorway...Or was it a smirk?

School was out for Christmas and Lorne agreed to take Tommy along for the ride. He could use the extra set of hands. His plan was to drive to Corpus Christi, unload the trailer and be back in time for our annual family gathering...Christmas Eve at his grandparents' in the country. This was an encounter I dreaded like the chicken pox, the covered whispers and huddled stares as word of our separation spread like wildfire. But I was fighting to save my marriage; I only prayed I was strong enough to pull it off.

Tommy trotted after Lorne like a puppy expecting a treat, hanging onto his dad's every word. I knew he missed Lorne, but that was Shirley's fault, not mine. Maybe things would have been different if Tommy still lived with us. But that was another lifetime. I followed them through the house feeling useless and defeated.

In the hallway, Tommy glanced back over his shoulder and our eyes met. A twisted grin contorted his young, unblemished face, clearly flaunting victory...his dad was moving out. Crushed, I turned away, blinking back a rush of tears. Who knows, maybe Tommy was still mad because I made him sweep the kitchen floor.

I promised myself I wouldn't cry. But that was easier said than done, standing in the shadows watching my life being torn out from under me.

Lorne and Tommy struggled to shove the massive brown couch out the front door. Muffled curses echoed down the hallway. My husband was leaving. I had no idea how I would survive without him. Waves of nausea churned in my stomach.

"Sorry, Baby," Lorne said, nearly bowling me over, "but you need to stay out of the way."

The monster crate he was wrestling with contained the base of our driftwood coffee table…a token of our first night together.

I felt abandoned. My hands were tied. From now on this would be my life. Submerged in self pity, I watched from the kitchen as they stripped pieces from my home like boiled chicken from a carcass.

As I stood watching, I recalled a night two months earlier.

Lorne had come home in a highly agitated state. Normally alcohol subdued him like Valium but not that night. He paced the floor ranting and raving about his boss and how they were screwing him out of his territory. I recoiled in the corner of the couch not saying a word. He paused at the coffee table, bent over and abruptly lifted the heavy plate-glass top, that in turn, propelled my spider plant across the room like a paper airplane…and then he dropped it. The heavy piece of glass hit the solid driftwood base at just the right angle. It exploded. Shards of glass went everywhere. Unruffled and grumbling, he staggered off to bed leaving me to clean up the mess.

The next morning, Lorne noticed the glass top on the coffee table was missing. He wanted to know what happened. I told him but he refused to believe me. This was when I first learned of his blackouts.

I was still standing in the kitchen gazing out over the backyard when Lorne came up behind me. He touched my shoulder. I turned…my eyes were brimming with tears. Gently he wrapped me in his arms and held me close; the soothing warmth of his body enfolded me. I ached with a dreadful sadness not knowing what lay ahead or if we would ever again live together as man and wife.

He held me quietly for some time. Then lifting my chin he looked into my eyes. Smiling tenderly, he wiped a tear from my cheek with his finger.

"Baby, don't be sad," he said softly. "I'll be home every other weekend, I promise. And you can drive down to see me whenever you want. It'll be fun. It's less than a four hour drive. Besides, we can talk every night on the phone and the company will pick up the tab."

"I know." I struggled to find my voice. But I knew him better than he knew himself. "I'm just going to miss you so much."

"I'll miss you too," he said, squeezing me tightly, "more than you'll ever know. Please tell me it's okay, please?"

"It's okay, Lorne," I whispered, lying through my teeth.

Then he kissed me. It was a long kiss but it had to end. He stepped back, holding me at arm's length. "Baby, I love you," he said. I'll call you when we get in."

These were the last words I heard as I watched him leave. I ran my finger over my lips, my mouth felt hot and bruised. I stood motionless in the kitchen, tears spilling down my cheeks, wondering if I would ever feel that kiss again.

I tossed and turned for what seemed like hours. It was 3:00 a.m. when I rolled over, turned on the light and reached for a cigarette. I inhaled deeply, feeling the nicotine rushing through my body numbing my jitters. I had to stop smoking, but how? My life was upside down again and I was powerless. I flicked an ash into a disgusting mound of butts in the ashtray. My bed felt cold and empty. Even the light was no help. My mind and body ached for my husband, knowing he would not be crawling in next to me, drunk or sober.

I propped two pillows behind my back, picked up a book and turned to the tattered bookmark. But I couldn't concentrate. The children's father had flown into Houston to be with them for a few days and would bring them back on Christmas Eve. Right now I was alone with a suffocating loneliness I never felt before.

Tomorrow would be my first day as a "separated woman." What did that mean? That my husband doesn't want to live with me anymore? I tried being a good wife, loving and understanding through all the shit he dished out. Anger raised its vengeful head but I was too pathetic to deal with it. I was sure Lorne loved me and our love life was good...when he was around. I never nagged about things around the house that needed to be done; I just did them myself...which was getting pretty damn old. If only my anger could save me. It was rough working full-time, running a house and caring for a family alone. All Lorne had to do was go to work. It wasn't fair. Was it too much to want a normal life with a loving responsible husband? My children were my reasons for living and they were everything a mother could want.

Lorne was a Vietnam vet. He made it home safely with a box full of medals, including two Bronze Stars that sat in the back of a dresser drawer. Only Lorne knew what he went through to receive those honors, but the wounds to his mind refused to heal. They festered like gangrene, chewing away his sanity and tearing our marriage apart. But I refused to give up. Lorne was the love of my life and I would fight to the end...whatever that might be.

I lay in the dark, staring into nothingness, feeling lost and alone. Unconsciously my hand moved to my lips, tears spilled onto my pillow. I ached for my husband. The agonizing pain cut through my body like a knife.

Suddenly the children's faces filled my mind, reminding me of my gifts from God, and I knew I must fight to survive for them.

38

Survival is an art

My life felt hideously empty. Lorne was gone and I felt like a cripple.

In the light of a new day I yanked the covers over my head. The pain was unbearable. All I wanted was to crawl into a hole and hide from a world where I no longer fit. Yet another part of me knew I couldn't give in. I had to fight back. This was my life and I had to be strong for my children.

I walked into work with my head held high and my shoulders back; makeup covered the dark circles under my eyes. Unknown to all, I carried the burden of still another secret. A secret I was too ashamed to admit to anyone, even my family. My husband had left me.

Pretend was the name of the game I had to play until I could figure out how to live again. I needed to focus all my energy on work and caring for the children's needs. These were my first priorities.

"Lorne was transferred to Corpus Christi," I calmly explained to the children as I watched their reactions. "And rather than pull you out of school, we decided it was best for us to stay in Houston until he figures out if he likes it there."

I had no idea if they believed me, but they went along with the story.

Survival is an art. A skill learned by a determined mind. And time itself has a way of dulling intense pain. It is said, *"When God closes one door, He opens another."* I only prayed I could find the other door. Refusing to admit that my marriage was failing, I tiptoed through lies, acting as though my life was normal.

The distance separating Lorne and me actually gave me room to breathe, that is, whenever I wasn't having pity parties. It was hard, but a welcome change from the daily stresses I was used to. And day by day I grew stronger. I missed him terribly, but still blamed him for nothing: Vietnam and alcohol were the culprits.

Every other weekend Lorne drove back to Houston like he promised. Well, almost every other weekend. But his phone calls in between visits were disturbing. I soon learned that if the phone rang after 8 p.m. he was drunk.

"Baby, I sure miss you," he would slur in my ear. "Don't know what I'd ever do without you."

At first his calls upset me, but soon I simply let him talk and blow off steam while I cleaned up the kitchen, loaded the dishwasher and wiped down the stove. I was in love with Lorne and wanted to help him, yet as I grew stronger I could see things more clearly. Lorne took everything too personally; he felt everyone was out to get him. And his isolation didn't help.

To disagree with him would only enrage him. But no more, I vowed never to live like that again.

Reading became my passion, the library my source. I'd lug home mountains of books on anything that caught my eye: the Vietnam War, Self-Help, Psychology and books on Gardening. I couldn't read fast enough. At times I wished I had two heads so I could get through more books; Meditation, Cooking, Photography, Health—my thirst was unquenchable. Every night I fell asleep reading. This became my life.

The weekends Lorne came home seemed more like dates. A home cooked dinner, wine and light conversation. But more often than not Lorne was venting. Afterwards we'd make love and fall asleep in each other's arms.

39

This feeling...*happiness*

April 1981

I tossed my suitcase into the trunk of our red MG Midget, closed my eyes and inhaled deeply. Spring had finally arrived with an intoxicating fragrance of its own. The weather forecast was for clear skies all weekend and I was making my first trip to Corpus Christi...alone.

Unsnapping the convertible top, I stuffed it down behind the seat, then I stretched the black tarp over the metal frame and snapped it into place. Giddy with anticipation, I backed down the driveway into the street. The children were staying with friends for the weekend and I was as free as a butterfly in the open sky.

The brisk wind tousled my hair and plucked cobwebs from my mind, while backcountry roads raced beneath my tires, drawing me closer to Lorne. It had been a long time since I had this feeling...*happiness*...a word absent from my vocabulary. I pretended I was happy for the children's sake, but my broken heart held only sadness.

After an hour into the trip, traffic slowed to a crawl; I was stuck behind a caravan of eighteen wheelers. The two-lane, winding road made it impossible to pass. Trapped and disappointed, I slouched behind the wheel, pouting like a four-year-old.

Suddenly a muscle-bound arm reached out of the window of the truck blocking me, motioning me to pass. I peeked around the metal monster. It looked clear, but I wasn't sure. A toot on his air horn got my attention; the zealous arm thrashed. With a prayer I edged out, hit the gas pedal and passed, squeezing in front of the trucker. His bright lights flashed in my rearview mirror. Sticking my arm high overhead, I waved gratefully.

Then to my surprise, each truck in the convoy waved me on when the coast was clear, passing me along on their CB radios like a giant game of leapfrog.

Lorne's apartment was small and cluttered. It was strange seeing our furniture in his tiny one-bedroom flat. Papers and boxes were scattered everywhere. Not much had changed; Lorne hated paperwork. He hated doing expense reports and income tax even when the government owed us money. But I didn't care what the apartment looked like. I came to spend time with my husband and that was all that mattered.

We made love in the middle of the afternoon, and Lorne was sober and made me feel loved.

"Hey, Baby, are you hungry?" he hollered through the bathroom door.

"I'm famished," I called back, stepping out of the shower.

"Good, cause I'm taking you to my favorite seafood restaurant," he said cheerfully.

I smiled, tingling with new life…fresh blood pumping through my veins.

Lorne took me for seafood as he promised, but it wasn't what I had expected. It was a bar…his regular hangout. The food was good but I felt uncomfortable and out of place. He introduced me to some of his friends but I didn't know what to say to them.

Around Lorne I reverted back to the needy, insecure woman he left behind. I detested that woman. Weak, vulnerable, lacking self-esteem, and yet I was helpless to do anything about it. Being back in Lorne's arms seemed to heal my heartache something I could not do alone

40

Starting to worry

June 12, 1982

Lorne was late...but that was nothing new.

It was the weekend before my birthday and I could hardly wait. Lorne had taunted me for weeks with his big surprise, and even though I begged he refused to give me the tiniest hint. He loved to tease me. The children were in Chicago with their father for the summer, the house was ours. I primped for hours—a bubble bath followed by a pedicure using my favorite color, Bordeaux Red. I even splurged on a silk teddy in a lovely shade of robin's egg blue, biting a hole in my already strained budget.

"Brrring..."

"Brrring..."

"Brrring..."

I dropped the garden hose in the middle of the backyard and sprinted across the lawn into the house.

"Hello?" I said breathlessly.

"Hi, Baby," Lorne said, his voice raspy.

"Lorne, where are you?" I asked. "I thought you'd be home by now. I was starting to worry."

"Well, I've got bad news."

There was silence on the other end of the line. I stopped breathing.

"I won't be coming home this weekend." Lorne paused. "I'm in the hospital."

"What?" I gasped in disbelief.

"And before you go jumping to conclusions," he interrupted, "I'm going to be fine."

"Lorne, what happened? Is anything broken? What can I do?" I rattled on. Panic squeezed my heart. "I'm so far away. I don't know what to do."

"Baby, calm down," he said meekly. "I was in a car accident." He paused. "Carl, a friend of mine, asked me to take pictures at his rehearsal dinner which I did. The place was on the other side of the island. On the way home I guess I fell asleep at the wheel. But to make matters worse I was driving the company truck."

"Oh, Lorne," was all I could say.

"The next thing I remember I was lying in the street looking up at some guy I never saw before. It seems I wound up straddling the guardrail on Bay Street Bridge, rode it like a monorail until a concrete piling got in my way. They said the truck teetered on the railing until this guy pulled me out."

"Oh my God," I whimpered, sliding down the cupboard to the floor, my knees pulled up to my chin.

"I don't remember much but from what I'm told my face whacked the steering wheel when I hit the piling. At the same time the gas pedal plowed through the floorboards crushing my right foot. The doctor says they can't do surgery until Monday. They called in a specialist but he's out of town."

"Oh, Lorne," I said, resting my forehead on my knees.

"To be honest, other than some prize fighter bruises, I was lucky." He hesitated. "But the truck is totaled and so is my ass when word gets out."

"Are you in pain?" I said, reeling from the visions in my head.

"They've got me on some good drugs," he said with a chuckle. "I hardly feel a thing. The doctor says I'm lucky to be alive. I could have flipped over the guardrail into the Bay and drown!"

"Thank God, you're all right," I said, feeling sick to my stomach. But one question was eating at me and I had to ask.

"Lorne, were you drinking?"

The silence was numbing.

"Nancy, I wasn't drunk," he said honestly. "I had a couple of drinks at dinner. But I was taking pictures and that requires both hands. I was fine when I left the party maybe just somewhat exhausted from a rough week on the road"

I wanted to believe him but his past was too real. Now was not the time to get into it.

"Lorne, I'm coming to Corpus Christi," I said, pulling a pen and paper from the kitchen drawer. "What's the name of the hospital and your room number?"

When I hung up I called Lorne's mother.

"I'm going with you," Joan said, after she heard the news. "I'm driving and won't take "no" for an answer. I'll pick you up at nine tomorrow morning."

Sleep was impossible. Each time I closed my eyes I saw Lorne slumped over the steering wheel unconscious and bleeding, teetering on the railing of a deserted bridge. Suddenly the truck tilts forward, slowly plunging headfirst into the inky black water, slipping out of sight unnoticed under a layer of bursting bubbles.

Frightened and shaken, I stared at the moonlight peeking through the slanted blinds. *"Thank you, God,"* I whispered, making the sign of the cross, *"for sparing his life again."*

41

My heart sank

June 13, 1982

The morning sky was crystal blue and the highway was deserted. With a tank full of gas, Styrofoam cups full of hot coffee and a box of Hostess chocolate covered doughnuts on the seat between us, we pulled out of the gas station.

Back on the road, Joan set the cruise control at seventy. "Keep your eyes open for the Highway Patrol," she said. "I hear they're pretty heartless along this stretch."

Munching on forbidden doughnuts, we chattered nonstop for well over an hour, mostly about Lorne. Joan was the only person in the world I trusted with my pain. She knew how much I loved her son and only wanted the best for him, even if he didn't want it for himself.

"Pssssssssss…"

Suddenly billows of a white steam gushed from under the hood engulfing us.

"Now what?" Joan sighed, slowing to a crawl.

My heart sank. Opening the window, I flailed at the fog, verbally guiding Joan to the shoulder, fearing we would topple into a ditch. The car finally stopped. I stepped out, hands on my hips and looked around. We were in the middle of nowhere.

I walked to the front of the car, pulled the latch and raised the hood, peering helplessly at a wet greasy engine. I shook my head. And to think we decided to take Joan's car because mine was always breaking down.

Off in the distance a thundering roar rumbled across the flatlands, scattering flocks of birds in every direction. Flashes of light hit my eyes as a truck the size of a locomotive came into view. Bright sunlight danced from its chrome exhaust stacks mounted on its roof like a giant pair of Texas Longhorns.

We watched the truck draw near, realizing not a single car had passed our way. Airbrakes screeched as the massive machine veered off the road and came to a stop behind our car. The door swung open.

"Hey there…are you ladies all right?" shouted the driver, stepping down from the cab.

Weathered and wrinkled, he looked like he should be riding a Harley. A silver gray ponytail tied with a piece of leather reached half way down his back. Curious tattoos adorned his arms. *Born Free* stretched across his crumpled tank top while a cluster of keys tugged at his jeans, pulling them lower with each step.

"Yes, we're fine," I replied, "but our car died."

"Step aside," he said, waving his arm. Hoisting his jeans, he leaned over the fender while I explained our dilemma.

"Looks to me like you overheated," he said, nodding. "First, she needs to cool down. Then you need to find a gas station an' fill her up with water." Again he hoisted his jeans. "Keep a keen eye on that temperature gauge. If she starts overheatin,' you need to stop and let 'er cool down again."

Half an hour later…I was driving…my mission…water!

"Damn it," I said, banging my palm against the steering wheel. The needle was creeping back into the red zone.

Once again we sat on the shoulder waiting. I was on the brink of tears.

"Why is this happening?" I whimpered pathetically. "It's all like a bad dream and I want to wake up."

"Everything's going to be all right," Joan reassured me. She reached and stroked the back of my hand.

Two more pit stops and hours later, the crippled car arrived at the only water pump within a hundred miles. Or so it seemed. I raised the hood and stretched the hose to reach the car. Relieved, I indulged in the sweet sound of gurgling water rushing into the radiator. Next door was a restaurant. We agreed to grab a bite before getting on the road. Lorne wasn't going anywhere without us.

Food defused our frustration. Feeling relaxed and nourished, we laughed about our adventure on the way to the car, anxious to get back on the road.

However, in less than half an hour the car was engulfed in steam…again.

"Damn it," I snapped. "Why is this happening…today of all days?"

I pulled off the road, not a house in sight.

"I don't know what to do," I stated. "We never thought to buy extra water."

"Guess we'll have to wait until it cools down," Joan said calmly.

"Hooonk...Hooonk," the piercing air horn shattered the silence. We looked up, eyes wide in disbelief. Coming down the road at full speed was the same truck that stopped earlier!

Waylon Hawkins lived in Pittsburgh, owned his own rig and was headed for Corpus Christi to drop off a load of electronics. He had driven all night and decided to pull into a rest stop for some shuteye after he left us. We must have passed him along the way.

After surveying the damage, Waylon stood up. "This puppy's had it," he said shaking his head. "How 'bout a lift to the hospital?"

"Oh we couldn't impose," Joan said.

"No trouble, Ma'am," Waylon assured us. "This guy I know in Corpus owes me a favor. He'll tow your car to town for free, fix it and you can pick it up in the morning." He handed me a business card.

"Excuse us a minute," I said, dragging Joan by the arm behind the car. Waylon nodded and wiped his greasy hands on his bandana.

"What do you think?" I whispered, looking back over my shoulder. "He looks okay, yet everything I read warns women against taking rides from strangers. On the other hand not a single highway patrol car has passed us this whole trip," I said. "And if we think positive, there's two of us and only one of him."

Joan gazed across the field, her designer handbag tucked neatly under her arm.

"Or we could stay put and wait for the sheriff's department to find us?" I stammered, on the verge of tears.

Joan turned, looking me straight in the eye. "I think we'll be safe," she said, a gentle smile softening her face. "I have a good feeling about him."

"And I've had karate," I said, smiling sheepishly, "even though I've never had to use it." I hesitated. "Okay then . . . it's a plan?"

"It's a plan," Joan replied.

42

Two scared rabbits

Corpus Christi, Texas

Every square inch in the cab's interior was covered in Playboy centerfolds, naked ladies leaving nothing to one's imagination. Red ball fringe outlined the cab's massive windshield, rippling in waves with the vibrating engine. A blue plastic lei draped the rearview mirror, while a double jointed hula dancer wiggled on the dashboard. It looked like a brothel on wheels.

Wide-eyed and nervous, Joan and I glanced at each other. Waylon grinned and chewed on a toothpick. His huge hand grabbed one of the dozen gearshifts sprouting from the floor.

I cringed as I visualized headlines, *"Partially clad bodies of two women discovered in ditch on outskirts of Corpus Christi."*

"You ladies ready?" Waylon interrupted, over the roaring engine.

Huddled together on the passenger seat like two scared rabbits, we nodded in unison.

You can't judge a book by its cover.

Waylon Hawkins was nothing but a gentleman. In fact, he was educated and well-read; a man who thrived on the adventure of an open road.

Curious, I asked about the nude pictures surrounding us.

"Well," he said, rubbing his chin, "I'll tell you this. The open road is a lonely place and these pretty ladies keep me company. Besides I just love looking at 'em, makes me feel young."

Less than an hour later, Waylon hit the air brakes and rolled to a screeching halt in front of St. Mary's Hospital. The white metal sign caught in the headlights read, *"Quiet."*

A startling full moon lingered in the clear night sky and the street was empty. Off in the distance the thunder of crashing waves echoed through the mist. I helped Joan down from the cab. Waylon stepped forward, setting our luggage on the curb.

"We can't thank you enough," Joan said. Reaching into her pocket she pulled out a small roll of bills, extending her hand.

Waylon pushed her hand aside, and then bowed. "For you ladies it's been my pleasure," he replied, moving into the shadow of his truck. "And good luck to you."

It was nearly midnight when we walked into the lobby of St. Mary's Hospital, lugging our suitcases and asking to see Lorne.

"I'm sorry, but it's way past visiting hours," said the nurse behind the desk, peering over her steel-rimmed glasses.

"We've been on the road all day. Fifteen hours! Could we just see him for a minute?" I pleaded.

"That's impossible," she insisted, "it's against hospital rules."

"Couldn't you make an exception…just this once?"

"Like she said," a sturdy starched nurse in white appeared out of nowhere, "it's against the rules." Stepping from behind the counter she blocked us like an army tank. "Besides he was given a sleeping pill at eight."

"But you don't understand," I said, clenching my teeth, fighting back tears. "Last night, my husband was in an accident. His mother and I left Houston at nine o'clock this morning and have gone through hell to get here," my voice quivered. "When our car broke down for the umpteenth time, we had to leave it at the side of the road and hitch a ride with a stranger driving a semi."

The heated commotion drew more nurses than flies on an elephant.

"And God only knows what could have happened to us," I grew louder.

Joan stood by our suitcases, her purse under her arm, her hands folded in front of her.

"Do you have any idea how dangerous that was?" I shouted. "We're exhausted, hungry and we have no car. We're not asking you to wake him. We just want to see him. Is that asking too much?" Tears welled in my eyes. I took a deep breath and firmly planted myself for the next attack.

A few minutes later we were ushered down a dimly lit corridor past the nurse's station to room 232...Lorne's room.

The door stood ajar. Light from the hall spilled across Lorne's bed as we tiptoed in. He slept soundly, covered in a thin sheet. The glow from an overhead nightlight illuminated his face; his head was turned sideways on the pillow, partially hidden in shadow. My heart sank. The left side of his face was badly bruised. His eye was a grotesque shade of purple, the size of a golf ball and swollen shut. He had a fat lip. And four inches of nasty black stitches seemed to be holding his forehead together. A sling covered his left arm lying across his chest and the lower half of his right leg was uncovered resting on two pillows; his toes were stained bright orange.

A long envelope was stuck between his first and second toe. It had my name on it. I took the envelope, leaned over to kiss Lorne on the cheek and then left the room. Joan followed close behind.

In the hallway, I examined the envelope as Joan looked over my shoulder. Lorne had drawn a crude map to his apartment; instructions were scribbled along the bottom and up the sides. *"Spend the night at my apartment. There is food there also. Key is in philodendron flower pot. Do not clean up or straighten out any paperwork. Please!!"* This part was underlined 3 times. *"I Love You!!!"*

43

No other choice

June 18, 1982

I paced the sidewalk outside the hospital like an expectant father, checking my watch every few seconds; I was parked in a twenty minute zone. Where was he? Shrieking seagulls filled the morning sky, soaring wide out over the pounding surf. Today was my birthday and Lorne was coming home. What better gift could I ask for?

After the surgery on Lorne's foot, the doctors gave strict orders he was not to drive until the cast came off. There was no other choice. He was moving back to Houston after more than eighteen months in Corpus Christi. The thought of Lorne without wheels for eight weeks was not a pretty picture.

The sliding glass doors opened and Lorne appeared, propped in a wheelchair and looking a tad ragged around the edges. Squinting into the sun, he shaded his eyes with his hand. I waved. The nurse was at the helm, steering him in my direction. Lorne smiled brightly when he saw me and waved back. Joan walked by his side, cradling a bouquet of flowers she had bought on the way to the hospital.

"Hi Baby," he said meekly when they reached the car, "Happy Birthday." He took my hand. "I'm sorry how this worked out. It's not how I planned."

"I know," I said, kissing him gently on his swollen lips. "You're alive and that's all that matters."

Opening the car door, I helped the nurse lift Lorne into the back, carefully placing his leg on the seat. He looked miserable propped against the door. He wore a loose three-button shirt, khaki shorts and a mummy-like cast from his groin to his bright orange toes. By now his bruised face was multicolored, his swollen eye had opened a crack and the jagged black stitches crossing his brow looked like tiny *Tonka* tire tracks.

"Where to?" I asked, watching Lorne in my rear view mirror.

"How about some real food," he grumbled, sounding like his old self. "That stuff they feed you in the hospital tastes like cardboard. Marie Callender's is just up the street from the apartment."

"Sounds great," I said with a smile, pulling away from the curb.

Lorne hobbled his way to a table on his crutches, tilting precariously close to a waiter balancing a tray of dishes. I restrained my urge to run to his rescue, knowing he would be annoyed. Besides, he had to learn how to do this himself. He'd be on crutches for the next eight weeks.

By the time lunch was over Lorne's mood had changed.

"How about a trip to Padre Island?" he volunteered out of the blue. "It's your birthday," he said smiling. "We can leave for Houston later."

"Really, are you sure you're up to it?" I squealed, not wanting to appear selfish. I loved being near the water more than any other place, and Lorne knew this.

The decision was made. Brief stop at the apartment, Joan and I pulled on swimsuits under our clothes while Lorne waited in the car. Then, grabbing a few supplies, we dashed downstairs. I pulled a frosty coke from the cooler, opened it and took a sip, then passed it back to Lorne. If only life could be this simple all the time.

Summer cottages speckled the landscape, their railings draped with brightly colored towels. Lazy sun-faded canoes and kayaks rested under shady porches, while happy children clad in swim suits played football in the sand. To me this was heaven. Across the road, clusters of tall wild grass clung to the dunes, bending in the breeze as ridges of white caps lapped the sandy shore. I rolled down my window to welcome the fresh salt air. Taking a deep breath, I let out a sigh.

"What a glorious day," Joan said, mesmerized by the view. "I can't remember the last time I was here."

The beach was deserted. Driving along the packed sand left by the high tide I picked a spot and parked. Then I pulled lawn chairs from the trunk and set one next to the car facing the water for Lorne. I helped him get comfortable, propping his injured foot up on the cooler as Joan walked out onto the sand. I leaned down and kissed him.

"Thanks, Baby," he said, taking my wrist, "for everything." He looked up, dark sunglasses covering his eyes.

I smiled down on my husband and the breeze ruffled my hair. I turned to gaze out at the sea. Rows of rolling surf dashed against the gray-white sand glittering in the sunlight. The cries of seagulls surrounded me. Standing barefoot in the sand, I closed my eyes lifting my face to the warm afternoon sun.

"Hey, birthday girl, I've got a surprise for you," Lorne said, breaking the spell.

I turned quickly. A large box wrapped in silver paper and tied with a white satin ribbon sat on his lap. Lorne was beaming. Joan must have been in on the surprise.

She left us alone, giving us the moment.

"Oh, Lorne," I said, sinking to my knees in the sand beside him.

I looked up at my husband smiling as I untied the ribbon. Then carefully I lifted the lid of the box.

"Oh, it's beautiful." I could only stare.

Then gently I slid my fingers over the camera in the box. It was a Canon 35mm top of the line with all the attachments. For years I had talked about photography and wanting a camera to do black and white stills, artistic shots of my own. Photos I could enlarge and frame and hang on the wall. But there was never enough money for anything so extravagant. Yet Lorne never forgot.

For the next few hours I indulged in happiness. Joan and I waded out into the water laughing and giggling like best girlfriends, while Lorne sat on the beach and watched. Later he took the first shots on my camera. I was feeding a flock of seagulls circling over my head, enchanted as they dared to dip and snatch bits of food from my finger-tips.

I savored these precious moments...hiding them away in my heart for when things got rough again...and I knew they would.

44

Sign of codependency

Houston, Texas

Having Lorne home again was no easy task. But I was stronger now.

It was hard to believe almost two years had passed since Lorne first moved to Corpus Christi. In the beginning I was a wreck without him. With no identity of my own I felt like only half a person. According to a book I was reading, *Codependent No More* by Melody Beattie, this was a sign of codependency. A new word was added to my vocabulary.

Spending time alone does different things to different people. Once I stopped the pity parties, which often appeared out of nowhere, I began to enjoy the tangy taste of independence like a tart green apple. My new lifestyle began to feel normal and routine. I felt like I fit in for the first time in a long time. Sure it was hard juggling work and the children's needs, and money was always in short supply, but a feeling of peace and satisfaction lulled me to sleep at night knowing I had had a good day.

Now Lorne was home again.

He was unpredictable. I never knew from one moment to the next what might be lurking in the shadows waiting to pounce. But having him home was all I ever wanted, all I ever prayed for. Lorne was my husband, the love of my life and he belonged at home...home where I could care for him in sickness and in health.

It was true...living without him all those months was peaceful, but he had left a hole in my heart. I missed his contagious smile and spontaneous joy, like the day he spotted a butterfly drying her wings in the sun. I missed eating warm wild blackberries picked from a bush, our fingers and tongues stained blue. I missed riding on the back of the wind, my arms wrapped tightly around his body, my life in his hands. I missed sitting spellbound at his feet listening to tales of Jupiter and her four moons, or simply rocking him in my arms when he woke from a nightmare. I missed the warmth of his body in the night and the touch of his kiss. I would have done anything to get him back. Why now did I feel so restless?

Life moved on and new routines fell into place. Each morning Lorne was picked up by a coworker for the duration of his recovery. He walked without a limp which the doctors had suspected but complained of constant pain when it rained, which it seemed to do daily. Once the doctor signed his release the company gave him a new car.

Meanwhile, Lorne toyed with the idea of moving to the country, owning a piece of land where we could build a home, plant a garden and leave the city behind. Searching the countryside, we uncovered Eden. It was a full acre with a scenic hill, scattered trees and a creek running through the property. We met the neighbor quite by accident when we were stalked by his runaway cow.

Lorne was excited.

That evening he sat at the kitchen table sketching floor plans. The house would be built into the side of the hill with all the rooms underground limiting our need for air conditioning.

The front of the house, entirely glass, would overlook the creek with a huge stone indoor/outdoor fireplace on the patio.

"I think we should name it *Hillhouse*," Lorne said with a grin.

And once we agreed on a dollar amount, we put in a bid on the property. But we lost...someone came in six thousand dollars higher.

Old habits are hard to break. Disappointment tossed Lorne back into the heap. Drinking and staying out late became his normal way of life again. For me it was like an episode from the *Twilight Zone* and I had been pulled back in time...except this time I wasn't afraid. I knew I could survive without him, even though I didn't want to. Resigned to the fact that Lorne was an alcoholic who refused to admit it...I backed off once more.

45

His optimism was electric

December 18, 1984

The phone call came a week before Christmas. Lorne was offered a job in California.

A friend in the industry was looking for someone in sales with his field of expertise, experience and knowledge of high pressure valves used on oil rigs. It was an answer to my prayers. A fresh start someplace far away...away from the hell we'd been living with for such a long time. Lorne's optimism was electric; he was like a new man. He hadn't been satisfied with his current employer or the territory he had been given. The new company offered a higher salary, a new company car and moving expenses. But there was one stipulation...he had to be there by January third.

So, it was the day after Christmas.

Our little red MG sat at the curb, stuffed like a holiday turkey ready to go, shrouded in a pounding Texas downpour. Lorne decided to drive our extra car rather than haul it behind a moving van. This way he could take more clothes and personal items. But I was worried. The MG lost its reverse gear a month earlier and Lorne never found the time to get it fixed.

"Baby, I'll be fine," he reassured me, digging through his toolbox on the garage floor. "I'm aware of the situation...and I promise....I'll only drive forward." He flashed a devilish grin over his shoulder. "Cross my heart," he said crossing his heart with his index finger.

"I just worry," I said, smiling warily. "California seems so far away."

Lorne came up to me clutching a fistful of dirty tools. He pulled me close with his free arm and planted a wet kiss on my lips. "Besides," he whispered an inch from my nose, "the company will have a brand new Ford Taurus waiting for me when I arrive." He squeezed past me into the kitchen. "I wonder what color..."

Later that afternoon Lorne stood in the hallway holding me in his arms.

"It's time to go," he said. Then kissing me quickly he opened the door, yanked his jacket over his head and charged down the driveway like a wild bull through the sheeting rain.

The children and I huddled on the porch waving. He revved the engine, reached out the window and waved. He beeped his horn and pulled from the curb, water waking behind him. I watched his taillights fade into the storm. Fierce lightening crackled across the sky.

Our plan was for the children and me to follow once the house sold…but in 1985 the Houston real estate market was flatter than a tortilla.

Lorne called almost every night. Sometimes he was drunk yet I chose to overlook it because I missed him. Once a month the company paid for him to fly home. Those weekends were special but never long enough. On Valentine's Day he brought me a velvet heart-shaped box of chocolates. And when the weekend was over and Lorne was gone, I was content knowing we would all be in California soon…and this distance between us would all seem like a bad dream.

But the months passed without a single offer on the house.

46

My insides recoiled

April 1985

Lorne flew home in the middle of April. We spent the weekend totally absorbed in each other. I made potato salad at the kitchen counter and Lorne grilled steaks outside while we discussed our future plans in California through the open patio windows.

Sunday evening Lorne was supposedly packing to leave when he called me into the living room.

"What is it?" I asked from the doorway.

"Come sit down," he murmured softly. He seemed ill at ease standing in the middle of the room as I settled onto the couch. "Nancy, you must know how much I love you," he said as he began to pace the floor.

"Yes." My insides recoiled. The monkeys were stirring.

"Well," he began as he stopped in front of me with his head down. "I want a divorce."

Shocked, I couldn't speak.

He stammered out an explanation, saying it wasn't my fault. He loved me but just couldn't cope with the responsibilities. He didn't know why, but being a husband and father was too much. He needed to be alone. He promised to go on sending money and we would work out the details later.

"But why didn't you say something before now?" I whimpered in betrayal. My knees felt disjointed as I struggled to stand and face him. "Why did you lead me on?"

"Because I really do love you, Nancy, and I didn't want to spoil the weekend," he replied, tears glistening in his eyes.

I was broken. The last ten years had taken their toll. There was no fight left. Plain and simple the battle was over.

August 30, 1985

Four months later, Lorne was back.

It was Labor Day weekend...he had changed his mind.

"Baby, I'm sorry for everything I've put you through. Can you ever forgive me?" he pleaded. "I love and miss you so much, I'm miserable...I don't want the divorce."

I was stunned and confused. "Lorne, I just don't know," I said, my hands folded in my lap. I still loved him and always would, but I was terrified he'd leave again...and I knew that could destroy me.

"Please say you'll come to California," he begged, sitting down next to me. He took my hands. "Things will be different this time, I promise. Please say yes?"

The torment in his eyes broke my heart. What should I do? I knew how much he loved me but his demons still stood between us. I had to think.

September 2, 1985

Lorne flew back to California on Labor Day evening…without an answer from me.

And, as fate would have it …three hours later the phone rang. Our real estate agent had a signed offer he wanted to bring by.

"Mrs. MacMillan," he said warily, "there is one problem."

"Yes, what is it?" I asked.

"The family wants to be in before school starts."

That was only six days away! Could it even be done? Now I must make the hardest decision of my life.

47

When it rains it pours

One thing about Texas…when it rains it pours. The water comes down in buckets and windshield wipers are useless. All you can do is attempt to follow the fading red taillights in front of you and pray you don't end up in a ditch. Facing the hardest decision I've ever had in my life was like being on that road with no one to follow…I was alone and I had to figure out which direction to turn.

Fall classes had already started at the University of Houston where Cory and Tiffy were enrolled. They had worked diligently to earn their tuition by waiting tables after school and on weekends, determined to a have a college education. I raised them to be strong and independent and to go after what they wanted no matter what stood in their way. Unfortunately, the university imposed a deadline on all refunds…and we had passed the point of no return.

And where was Peter when this was going on...Peter, their father, the Ohio State graduate? Stuck with his head in the sand like an ostrich, he claimed he couldn't help with college expenses. He wasn't asked to pay all the costs...but anything would have been better than nothing to ease the burden on the children. What could I do? But that hadn't stopped Cory and Tiffy. My heart ached with pride.

Cory, now twenty-one and a natural whiz at mathematics, was in his third year of accounting. He was busy wading through the red tape of changing classes and was picky about his professors. He had a handful of favorites. Tiffy had celebrated her nineteenth birthday a week earlier and was over her head in first semester fundamentals and still vacillating about a major.

Just as everything was finally moving forward...for a change, what happened? The crazy world turned upside down again. I agonized over my quandary. An attractive young girl starting college should have her mother nearby. What was I going to do?

I was still up when the children got home from work; they both worked the late shift and went straight to their rooms. I didn't say a word about what happened. I needed time to think. I had no idea what to do. Torn between my children and my husband, my dilemma was staggering.

It was late when they finally turned out their lights. I dragged a lawn chair out to the middle of the backyard and sat staring up at the stars, smoking one cigarette after another. The night air was warm and still. The broad bladed grass felt cool under my bare feet. What was I going to do?

There was no easy answer. I loved Lorne deeply...but I loved my children more. I raised them to think for themselves and to go after their dreams, but was I ready to let them go? Lorne needed me...the children needed me...who needed me most? This was too hard...too painful...I had no idea what to do. Tiffy and Cory were seldom around anymore. When they weren't at school or at work, they were out with their friends...and someday soon they would leave me altogether. Then what would I have?

Dear Lord help me, I prayed tearfully into the vast night sky.

September 3, 1985

The outcome was heartbreaking. A veil of sadness filled the house as immediate plans were made for the children to remain in Houston. They talked about moving to California the following summer, easing our feeling of panic. There was so much to do and so little time. We couldn't talk about our final separation…our last day together…the pain was too great.

It was agreed that Cory would move in with my father and stepmother in the next county, while Tiffy begged and pleaded to be allowed to live with her best friend. After many phone calls our families agreed.

September 7, 1985

Lorne flew home two days before the movers were due. This was the day I would have to say good-bye to my children. Still dazed, we went through the motions like robots doing what needed to be done but not talking. Everything had happened so fast. All too soon the clock on the wall said it was time. Our final farewell had arrived.

It was dusk when my children left.

I stood at the curb. My heart was breaking while I watched my only daughter climb into the car clutching the tattered pink bunny she had loved since she was little. She looked out the window; her big eyes brimmed with tears. A choking knot filled my throat as I waved goodbye. My lips formed the words "I love you." Hers did the same. Scalding tears burned my cheeks yet I tried to stay strong for her. The reality of our separation was hard to grasp. Our eyes met and locked one last time as the car pulled away…ripping us apart. I was numb. I stood waving, blinded by tears, trying to release my baby girl. We'd been together since her birth. I didn't want to think of the empty tomorrows. I stood at the curb crying as I watched her car disappear out of sight.

Minutes later, Cory walked down the driveway and shook Lorne's hand. I noticed how young and innocent he looked as they talked, so vulnerable. Then he turned, smiling impishly. He put his arms around me and gave me a big bear hug, lifting me off the ground. This usually made me chuckle...but not today.

"I love you, Mom," he whispered in my ear.

I took his face between my hands and kissed his lips. "I love you, Cory," I said, looking tearfully into his eyes. Neither of us could say another word.

Standing at the open door of his little blue Honda, he looked at his basket ball hoop mounted on the garage and then his eyes slowly moved over the house and the neighborhood before getting in. The car was crammed to the ceiling with his worldly possessions. Flipping on a new sound system housed in the trunk, Cory backed down the driveway, music pouring into the street. He beeped twice driving off into the darkness.

I continued to wave long after Cory's taillights vanished, not wanting to release him, tears burning my eyes. Lorne was waiting when I finally turned around. He put his arm around my waist. We walked in silence back up the driveway and into the house.

It was as quiet as a tomb. The stillness was consuming. This had been our home for the last eight years, for better or for worse, but the life and love were gone. Now it was only a house, dead and hollow. Or was I the one who was dead and hollow?

Dear God, what will I do without my children? What will my children do without me? We've been through so much and have never been separated. Please watch over them and keep them safe. Amen.

48

Struggling with my decision

September 11, 1985—Somewhere in Texas

Still struggling with my decision, I stared aimlessly through the bug splattered windshield of my dusty brown Nissan 280ZX. Two days on the road and the landscape had grown monotonous. A tiresome sea of empty fields lapped at the edge of the asphalt. Vast acres of sun drenched meadow crisscrossed with rusty barbed wire fencing reached out to meet the horizon. For all I knew we were going in circles. Occasionally a few stray cattle napped in the shade of a lonely tree. Sometimes a rusty old tractor rested in a pasture of waist high weeds. The endless blue sky was cloudless and clear as hungry vultures sailed the air currents in search of their next meal. After fourteen years in Texas I was finally leaving.

Lorne sat behind the wheel. A look of pure contentment softened his handsome rugged profile. I smiled to myself. This must be what "happily married" felt like. It had been years since I had seen him this relaxed, this normal. I only hoped it would last. It was strange, but driving my car seemed to calm the beast that lived within him. The demons that walked in his shadow were at rest...at least for now.

My eyes lowered and I noticed that the speedometer edged past eighty.

"Honey, please slow down," I said, laying my hand on his leg.

"Sorry," he said, grinning sheepishly. "Guess I got carried away."

As I gazed out the window, my mind wandered back to the day I got my car.

In those days I was stuck driving an old Ford Thunderbird that Lorne just had to have. "Baby, it's a Classic," he said, patting the fender as if it were an old Army buddy. "They don't make 'em like this anymore. It's the kind of car a man would be proud to be buried in."

And bury is what I wanted to do with it. I hated that car. It was the size of a school bus and constantly breaking down, leaving me stranded in the middle of nowhere...easy prey to any pervert on the loose.

One evening Lorne picked me up from work because the Thunderbird was in the shop again. On our way home we stopped at a local Nissan dealership. Browsing used cars had become a hobby, so knowingly I strolled ahead leaving Lorne to analyze sticker prices taped to the windows.

I was off in another world when he crept up behind me and grabbed me by the waist.

"If you could have any car in the lot," he whispered in my ear, "which one would you pick?"

I whirled around. "Lorne, don't you tease me. You know how much I hate driving that Thunderbird."

"Just humor me," he said, grinning down at me.

What harm could it do? The search was on while Lorne tagged along like a playful puppy.

Then I saw it—a rich brown Nissan 280ZX Turbo with T-Tops parked against the fence, dazzling like liquid chocolate under the bright overhead lights. It was love at first sight.

"That's the one!"

It was a few years old with less than five thousand miles on it. Lorne and the mechanic on duty went over it with a fine-tooth comb, and, to my amazement...he bought it on the spot.

His words still echoed in my ears..."Baby, you deserve this for all the years you've put up with me."

This sudden move to California was to be a new beginning, a time to start over and leave the past behind. Lorne promised. A place where we could build our marriage the way it should have been but never was. A new beginning...words I thought I would never hear but wanted to believe. Fewer than five months earlier Lorne had asked for a divorce. He wanted to be free. He didn't want the responsibilities of a wife and a family. He said he couldn't handle it. And now here we were...ready for one last try.

49

Guilty for doubting him

"Baby, are you ready for dinner?"

The sound of my husband's voice plucked me back to reality.

"Sure, any time you are." I sat up straight. Hostage to my seat belt I stretched from side to side trying to relieve the tightness in my back and shoulders. "Any idea where we are?"

"Van Horn," he said. "It was posted on a sign we just passed."

In the distance was a tiny town perched at the base of a vivid sunset dipped in swirls of lavender, magenta and ravenous pink. A sign along the road pointed to food and gas at the next exit. Lorne turned off the main highway and headed towards the small cluster of buildings on the horizon, clouds of dust billowing in our wake.

The town was the size of a shoebox. Old wooden buildings lined the dusty deserted streets. Rusty relics cluttered the sidewalk outside a gloomy antiques store; chipped and faded letters crossed the dirty front window. Where was everyone? A shiny new Coke machine sat under the eaves of a dreary gas station like a rocket waiting for fuel. I leaned forward. Buckled boards covered the windows of a two-story building engulfed in weeds; a flashing red sign shaped like a buffalo was the only indicator of life. Then I shuddered. Posted at the top of the sagging steps a hand-painted sign read, *Trespassers Will Be Shot.*

The only restaurant in town was rundown and weather beaten like she'd been lost at sea for years. But a sign in the window read *Mom's Home Cooking* and we were starving.

Lorne pulled next to an old green pickup; a shot gun sat boldly in a rack mounted in its back window. Chained behind the cab, a mangy black dog danced on his hind legs, barking fiercely. Lorne walked around the car, opened the door and reached for my hand. Our eyes met, I looked down. After all these years I felt shyness with this new man he promised to be.

Lorne led me across the parking lot and up worn wooden stairs to a covered porch. It was hard to believe he was really back and this was not a dream.

The pungent aroma of barbecue laced with stale cigarette smoke drifted out through the screen door. Stepping inside, we were greeted by a hodgepodge of flashing neon beer signs covering the walls like pop-art.

High-backed wooden booths upholstered in worn, red vinyl nestled under the dirty front window. Tables covered with red plastic checkered the middle of the room. Dingy ceiling fans whirred over the clatter of dishes from the kitchen.

"Help yourself to any seat y'all want," called a burly man from behind the counter; a soiled apron encircled his bloated belly.

I led the way to a booth in the back, Lorne at my heels. A few of the locals looked up. Sliding in on one side, I reached for two grease-stained menus propped against the window, passing one across the table. The voice of Kenny Rogers filled the room from a yellowed jukebox in the corner.

"Wonder if they know how to grill a steak medium rare?" Lorne mumbled, scanning the menu.

This will be our last day in Texas, I thought, gazing out the window and watching the sun slip out of sight. A scruffy-looking mutt slept peacefully on the porch, his face buried between his paws.

"Have ya'll decided?"

Our waitress was as skinny as a chicken bone. She was dressed in tight-fitting jeans and cowboy boots, a shock of red hair pinned on top of her head. She looked like she lived a hard life, but her dimpled smile was a charmer.

Once she scribbled our orders on her pad she left the table.

"How are you feeling?" I asked, unfolding a paper napkin in my lap. "We've covered a lot of miles today."

"Great, now that we're back together," Lorne said, leaning forward. He reached for my hands across the table, our eyes locked. His half-crooked smile tugged at my heart.

"No," I said grinning. "I mean, aren't you tired of driving? After all, we've been on the road for two days and you haven't let me drive once. I'm actually a good driver you know."

He would be crushed if he could read my thoughts. I loved him so much but had no idea what lay ahead. And I was more than a little scared.

"No, I'm not tired of driving," he enunciated with a broad grin, "but you're changing the subject." He squeezed my hands tightly. "Baby, I've missed you so much."

"Me, too," I said softly, feeling guilty for doubting him.

Breaking his gaze, my eyes lowered to his hands, his beautiful, strong hands. The hands I loved and longed for all those lonely nights that he was away. I could feel his heat penetrate my skin but I could not escape the images of my children leaving. How could I share my pain? It was too raw and at times unbearable. And the same question kept floating to the surface. Had I made the right choice?

"Baby, I can't wait to get you to California," he said, excited as a schoolboy at recess. "You're going to love it. And wait until you see the beaches."

I smiled warily. Seeing him this happy was rare indeed. His eagerness seemed to ease my anguish...but now only time would tell.

"It's going to be wonderful," he said leaning closer. "Baby, I love you. Thank you for giving me another chance; I know I don't deserve it." His smiling blue eyes said it all.

"I love you, too," I said, shifting my feet under the table.

Lorne put cream and sugar into the steaming cup of coffee set in front of him. Settling back into the booth, he drew a pack of cigarettes from his shirt pocket and reached for his lighter. It looked like any stainless steel Zippo. But this lighter was special. One side was engraved, SGT MAC MILLAN, Vietnam, 70-71. On the other side, RECON 1/46...Live by Chance, Love by Choice, Kill by Profession.

I wanted to believe Lorne, but the past screamed in my ears. I knew he meant what he was saying, but his words were too familiar. The love we shared was strong, but was it enough...enough to pull him from the pits of hell? Tormented by the past, he could not keep his demons buried.

A leather-skinned cowboy dropped a coin in the jukebox, punched a few buttons and walked away. Soon Barbra Streisand's *"Memories"* swelled up from the past, reeling me back in time. This was our song—the song I played a thousand times while Lorne was gone, weeping to the words long after the children were asleep. As I stared out into the soft newness of night, haunting visions flooded my memory.

50

One last chance

The restaurant was deserted by the time we finished eating. A young busboy cleared the tables, loudly stacking dirty dishes in plastic tubs. I stared into the night through Lorne's reflection distorted in the dark glass. He raised a cigarette to his mouth and inhaled deeply. Leaning his head back against the booth, he formed a circle with his lips, releasing milky white smoke rings that hovered like halos. Once again my life had turned upside down. Lorne and I were back together as husband and wife. It was still new and hard to believe, but the journey had only begun. Bound for California to start a new life, we were much like the pioneers in covered wagons, except we used a moving van. Centuries stood between us, yet we had one thing in common, neither knew what lay ahead.

"Can I get y'all anything else?" inquired our skinny waitress. "Maybe some dessert, a piece of pie?"

Lorne looked up and smiled. "No thanks," he said, leaning forward, crushing his cigarette in the ashtray. "Just another cup of coffee for the road, please."

God did answer prayers. For almost two years I prayed for one last chance. And here it was. But there was a price to pay, I was sure of it. And I was scared. With ten years of marriage, our love was stronger than ever, but predators from Lorne's past prowled in the shadows waiting to devour him. He had to break free. He promised he would. And I wanted more than anything to believe him.

I read a famous quote about there being nothing to fear but fear itself, but logic is impossible when paralyzing panic rises in one's throat like vomit, chasing that theory right out the window.

"Tonight we cross the Texas border," Lorne said, pouring cream into a Styrofoam cup of hot coffee. "Lived here most of my life and never realized how big it was until I tried to get out."

"You want me to drive for a while?" I asked, reaching for my purse.

"No, Baby, I'll be fine. Besides, I've had plenty of coffee to keep me awake." He left a tip on the table and slid out of the booth.

The night was crisp and quiet as we stepped out onto the porch. Shimmering stars filled the sky like a thousand fireflies. I shivered. Lorne put his arm around my shoulder and guided me down the steps and across the parking lot. Tumbleweeds edged in moonlight drifted aimlessly across the plain. I stood by the car gazing up overhead as he unlocked the door.

A Texas sky full of stars…what could be more beautiful? Blue diamonds, thousands of light years away. Lorne had been my mentor, expanding my mind to the wonders of the universe while sitting on a motorcycle in the middle of nowhere. I loved his stories of the stars traveling through space: where they came from, what they were made of and where they were going. How could I let him go without a fight?

Back on the road he settled in; he turned on the radio, lit a cigarette and cracked open the window. "Baby, why not tilt your seat back and try to get some sleep?"

"Maybe a little later," I said, searching the darkness surrounding us. "Right now I need to stay awake. I want to see Texas as long as I can. This is where my children live; tomorrow I won't be able to say that." I couldn't hold back the tears. "I miss them so much and it's only been two days."

"I know," he said tenderly, patting my knee, "but they're going to be fine. You wait and see."

He could never know how I felt…not in a million years. I was a woman but even more so I was a mother - two separate entities. I had made a heartbreaking decision, torn between my children and the man I loved. No woman should ever have to make such a painful choice

PART FOUR

Southern California

A new beginning

51

Cross my heart

September 13, 1985—Somewhere in California

California was like being on another planet. Timeless mountains hemmed the sapphire blue sky while five-story palm trees stretched high over housetops, enough to humble any girl who grew up in Ohio. It was more beautiful than I remembered.

Peter, the children's father, had been transferred to California when Tiffy was nine months old. We bought a house with a pool and proceeded to live the lifestyle of sunshine and parties. The children thrived in the environment, but the marriage did not. Entertaining was a way to fill my emptiness, that is until the guests went home and I was faced with reality. Peter and I had nothing in common except the children. The Sylmar earthquake in 1971 sent me into a tailspin. Our damage was minimal but I was scared...for my children. Fear of another earthquake haunted my dreams. Three little lifejackets hung on nails outside the patio door, but I knew they'd be useless when California slipped into the ocean like people from Ohio thought it would. I was so obsessed with this thought that I persuaded Peter to ask for another transfer. That's how we settled in Texas.

Jagged boulders hovered high over Interstate 405 as it carved its way through the San Bernardino Mountains. Rusty orange folds layered the walls of the freeway, revealing a bold snapshot of the earth's cooling long before the dinosaurs. I was entranced.

Lorne watched me out of the corner of his eye. "One of these days I'll take you exploring," he said in good spirits. "I'll bet we could find dozens of fossils in those walls."

I was fascinated with science, nature and the universe. I should have gone to college for a degree but chose to have my babies instead. Stacks of books littered my nightstand waiting to be devoured. Carl Sagan was an idol; I watched every episode of *The Cosmos* at least twice. This is what first drew me to Lorne, other than his good looks. His curiosity and his wisdom were far beyond average for someone his age. No man I had ever known saw things the way I did, except maybe my dad. And now Lorne was my mentor.

The blazing afternoon sun beat down on the steady stream of traffic crawling through the pass. I lowered the window and a blast of hot air hit me in the face. Quickly I closed it. Then I fiddled with the radio searching for a weather report.

"Its ninety-eight degrees in the San Fernando Valley," said a brisk male voice, "with more of the same due tomorrow. And if your animals must be outside be sure they have shade and plenty of water."

Heat or no heat I was content. God had answered my prayers and I knew He'd watch over my children as well. Lorne promised things would be different. I wanted to believe him. Believe our love would find a way to heal his wounds and let us start over.

Lorne crushed his cigarette in the ashtray, reached over and squeezed my leg. "Baby, we're almost there," his eyes twinkled. "Are you excited?" His hand slid up and down my leg, keeping his eyes on the traffic. "I've pictured this moment so many times...and now you're here."

I put my hand on top of his and turned to face him. "Of course I'm excited," I said softly. "Lorne, I love you so much and I want our marriage to make it. You know I'd do anything for you. I just don't want any more pain."

"Baby, I know, and I promise you won't regret your decision," he squeezed my hand. "Cross my heart." He grinned lovingly, making a cross over his heart with his finger.

Suddenly I froze. Looking out the window, a single word was sculpted into a grassy knoll in huge white letters...*VALENCIA*. It was the name of the city I addressed my letters to during the nine months Lorne lived in California without me. The nine months it took to sell our house...during which time he asked for a divorce.

I knew Lorne rented a room from a single woman in Valencia. He told me she was just a friend, nothing more. That's all I knew or wanted to know. The only thing that mattered was that he loved me and wanted to save our marriage.

52

Reality slapped me hard

Lorne had had only three days to find someplace to live before he had flown back to Houston. "Housing in California is sure expensive," he griped when I had picked him up at the airport. "There wasn't a whole lot to pick from, but we got lucky. I found a house in Canyon Country that we can afford and it's huge. But there is one problem...it's on the outskirts of town."

I had no clue where Canyon Country was...but no big deal. I'm flexible. The only thing that mattered was that Lorne and I were together. Besides I had the flair to turn any house into a home.

Lorne turned off at the Magic Mountain exit. It was a quiet neighborhood of tree -lined streets, where stately homes rested on lush lawns tended by gardeners and children pedaled tricycles down the sidewalks. The main highway traveled past small, fairly new shopping strips and a flowering park with a bike path. But all too soon I noticed a gradual change in the landscape. The luscious greenness was fading...and before long everything looked dry and dead.

Sierra Highway was a two-lane road at the bottom of a canyon where parched underbrush covered the terrain like mold on cheese. Cars lined up at a small gas station on the corner. We passed a grocery store where planks of wood were nailed across the front window. Vacant lots of overgrown weeds and a few small buildings were nearby. A drooping flag hung over the Elks Lodge. Up the road dusty camper shells were stacked like building blocks behind a chain link fence. A dirty brown dog barked fiercely as we passed. I could only stare. An old pickup was parked outside a seedy little motel; a sandwich board sign with bold red letters sat propped at the edge of the road.

Approximately a quarter mile from the motel we crossed a small bridge where Lorne turned left onto an unpaved drive. I had no idea where we were.

A giant pepper tree with its leaf-burdened boughs touching the ground blocked our way. Lorne made a sharp right into a circular driveway. A six foot, black wrought iron fence caged two large houses that were clearly built by the same builder and dwarfed by the windswept mountain rising behind them. We drove through the open gates of the house on the end.

"This is it, Baby," Lorne said, sounding pleased with himself, "our new home. I'm going to unlock the door. You take your time." He leaped out, bounding up the driveway like a kid.

Reality slapped me hard. This was not what I had pictured. The house was ugly. It made my skin crawl as if something evil lived there. I felt the urge to run before it was too late...but where to?

The single story structure was one dimensional like a child's drawing. The plain brown door sat between two forbidding windows. Under the windows, dirt stained the cream colored stucco like giant tears. The house was void of any landscaping, not a single bush or flower. The skeleton of a dead tree sat in the middle of brown, withered grass, a worn rope dangling from an overhead branch, once a child's swing...like something from a Stephen King novel.

Teetering on the edge of panic, I took a deep breath, then closed the car door behind me and looked around. The hum of a rumbling engine crept over the five-foot, cream-colored, brick wall running the length of the paved driveway, partially camouflaged by a row of twelve towering cypress trees, which were the only green vegetation in sight. I walked over to the wall, stepped on a rock and peeked over the top. Two semi-tractor trailers sat idling. From the look of the paraphernalia scattered on the ground, they were waiting to be washed. The Lord knew I was open-minded, but this was pushing it.

I walked up to the house, opened the screen door and from there things went from bad to very bad. I stood in shock. Stretched before me was the most hideous maroon carpeting I had ever laid eyes on. It seemed to be the length of a football field. The house was cavernous. A massive stone fireplace sat off to the right at one end of the living room, littered with mounds of charred ashes left by the last tenant. Thick dust covered everything. No one had lived here for a long time. Spiders dangled freely from complex webs anchored to the knotty pine paneling that covered every wall. A Boy Scout could have been the interior decorator.

I stepped into the spacious dining room that was the hub of the house. Two non-descript bedrooms flanked a bathroom large enough to hold an elephant. A long, narrow kitchen and a huge den in the back completed the space I was to call home. The kitchen windows faced the truck depot. Thank God, the giant cypress blocked the view but not the sounds.

Lorne hurried outside to check on the detached garage and workshop...home to his beloved motorcycle, leaving me to roam at leisure and to try to adjust to my surroundings.

Lord, help me.

I opened the closet door in the second bedroom. High on the wall was a small window with a latch. I grasped the handle and it opened, sending a chill down my spine. Anyone with a ladder could easily break in...through the closet.

But the room had another door. I cringed when I opened it. A dark narrow corridor led between the walls and I was certain it was filled with spiders. But if I was going to live here I had to know where it went.

Inching my way through the dark, I came to another door. It led to another bathroom; this one could accommodate two elephants. This was the strangest house I had ever seen. Brushing cobwebs off my clothes, I looked around. Knotty pine walls, ugly maroon carpet, a walk-in shower...and a powder blue Jacuzzi sunken in the center of the room like a koi pond. Nothing could surprise me now.

Or could it?

On the opposite wall, two powder blue sinks and a toilet sat next to yet another door that stood ajar. I walked over, flipped on the light and peeked inside. There was a cedar sauna built for two complete with lava rocks. I shook my head, unable to hold back the grin. Now I knew why Lorne picked this house...but did it work?

A third door in the two-elephant bathroom opened to a sunlit family room that could easily accommodate fifty people. Windows on two walls overlooked the concreted back area, a huge brick barbecue and of all things, a barber's chair. A mirrored bar with a brass foot rail straight from an old western ran the width of the room. Intricate spider webs glittering in the afternoon sunlight draped the dusty glass shelves behind the bar. If rooms could talk what tales could this one tell?

I looked out the dirty patio window. The Santa Ana winds had kicked up, whipping hot sand against the glass. Lorne and I never had parties. It was too difficult to plan anything with his problems and never knowing if he would show up. The only people to ever visit were family. They were aware but they just didn't know the gory details. Here there was no one.

Lorne tapped on the glass patio door and startled me. I let him in.

"Well, Baby, how do you like it?" he said, grinning. Leaning over, he kissed me on the lips, "Big, isn't it?"

"It's big all right, but it sure is dirty," I said, eyeing a giant spider skittering across the window sill.

"They told me it would be cleaned before we got here," he replied, walking over to the bar. Leaning on his elbows, he gazed into the mirror and propped his boot on the brass foot rail. "It looks like they didn't make it," he continued. "I'll call the leasing office as soon as we see a phone."

The furniture wasn't due for another two days. There was still time to have the house cleaned properly. What a contrast to our home in Houston where I raised my children for the last eight years. Thank God we were only renting.

This strange dwelling was going to take some getting used to. But I'd manage. After all, this is what I wanted, one last chance to start over...one last chance to do it right.

53

The other woman

The mystery was about to unravel. I knew I must steel myself to face the facts and let my female instinct turn in the verdict. Our furniture wasn't due for another two days, which meant Lorne and I would be staying in Valencia...in his rented room. I was about to meet the "other woman" living in my head. The woman whose house my husband shared for the past nine months.

My first glimpse of Maggie squelched any notion of an affair, putting my overactive imagination back in its box with a sigh of relief. Indeed, Maggie was an attractive redhead and single. Her pretty, unlined face was made up to the hilt. I guessed she was in her mid-thirties, open and animated. But the baggy sweater she wore could not hide the surplus weight rippling under her purple stretch pants. And one thing I knew about my husband...he was not attracted to overweight women, a flashback to his first marriage.

That evening we sat chatting.

"You know it's no problem for you two to stay here until you get the house put together," Maggie said, washing down a cookie with a Diet Coke. "That landlord is a piece of work. It's going to take an army to hose the place down...it's so big."

Maggie was one worry I could now cross off my list.

The next morning Lorne chased down the landlord only to find out he had been given orders not to hire a cleaning crew. It seemed the owner had put the house on the market and didn't want the extra expense. So I got the job.

Once Lorne and Maggie left for work, I took a shower, drained the last cup of coffee from the pot on the kitchen counter and loaded my car with Maggie's pail and broom. On my way to the house I picked up close to thirty dollars worth of cleaning supplies. I would need it all.

Musty cobwebs hung like curtains in every room. Gritting my teeth, I whopped them with the broom, squishing the spiders that broke loose by stepping on them…if I could catch them. I only wish I'd had a dollar for each one I terminated…I could have bought a new stove. It seemed the last tenants literally stole the stove. No one walks off with something that big by accident.

A thick layer of dirt covered every surface like volcanic ash; it was my worst nightmare. Down on my hands and knees I used a dustpan to scoop the charred cinders from the fireplace. Shimmering particles swirled freely in the sunlight irritating my eyes and lungs as I questioned who lit the logs I was now cleaning up after.

I had barely scrubbed through the first layer of grime when the moving van pulled up in the driveway and honked its horn…one day early. Whoopee. The movers were able to cram our belongings into a few rooms and the garage. I proceeded to clean like a crazy lady. All day I heard the rumbling engines outside my window. What was it going to be like when we finally moved in?

54

Someone stole the stove

September 28, 1985

Our new beginning in California had started off on the wrong foot…not to mention the fact…we arrived on Friday the thirteenth. Thank goodness I'm not superstitious. The house was hopeless. The acre of hideous maroon carpeting clashed with everything we owned. Even my most creative ideas could not pull it together. *Home Sweet Home* it would never be.

Our first morning in the house was somewhat unnerving to say the least. It was Saturday and before breakfast I had to rummage through boxes to find my cookbooks. Inasmuch as someone stole the stove, I would now have to learn how to cook all over again…in a microwave. I could hardly wait.

I stood at the kitchen counter chopping onions, my eyes burning. From outside, the annoying hiss of water from a high pressure water hose seeped in around the windows. Across the driveway behind the wall, cross-country grime blasted from the aluminum carcass that rolled in around midnight. Its laboring engine woke me from a sound sleep. I shuddered to think Lorne had signed a one-year lease.

Cooking in a microwave was going to take some practice. In the past I had only used a microwave to reheat leftovers…not cook an entire meal. My scrambled eggs sautéed with onions and mushrooms were on the dry side, but edible. Lesson learned, remove sooner. The bacon was burned beyond recognition and I buried it in the garbage. I discovered my toaster in a box with the cookbooks.

"Breakfast is ready," I called through the dining room while sipping my second cup of coffee.

"There's a full-page ad for the annual Gem and Mineral show," Lorne called from the living room after breakfast. "It's at the Convention Center all weekend. I've heard it's huge."

I had no idea what he was talking about but I was sure he knew.

"Let's drive into Santa Monica for a look?"

"Sounds great," I replied, hanging the dishtowel on a hook. "Give me half an hour."

I poured a capful of bubble bath into the hot water gushing into the deep, claw-footed tub, then stepped into the rising foam. It will be nice to get away. I was sick of the smell of Pine-Sol.

Traffic was bumper to bumper all the way to the Convention Center, but I savored every minute, letting California seep back into my pores. I loved California…that is, everything but the earthquakes.

Throngs of people stormed the entrance, dragging us along like a cattle drive. Inside the double doors stretched the largest jewelry showroom I had ever seen. There were hundreds of vendors. I stood in awe. Lorne watched with amusement while I explored, touching everything in sight.

Later that evening we sat on the couch sipping wine and watching TV.

"What would you think of owning a business?" Lorne said casually.

I turned to him and grinned. "Would I ever!" I exclaimed.

For years I had tried to find my niche as an entrepreneur while holding down a full time job. I had the drive and intelligence but nothing ever took off. Working for other people was like being a bird in a cage stifling the air I breathed. And Lorne knew it.

"And what did you have in mind?" I inquired.

"I've been thinking about a small jewelry business," Lorne said, tapping a cigarette from the pack. "We have some money from the sale of the house. I'd like to invest it."

I swirled the wine in my glass while studying the lamp light under its ruby surface. It had taken nine months to sell our house in Houston…the market was flat. We barely made a profit. Yet California seemed strange and unfamiliar; I dreaded the thought of looking for a job.

"Lorne, you know I've wanted a business forever," I said, watching his expression, "but we have to be sure it's the right one before we invest a thing."

"I agree," he responded. "Today I was talking with an older couple while you browsed the showroom. I'd like you to meet them. They'll be there tomorrow. We can go and chat. Let them answer any questions you may have and then we'll talk."

Later that night we shared the darkness with a love that bound us eternal. A love that roamed restlessly, deep within our souls, always present, waiting to be rekindled, the need to feel a complete oneness that was ours alone.

I lay the length of his body, my arm draped over his bare chest, listening to the slow rhythmic breathing of deep sleep. Outside the bedroom window, cries from the hills were magnified in the dead of night. Eerie cries like human babies echoed throughout the canyon. Soon the haunting howls of coyotes stirred the night air celebrating their kill...food for their cubs. Suddenly all was quiet.

The next day we became partners, investing our entire savings in a jewelry business, totally unaware of what lay ahead.

55

Heal our wounds

And life went on.

While Lorne was at work I was at home drawing up a business plan. It was exciting. The thought of working with my husband towards one common goal, believing this would heal our wounds and draw us closer. With our DBA (doing business as) in hand, *MacMillan and Wife Creations*, I began researching the Gem and Mineral Shows and where they were held. Before long I had shows booked up and down the state of California for any event I could talk my way into...as long as the entrance fee was feasible. I even stumbled on a show in my hometown in Ohio. I booked it immediately. It would be our first vacation since our honeymoon and a chance for my family to finally meet Lorne in person.

At the Convention Center I had been drawn like a rabbit to a garden, mesmerized by all the beautiful and unique neckwear. Items made of gemstones of every shape and size: turquoise, jade and lapis. The list was infinite: stones mixed with wood or brass or silver or colored glass. Like the stars in the sky, the combinations were endless. Ideas whet my creative juices. I knew I could do this. I located a supplier and began to work evenings, sketching each new design in detail with the eye of an artist.

I found my niche and for the first time in a long time…contentment.

Weekends were show time. Our display drew crowds and my designs were a hit. But this business was as unpredictable as my husband. Some shows were large; others small and so were our profits. The bottom line called the shots and soon I had to return to work full-time, which I did. But now I also had the details of running a business to contend with. The pressure was starting to build…for Lorne as well.

56

House from hell

November/December 1985

It was bad enough cooking without a stove but the furnace quit working in the middle of November leaving us without heat. I knew I couldn't take much more. A blazing fire only warmed the living room, leaving the rest of the house icy as an igloo. It definitely gets cold in California, especially in the mountains. Lorne haggled with the landlord, but the owner put his foot down. With the property up for sale he refused to buy a new furnace.

What could we do? We stopped paying rent!

The House from Hell…became its new nickname. We couldn't move because Lorne had signed a one-year lease. A lawyer was out of the question. We simply didn't have the funds. Our only solution: deal with it one day at a time.

It was the first week in December when I heard someone tapping on the front door. I went to open it and found a strange man stapling something to the wood. The red and white notice read, *Foreclosure Sale*. The next day two men did a walk through, jotting notes on their clipboards.

This was one time I was grateful the children weren't living with us.

Christmas 1985

My first Christmas without the children hurt deeply. During our separation we talked on the phone, but that wasn't enough for me. More than anything I longed to touch them, hug them, kiss their faces and look into their eyes. I ached when I thought about it, so I tried not to go there. This was my life...the choice I made. And somewhere in the back of my mind I knew we'd all be together again.

The holiday was approaching like a race horse. I tried to beat the crowds by shopping sales in between my job and running the business. Two weeks before Christmas, pleased with my bargains, I headed for the post office with a huge box addressed to my dad. *At least the children would have a nice Christmas with their grandfather,* I thought as I waited in line.

December 25, 1985

I called my dad on Christmas afternoon when I knew Tiffy would be there.

"Merry Christmas," I said, attempting to sound cheerful. "Are you and the children having fun?'

There was a silent pause on the other end of the line.

"Nancy, I'm sorry to tell you...your presents never arrived," he said solemnly.

The first Christmas I was ever separated from my children, the United States Post Office lost their presents. When I called to put a trace on the box, they assured me it would eventually show up. Months later, they officially declared the loss and sent me a check for fifty dollars. I had neglected to insure the box for the value of its contents. Now I was back at square one like a game of Parcheesi, and fifty dollars barely scratched the surface. I felt like a terrible mother. Tiffy and Cory finally got their Christmas presents in April.

57

"It's a surprise"

New Years Day 1986

"Where are we going?" I asked, unable to stifle my curiosity.

Lorne grinned, not taking his eyes from the road. "I told you it's a surprise."

After an hour's drive in holiday traffic, he turned off the freeway and soon we were twisting through the mountains. Over the guardrail the landscape fell away from the road. My stomach was in my throat.

"Look out the window and tell me what you see," he announced, his blue eyes smiling.

Other than a death-defying drop on one side, we were surrounded by acres of very tall pines. Peering through tree trunks, I only saw more tree trunks. There was nothing else to be seen, not even a deer.

"Tall pine trees and a very low guardrail," I replied, wondering what he meant.

"Let me know when you see something else," he grinned.

When we turned the bend…I saw the snow.

"Snow," I declared, anxious to stop and touch it.

The last time I saw snow, a freak snowfall covered Houston but it was only a dusting. Outside my window it was getting deeper and deeper the higher we went. I grew up with snow but hated dealing with it every winter. Living with it was different than playing in it.

Blinding sunshine bounced off the virgin snow as Lorne leaned into the trunk, retrieving a canvas bag he had stashed that concealed our jackets, boots and gloves. He had thought of everything.

Soon we were frolicking like a two kids, knee-deep snow spilling in over our boot tops. It was impossible to run while hurling snowballs fast and furiously. We laughed until our faces ached.

"Hey, I saw a huge sheet of cardboard lying next to the road," Lorne hollered, ducking my snowball. "Let's get in the car and go get it."

The rest of the afternoon we took turns flying down the hill on a giant sheet of cardboard, our jeans soaked and our feet frozen. Once we tried to double up only to land face first in the snow...where Lorne kissed me.

That evening we laughed over bread bowls filled with steaming clam chowder at a quaint little restaurant in the village. It was the ending to a perfect day...not easy to forget.

I remembered when the children were small.

Peter had rented a cabin in the mountains for a weekend. The children's laughter echoed through the tall snowy pines as they raced down the hill on an old black inner tube, their cheeks flushed from the cold.

Before heading home we disassembled our handmade snowman, gently placing him in the trunk of the car. Back in the valley, he was resurrected on the front lawn complete with a carrot nose, a smiley face, hat and scarf. And this is where he stood charming neighborhood children and the mailman until he was nothing but a puddle.

January 11, 1986

Much to my delight, Lorne had another surprise up his sleeve...a trip to Pine Mountain to view Haley's Comet. We would be joining an astronomy class from the nearby college.

We sat on the top of the mountain, swaddled in the black of night, peering through telescopes beyond the stars. The subject of our excitement can only be seen from earth once every seventy-six years, a once in a lifetime experience. Even though our view was head-on and the comet looked like a far-away sun, the experience was still heart stopping. My husband knew how much this would mean to me.

58

Children were part of me

"Hi Mom, it's your son Scott," boomed an eager voice in my ear.

"Scott, what a nice surprise," I said, grinning. Stretching the phone line to the dining room, I pulled out a chair. "It's wonderful to hear your voice. What's been going on?"

"Didn't you say I could come and live in California if I wanted?" he asked hesitantly.

Caught off guard...I let it sink in a few seconds before replying.

"Of course I did. Is anything wrong? Are you and your dad having problems?" I questioned with concern.

"Nah, not really," Scott sounded relieved. "I've been thinking about it a lot. And I think California would be a perfect place to learn about boats. I'm sure there are thousands out there with all that water. I'm half-way through college and I'd like to give it a try. Get a job, maybe working on boats," he chattered on.

"Okay," I said slowly. "Does your father know about this?"

"Yeah, he doesn't care," Scott said.

January 23, 1986

The House from Hell raged on. The owner wanted his rent. We wanted heat. It was a standoff like an old western movie.

It was a Thursday when we were served with an eviction notice. Lorne contacted a lawyer the next morning and explained our quandary. On Saturday there was no hot water.

We saw the lawyer on Monday. That evening the landlord came by and we signed an agreement. It stated we would pay half the rent past due, with the owner's signature promising to install a new furnace and hot water tank. Once completed, we would pay the balance.

The new furnace was installed on February thirteenth...three months after it quit working. As fate would have it, by then the cold weather was behind us. However, we decided we would still sue the owner.

February 1, 1986

I worried like any normal mother.

Scott waved goodbye to bone-chilling Chicago, which had been his home for a decade, and headed for sunny California. He bought a new red Volkswagen GTI with monies he earned during an internship at IBM and tips delivering Domino's pizza. My one worry...he was hauling his sailboat through blizzards and over mountains. He promised to call every day. In the meantime I wondered how Scott's moving in would affect Lorne. Only time would tell. But I wasn't about to turn my son away for the second time...my children were part of me.

February 7, 1986

Scott arrived safe and in one piece, elated with the prospect of living in California. Our agreement was a sixty-day trial. This would give him time to look around, check out the job market and get acclimated. After that he agreed to start paying rent.

59

Suicide alley

February 16, 1986

The soot-gray sky was dense with drizzle. It was a Sunday morning shortly after 6 a.m. and Lorne and I were traveling on Highway 126, a two-lane road snaking through the mountains, better known to the locals as *Suicide Alley*. We were on our way to a gem show in Ventura.

At a crest in the road, we noticed an old red car coming to a stop at the crossroad. It started to cross the highway...then stopped. Our speedometer read fifty. Lorne jammed on the brakes and the tires shrieked. The high pitched whine rang in my ears. Lorne fought to gain traction, but the car went into a skid.

"Baby, hold on," he hollered, savagely turning the wheel, trying to avoid hitting the car. Off to the right was a bridge spanning an open gorge.

"Dear God, help us," I prayed silently.

We hit the red car broadside behind the driver's door, sending it careening across the road head-on into a massive fence post. We spun out of control like a carnival ride, pinning me to my seat by centrifugal force. It felt like a dream as I gradually slid under my lap belt. I couldn't breathe; an excruciating pain cut through my chest.

When we finally came to a stop, we were facing the opposite direction in the other lane. Thank God it was early morning and there were no other cars on the road.

"Baby, are you all right?" Lorne asked with concern. Reaching over, he unhooked my seatbelt.

"I think so," I said, trying to sit up straight, pain searing through my chest.

"I'm going to see if I can help," he said. Opening the door, he rushed towards the other car, where there was no sign of life.

Gingerly I placed my feet on the ground; it was difficult to stand up straight. There was sharp pain in my chest each time I inhaled. I started towards the red car.

"Nancy, stay back," Lorne ordered. "The driver's hurt bad. I've been in Vietnam and know what to do but I don't want you to see this," he insisted. "I need you to go to that farmhouse and call 911. Tell them there are two women and a baby. The driver's unconscious, her head's split open, she wasn't wearing a seat belt. The other woman and the baby seem okay, just stunned. Please hurry."

I walked past the car without looking closely. I could see Lorne leaning over the driver. The farmhouse was at the end a long gravel driveway. Each breath I took caused more sharp pain.

Once the ambulance arrived, I was transported to the hospital along with the driver from the other car. The doctors said I had two cracked ribs caused by the seatbelt.

60

Hard time coping

March 1986

Lorne had a hard time coping with all that had happened during the past few weeks. He was more irritable than usual. But I understood. There were days when I myself wanted to scratch someone's eyes out.

He traveled more during the week, allowing him to flee some of the madness. He'd call me from the road to tell me how much he loved me, but when he was home he was back at the bars coming in long after I was asleep. What was I to do? To mention it would cause an explosion. Either way I couldn't win.

On the weekends when we had a gem show he was a different man. On the open road he was loving and happy. He was the man I fell in love with. And we talked. But the House from Hell was an evil place and there Lorne was someone else. I called him Dr. Jekyll and Mr. Hyde to his face but he only chuckled.

March 27, 1986

Lorne made his first court appearance as defendant in our lawsuit against Mr. Leonard, the owner of the House from Hell.

April 11, 1986

It was necessary for Lorne to make a second court appearance. He had to take off from work, which put him in a toxic mood. The landlord accompanied Mr. Leonard to present their side of the case...against us. Lorne was disgruntled when he came home that evening and he refused to talk about it.

"With my luck, we'll lose," he grumbled, heading straight for the liquor cabinet.

I didn't know if his lousy mood was due to the trial, or to the fact that he had put off doing our income taxes until the last minute. Now he knew he had a mountain of paperwork to wade through, including a new business mixed into the equation I was dreading the rest of the evening like a visit to the dentist.

April 23, 1986

"Brringgg..."

"Brringgg..."

I had just walked in the door from work, and dashed to reach the phone in the kitchen before it stopped ringing.

"Hello?" I said breathlessly.

"Hi Baby," Lorne said, three sheets to the wind, "guess what?"

"Lorne, where are you?" I asked, setting my purse and briefcase on the counter. "You sound like you've been drinking all afternoon." *It slipped out before I could stop it.* I bit my tongue and waited.

"I'm celebrating," he said cheerfully, ignoring my comment. "I called the lawyer this afternoon and he told me we won a judgment in the amount of nine hundred and fifty dollars. Isn't that great?" he boasted. "My luck is changing."

"Honey, I'm happy, too," I praised him. "I just wish you'd come home now."

"Baby, I'll be home in a little while," he said agreeably.

It was after midnight when he staggered into bed. When would this insanity stop?

61

A strange heaviness

May 1986

Our business was growing. Every weekend in May was booked, but our earnings were as unpredictable as the stock market. I scheduled the shows, kept the books, did the banking, inventoried product and purchased new merchandise. In the evenings, I designed and made one-of-a kind necklaces to sell. But with my full-time job I felt like a dog chasing my tail. Lorne traveled a few nights a week but was in the bars most nights he was home. Even so, I was way too busy to waste energy arguing so I let him be...suffering in silence.

May 14, 1986

I heard the front door close. Squinting at the clock on my nightstand, I saw it was after 2 a.m. Lorne tiptoed into the bedroom without turning on any lights. I pretended to be asleep but my eyes were adjusted to the dark. I watched him move through the shadows. Usually he would struggle out of his clothes, leaving a pile on the floor and crawl into bed. Tonight he made his way to my side of the bed and gingerly sat down on the edge. I didn't budge. Then I felt something...a strange heaviness on the blanket. It began to move.

"I brought you a present," he whispered close to my ear. The pungent scent of wine hung in the air. Then I felt something nuzzle my neck. At that moment Lorne turned on the light. A ball of white fluff stood on the pillow looking at me. I reached up and cupped the tiny puppy in my hands.

"Oh Lorne," I gushed with delight, "he's beautiful."

Lorne leaned down and kissed me lovingly. "I thought he'd be good company for you," he said, grinning from ear to ear. His gift was a hit.

How could I love someone so much and hate him at the same time?

May 30, 1986

I had booked a show in Reno but Lorne wanted to leave a day early and stop in Vegas on the way. I wasn't much of a gambler. I paid the bills and knew how much we didn't have. Nickel slots were fine until my twenty dollar limit was gone. But that night Lorne was on a lucky streak. He hit a thousand dollar jackpot amid a symphony of flashing lights and clanging bells.

In the pit of my stomach I knew he would lose at least half before we left Las Vegas. But I couldn't say a word…not without a scene. I knew better.

62

"Bail me out"

June 5, 1986

I rolled over, snuggling deep into my pillow. The distant ringing persisted. With eyes closed, I slipped my hand between the sheets, reaching for Lorne. The taut cotton was cold and empty. I bolted out of bed, racing to reach the phone in the kitchen before the caller hung up.

"Hello?" I said breathlessly.

"It's me," Lorne said, sounding annoyed. "I'm in Ventura County jail. I need you to bail me out." His speech was thick and sloppy.

I turned on the kitchen light. The clock over the sink read 1:50 a.m.

"Lorne, what happened?" I asked patiently, pacing the floor. But I knew the answer before he replied. The same old pattern…I was in for another long night.

"The cops pulled me over for drunk driving," he moaned irritably. "I told 'em I only had a few drinks but they didn't believe me. I was told to get into the cop car. They brought me here."

"Oh, Lorne," I sighed, running my hand through my hair. His belligerent attitude told me their observation was accurate.

"My company car is sitting on the edge of some orange grove on Highway 126," his tone softened. "They'll fire my ass if someone hits it. Baby, ya' gotta help me," he begged.

"Of course, I'll help you" I assured him like a small child, knowing I had no other choice. Lorne was my husband and my responsibility. "What do I need to do?"

I scribbled his directions on a piece of paper.

"And bring a hundred dollars," he added. "That should cover it."

"Okay," I agreed. "I have to get dressed; it'll probably take me an hour to get there."

"Fine," he snapped. "Just hurry, I don't like this place."

I pulled my nightgown over my head wondering when the nightmare would end. Lorne was getting worse. I never knew what to expect. He had never been arrested before…at least not that I was aware of.

I tugged on a pair of jeans and grabbed a warm bulky sweater from the drawer. In the back of the closet, I pulled a shoebox encircled with a fat rubber band from the shelf. I lifted the lid and removed seven twenty-dollar bills. Folding them in half, I shoved them in my pocket. This was business money I hadn't had time to deposit. God only knew if I would ever get it back.

63

Spiraling out of control

Highway 126 scared me, especially at night. I hadn't been on this road since the accident, but it was the quickest way to Ventura…I had no choice.

The narrow, winding two-lane road slithered through the dark mountains linking the San Fernando Valley to the City of Ventura, cutting hundreds of acres of citrus groves in two. A double yellow line snaked ahead of me. This was *Suicide Alley,* named for the mangled bodies pulled from wreckage caused by fools who passed illegally.

My eyes were fixated on the double yellow line. I was virtually alone in the dark in the middle of nowhere. White ghostly trees jumped into my high beams at every sharp curve like they might want to eat me.

My husband's illness was spiraling out of control. Tonight he was arrested for drunk driving. It was bound to happen. For years I lived in fear he would wrap himself around a tree, or worse yet…kill someone else. Could this be a wakeup call, a blessing in disguise? Maybe now he would admit he was an alcoholic and seek help.

The luminescent clock on the dash read 2:44 a.m. when I reached Ventura. The trip took less than an hour. I never passed one car on the road. Everyone was in bed asleep, where I should be. As I neared the courthouse, a metal sign pointed me to "parking in the rear" of the building. A few lonely cars sat under the bright security lights. I pulled into a space by the door and turned off the ignition. A three-story wall of black opaque windows rose like a monolith in front of me. I got out of the car and headed up the walk, unable to shake the eerie feeling I was being watched.

Inside, the spacious sterile gray room enveloped me; metal folding chairs lined the tiled floor like an army of tin soldiers. A disheveled young man huddled in debate with an older couple, their heated whispers lost in the vast room. Posters for bail bonds plastered the walls, *Just a Phone Call Away, Open 24 Hours.* On my left was a bank of pay phones that waited in silence. This was a first for me. The whole setting was surreal.

I walked across the floor towards a long glass window on the other side of the room. Approaching, I noticed a solemn middle-aged woman writing in a log.

"Excuse me," I said, setting my purse on the counter. "My husband called and told me he had been arrested. I came to bail him out."

The woman looked up. I felt a flush of embarrassment rush across my face.

"What's his name?" she asked matter-of-factly.

"Lorne MacMillan," I replied sheepishly.

The woman pulled another book from a shelf under the window. She began leafing through the pages and then she stopped, her finger resting on a name.

"Yes, I show him here," she said, without lifting her eyes from the page. "In order to release him into your custody I need to collect two hundred dollars in cash along with proof of ID."

"I only brought one hundred and forty dollars with me," I replied. "Can I write a check for the balance?"

"No," said the woman firmly. "Cash only."

"I live in Canyon Country," I said, totally frustrated. "It will take me an hour to get home and another hour to get back."

"We'll be here," she said coldly. "We don't close."

I picked up my purse, turned on my heels and briskly walked to the door. I was furious with Lorne for putting me in this position. I should let him stay put for a while. Give him something to think about.

"It's five minutes to five and we're in for a glorious sunrise," cooed a sultry soft voice over the car radio. "The streets are still quiet in paradise…"

Paradise…yeah right, I thought sarcastically, pulling into the same parking place I occupied two hours earlier. I was exhausted. Lowering my chin, I closed my eyes, slowly massaging my throbbing temples. On the way home I stopped for coffee, adding a pack of cigarettes to my bill. Tilting the pack, I peered inside. A fourth…no, it was half empty. I let out a deep sigh irritated by my lack of will power. On New Year's Eve I quit again, for the umpteenth time. Bingo…another crisis.

I entered the big double doors and headed back to the cashier with two hundred and fifty dollars bulging in my pocket.

"Excuse me," I announced at the window. "Remember me?"

"The name, please," the woman stated, a blank look on her face.

"Lorne MacMillan."

Flipping pages in the log, she stopped. "Oh yes," she muttered, continuing to read. "I'm sorry to say we found some outstanding parking tickets while you were gone. His bail has been increased to three hundred and fifty dollars."

I wanted to cry. Leaning wearily against the counter, fatigue crept over me like a virus. I had never felt so tired. All I wanted was to lie down.

"What do I do now?" I asked, teetering on the verge of tears.

"Get a bail bondsman," the woman said, pointing in the direction of the pay phones.

I walked along the wall, studying the collage of posters. The more I read the more confused I became. I had no idea how to pick such a person. Too tired to think, desperate and overwhelmed by the whole ordeal, I decided on a woman by the name of Jennifer Cook. Instinct told me I could relate better to a woman than the male prototypes seen on TV. Jotting her number on a blank deposit slip, I went to a pay phone and inserted a quarter.

The phone rang six times before a scratchy female voice crackled, "Hello?"

"I'm really sorry to wake you so early," I said, apologizing. "My name is Nancy MacMillan; I'm at Ventura County Jail. My husband was arrested for drunk driving and I don't have enough cash to get him out. Can you help me?"

"Was your husband in an accident?" she asked with a sound of authority in her once sleepy voice.

"No," I said, "just drunk."

"I'll meet you there at eight o'clock," she said. "And don't worry."

Two more hours...I decided to wait in the car. It was definitely more comfortable than a stiff metal chair. Back in the car I started the engine and pulled to the middle of the parking lot. I checked that both of my doors were locked and then reclined my seat and closed my eyes. Fatigue numbed my senses like Novocaine, but I knew I must not fall asleep.

Behind closed eyelids my mind wandered. Nothing had changed but our address. Lorne was doing what he had always done, exactly as he pleased. But why should he change? He knew I loved him; he had me wrapped around his little finger. Thank God, my family couldn't see me now...parked outside a jail with my husband locked inside, waiting for a bail bondsman. How in the world did I get into such a predicament?

At 7:30 a.m. I pulled my seat upright and cocked the rearview mirror. My back ached and my eyes burned from lack of sleep. The harshness of daylight revealed clownish black smudges under each eye. I pulled a tissue from my purse, wet it with saliva and rubbed until the black disappeared. A dab of gloss, a hint of blush, and a comb through my hair. Readjusting the mirror, I started the car and drove to a parking spot in front of the door.

As I headed up the walk, sharp tapping echoed from the sea of black glass overhead in every direction. I looked up and realized I was being watched like a goldfish in a bowl. The black glass concealed leering eyes of prisoners above me. Repulsed by the idea I hurried inside.

Jennifer Cook arrived at ten minutes after eight. She was an attractive, energetic woman, young enough to get by on little sleep and still look terrific. After a brief exchange of words, I was handed a stack of papers to sign. I skimmed the pages, too tired to comprehend what I was reading. I signed where I was told, then watched Ms. Cook walk across the room and talk with the woman behind the glass. She returned shortly with a satisfied look on her face.

"Everything's in place," she said, handing me something that looked like a receipt. "He should be out in half an hour; they're having breakfast right now."

I was too tired to respond.

"One last thing...just be sure he shows up for his hearing. It's very important he doesn't skip bail."

"I will," I said automatically, "and thank you." But in the back of my mind I knew I had no control over Lorne. If for some reason he chose not to show up, there was nothing I could do to make him.

We shook hands and then Jennifer Cook headed out the door, while I sat down in a stiff metal chair...to wait. Once again I was waiting for Lorne. It seemed like I had spent half our married life waiting for him. No matter what he did I came to his rescue.

It was almost 10:30 a.m. when the door opened and Lorne appeared. I stood. His eyes lit up when he saw me. Crossing the stark tiled floor, he looked as confident and self assured as ever. No one would ever know he had spent the night in jail. When he reached my side he leaned down and kissed me warmly.

"Thanks for coming," he said softly. "Now let's get out of here." He put his arm around my shoulder and we walked towards the double doors and out into the startling sunshine of a new day.

"We played volleyball up on the roof this morning," he said, pulling out onto the highway.

"That's nice," I said wearily. *Great, he played volleyball while I was condemned to a stiff metal chair all morning trying to stay awake.* I tilted my seat back slightly. First things first; we had to find his company car. Hopefully it was still where the police left it and unharmed.

I turned to look at Lorne. He lit a cigarette and offered me one. I shook my head. All these years he was still as handsome as the day we met. I loved him so much, but when would my life get better? Turmoil and crisis, never any peace. But what could I do about it? I was trapped.

Lorne reached up, flicking his ash out the crack in his window. I noticed something; it looked like the plastic ID bracelet they gave him in the hospital. When he put his hand back on the steering wheel I looked closer. This one read, "Ventura County Jail."

64

Something had to change

Scott slipped into the California lifestyle like he was born there. Within two weeks of his arrival he had his dream job...or so he thought...repairing sailboats. Wearing shorts and deck shoes to work was liberating compared to the confines of a rigid three-piece suit. And he liked what he did...but the pay was lousy.

When he wasn't working, he tested his wings. He sailed at Dana Point, panned for gold on Mount Piru and drove to Las Vegas, expounding about how he gambled at a table while sitting in a swimming pool. He dated a receptionist from my office named Cori and attended a Grateful Dead concert. But before long Scott realized how expensive it was to live in California.

May 26, 1986

Scott made the decision on his own to return to Ohio State and complete his degree. He left for Chicago towing his sailboat with zero snow in the forecast. His best friend was getting married that Saturday. Gord would be the first to leave the pack, and his wedding party wouldn't be complete without Scott.

Before leaving for Chicago, Scott bought a used Volkswagen. They were cheaper on the West Coast and rust-free, unlike the corroded jalopies back east. He scoured the newspapers, made a few phone calls and finally found the one he wanted. He left a down payment until he could fly back the following week to claim it.

June 2, 1986

I picked Scott up at the airport and the next morning we drove to Ventura to collect his newly acquired car. Primer gray and splotchy. Scott loved it. He called it his *California Suntan* car.

June 16, 1986

I waved goodbye to Scott once again, knowing this time he was ready to become a man.

June 30, 1986

Lorne was due in court at 10 a.m. on the DUI (driving under the influence) charge. He arrived on time and accepted full responsibility. *Thank*

God. And it didn't take long. The judge slapped him with a hefty fine, seven hundred and fifty dollars for a first offense. He lost driving rights for sixty days, other than traveling back and forth to work, plus mandatory driver's education classes once a week for two months.

The huge fee stung. There went the thousand dollars Lorne won in Las Vegas that was basically already gone. I was upset over his lack of concern for my well being. Something had to change...and soon.

65

"I've lost my rights

July 4, 1986

Life may be a bowl of cherries for some but I got all the pits.

Lorne had been in a foul mood since the day of the trial, blaming all his problems on the judge. However, I wasn't siding with him this time.

"Throw some stuff together, so we can go camping," he thundered from the living room during a commercial.

That did it, I had enough.

Dishtowel in hand, I marched into the living room, stopping at the end of the couch.

"I don't want to spend a weekend in the mountains when you're in such a bad mood," I said crossly. "Besides, I would have to drive and that's a long trip."

"I can't drive or I'd be out of here," he yelled, glaring back at me.

"I'm sorry, Lorne. I can't do it," I said calmly. Turning on my heels, I went back to the kitchen to finish making breakfast.

Lorne stood up and stormed over to the liquor cabinet. He squatted, holding onto one door while he rummaged through the contents. He pulled out a bottle of Remy Martin cognac that we had been saving for a special occasion. From the kitchen I watched him tear off the top, put the bottle to his lips and drink heartily. He took the bottle with him back to the living room.

I bit my tongue, holding my words intact.

When I finished making breakfast, I carried our plates to the living room and set them on the coffee table. When I went back to the kitchen to pour coffee, I heard a horrendous crash. I reached the doorway in time to witness a second plate of breakfast sail across the room into the fireplace. Lorne stood holding the bottle of cognac in his other hand.

"Lorne...Stop! What are you doing?" I hollered, tears rushing to my eyes.

"I want to go camping but I'm stuck in this damn house," he yelled back at me. "Between you and that judge, I've lost my rights. I fought in Vietnam! It's the Fourth of July and I have rights!"

Wide-eyed and frightened, I slowly backed up. It was then I watched the bottle of cognac fly across the room and explode in the fireplace.

"Lorne, you're scaring me," I whimpered. "I have to call the police. I don't know what else to do."

"I don't give a damn who you call," he bellowed from the other room.

Terrified, I dialed 911.

By the time the police arrived, Lorne was watching TV like nothing had happened. But the evidence was obviously heaped in the fireplace. One officer asked me to step outside while another officer went inside to talk to Lorne. After all was said and done, the police asked Lorne to promise to settle down, and threatened jail time if they were called out again.

That evening, Lorne tearfully begged forgiveness for scaring me, promising never to do it again.

The following day we took off for Sequoia National Park. We camped in a tent, cooked out over an open fire, hiked to a secluded waterfall and made love under the stars. The man I fell in love with was back by my side. But so were Dr. Jekyll and Mr. Hyde.

66

Pitted with potholes

Time passed...and our yellow brick road became pitted with pot holes...a few big enough to swallow a horse.

After hours of pain-staking research, I finally finished making the phone calls needed to fill our gem show schedule through the end of the year. With the holidays approaching, I expected an increase in sales that would help cover Lorne's bar bills.

He still traveled a few nights a week, hitting his local haunts when he was back in town. Once in a blue moon, he'd come home at a normal hour like regular people. It seemed strange but nice. I was again getting used to Lorne being gone during the week, whether out of town or out drinking. I liked the peace and quiet much better than his surly moods. And I was there for him when he awoke from a nightmare.

The House from Hell remained our main contention. The problems weren't my fault, but I was Lorne's nearest target. There were days when I just wanted to strike a match and burn the damn thing to the ground.

July 11, 1986
I was standing at the kitchen sink when the phone rang.

"Hello?" I said, as I scooped Puppy Chow into Benji's red plastic bowl.

"Mom, guess what?" Tiffy's sweet voice always brought a smile to my face.

"Ahhh...you got an A on your chemistry exam?" I replied with a grin.

"Mom...you know I don't take chemistry," she said impatiently. "I got my braces off a week early!"

"Congratulations, I'm thrilled for you!" I replied to the joy in my daughter's voice. "Is your smile gorgeous now?"

"It sure is. I can hardly wait for you to see."

My children learned at an early age that life isn't just fun and games. They all had jobs as soon as they were able, saving mostly for college, which was hard work. It filled my heart when they found a speck of happiness...they deserved so much more.

October 10, 1986

Cory went to work for an armored truck company, having missed the deadline for enrollment at the University of Houston. It was then he decided to move back to Ohio to finish college at Ohio State where his father graduated.

67

Not a good idea

Early December 1986

If it wasn't one thing, it was another.

The 280ZX had a dead battery for three days in a row. Each morning Lorne got up to start my car with jumper cables before he left for work, mumbling and grumbling like a senile old man. Buying a new battery would have been a whole lot easier.

"Baby, I've been thinking about your car," Lorne said one evening, walking through the door at a decent hour.

"What about my car?" I asked, glancing up from my book.

"I think we need something bigger for the shows," he said, dropping to the couch. "The Z car's packed to the hilt. If we had a truck we could buy more tables and enlarge our display."

I loved my car and we sure didn't need more tables. We didn't sell enough to cover our current display. This was not a good idea.

"Won't that be more expensive?" I asked diplomatically, as I set my book in my lap.

"We could take a few thousand from the business and use your car as a trade in. The payment shouldn't be too bad."

He had it all figured out as usual.

"Before you say no," he jumped in, "let's go take a look. I'll be home early tomorrow. We can drive into the valley and see what's out there. How about it?"

"Lorne, I'll go...but I just don't know," I said cautiously.

The vehicle he wanted was a white panel truck without any windows, and double doors that opened in the back. I would have to back up by using only the side mirrors which seemed dangerous to me. What's more, it looked like a bread truck without a loaf of bread painted on the sides.

When we got home I told Lorne just that.

"Besides, the car is mine," I continued, my voice shaking. "You said I deserved it and I'm keeping it." I took a breath. "And with all the problems we're having, if we ever do split up, I'll be left driving a bread truck that I hate...plus payments for the next five years...no way!"

After all these years I finally stood up to Lorne, but now I was afraid of the consequences. He was livid when he stormed out the door.

December 25, 1986

I was miserable...another Christmas without my children. Lorne suggested a trip to Catalina—a mini-vacation, he said. We could spend the night and it would be a fun way to take my mind off missing the children.

Reluctantly, I agreed.

The small boat to Catalina crashed against the angry waves churned up by the chilly wind, forcing everyone to stay inside until we reached the island. Lorne had booked a room at a quaint little hotel perched on the side of a hill. It was too cold to swim, so we rented a cart to tour the island. It didn't look like Christmas there, but my heart knew it was.

The two days were peaceful, but something inside of me felt different...was it because I finally stood up to him? I wasn't sure.

68

Soothing my weary soul

January 1, 1987

"What a gorgeous morning," I remarked, walking up the driveway clutching a hot cup of coffee. "We should drive out to Point Dume for a walk on the beach. What better way to start the New Year?"

Lorne stood up, placed his hands on his hips and looked around the garage.

"Baby, I just started going through this mess and I'd really like to finish while I'm still in the mood."

"Okay," I said weakly, handing over the coffee. It was then I decided to go alone.

I removed the T-tops from the roof of the car, stacked them in their case, zipped it shut and closed the hatch back. As I backed down the driveway, I beeped, waving through the open roof. Lorne looked up. I hoped my exodus wouldn't leave him stewing all day, but I worked hard and needed a break. Anyway, I'd find out soon enough. In the meantime I planned to savor every moment.

The drive along the PCH always moved me—cradled between a mountain on one side and a parade of beach homes on the other. Where does a woman meet a man willing to give so much? Something I could only wonder about.

The pounding surf sounded like God speaking to me, letting me know He was near. Sand-pipers raced after the receding water; their long skinny beaks preceded them like a blind man's cane. Bits of sand sparkled in the sunlight.

Rolling up my pant legs, I inched closer to the water, bracing myself for the first icy fingers grabbing my ankles. It was heart-stopping, the perfect way to start a new year. I wished Lorne was with me; he could use a change.

Yet during the times we lived apart I found a quiet peace being alone. It opened up a beauty to me I rarely saw otherwise.

Strolling barefoot along the shore, I watched waves mound like a monstrous sea serpent slipping beneath the surface. Its razor sharp spine would rise then curl and crash with a muffled roar. The churning surf drenched my pant legs and salty mist filled my lungs. White-winged seagulls screeched overhead, soothing my weary soul.

The House from Hell remained hostile. One evening the washer backed up and sent milky white foam swirling across the kitchen floor. The new owner sent a plumber who tried to clear the blockage and found that a part had to be ordered...another two-week delay. What next?

The Santa Ana winds were kicking up. I could hear sand pellet against the windows. It was a weekend with no shows and Lorne was home. There were only the two of us rattling around in an old cavernous house, each longing for how it used to be but neither knowing how or where to find the key. However, the moment was a gift. Wrapped in each other's arms, we found the love that bound us forever and a quiet peace we so desperately needed. It was a melding of two troubled souls, whose future could only be determined by God.

The days and weeks passed unnoticed. Nothing was different...except me. Lorne's pattern had not altered other than he slept on the couch more often. He may have thought this action would mask the time he came in, but I always heard the front door. Because he chose to sleep on the couch rather than to disturb me, I lost track of his nightmares.

Feeling brave one evening I approached him with the topic of Alcoholics Anonymous. He laughed out loud, stating he could quit any time he felt like it. And he didn't feel like it. But I knew Lorne better than he knew himself.

69

"...living in our garage"

February 25, 1987

Scattered bills covered the dining room table like trash after a football game. I sat with my head in my hands. Lorne's spending was out of control; his bar bills were unspeakable. If only I knew how to break this cycle.

I was attempting to make a dent in the pile when the phone rang.

"Mrs. MacMillan?" It was the landlord.

"Yes," I said cautiously, surprised by his stiffness.

"I'm calling to tell you that I'll be running an ad in the newspaper next week to rent the room in the garage." He took a breath. "I need the area cleaned out right away. Give me a call when it's ready and I'll come take a look."

I was speechless...a total stranger living in our garage?

The next day, Lorne returned from a convention in Vegas and hit the roof.

Later that night I dragged myself out of a warm bed to answer the phone, knowing full well who it was. Alexander Graham Bell had no idea what a pain in the butt his invention would become.

"Hello?" I said, shivering in the dark.

"Hi Baby," Lorne said with the charm of a drunk. "I'm at Poppi's. I'm too drunk to drive home. Will you come pick me up?"

"Oh, Lorne," I sighed reluctantly. "Of course...I'll pick you up. I have to get dressed, I'll be there shortly."

"Thanks, Baby," he drawled slowly. "What would I ever do without you?"

This was the first time Lorne had called for a ride, I thought as I got dressed. What else was waiting in the wings?

70

Fight or flight

March 1987

Life is seldom what we think it will be and sometimes it's hard to settle for what we get. The thought of a total stranger moving into our garage turned my stomach.

Fight or flight. Backed up against the wall, Lorne and I knew it was time to escape the House from Hell. A thirty-day notice gave us less than a month to find a place to live. The clock was ticking. I devoured the want ads like dark chocolate in search of a better paying job, sending my resume to anything with potential and scheduling interviews on every call back.

March 30, 1987

"Nancy, we need to talk," Lorne announced, strolling in before sunset.

I met him in the living room, "What's up?"

He leaned down and kissed me quickly. "I've been thinking," he said as he headed for the couch. "Come sit down."

My gut reaction was panic.

"I can't believe how expensive housing is," he said, lighting a cigarette. "And most apartments won't take dogs." He looked at me strangely, then turned away. "I think the best solution would be for you to get your own place."

I stiffened. Once again my world was crumbling out from under me and I had no place to run. "You want a separation . . . is that it?" I asked in a mere whisper.

"Nancy, I love you," he said, "but it's just too hard for me to live with another person." Lorne's eyes were heavy with regret. "I don't know why. I wish it weren't this way but it is and I am. It's not fair to you. I feel so guilty but I can't do anything about it."

I stood up. "I see," I said, fighting back tears. Suddenly I was tired of all the games and trying to hold our marriage together single handedly. I walked over to the liquor cabinet, pulled out a bottle of Merlot and walked to the kitchen.

Lorne followed me. "Baby, I'm sorry. I don't know what else to say." He stood staring out the window. "I looked at a used RV today; I could live there with Benji," he paused. "We could use it for the out of town shows…save the cost of a motel."

He had it all figured out again as usual.

"And where am I supposed to live?" I asked weakly, feeling vulnerable and alone. I sipped my wine while trying not to cry.

"In a place of your own where you don't have to put up with me," he said, trying to sound light hearted.

Later that evening, Lorne sat at the dining room table filling out a loan application for an RV . . . one that he already decided upon.

March 31, 1987

Our thirty-day notice surprised the landlord. That same day Lorne applied for a bank loan and arrived home for dinner in extremely good spirits.

"I plan to reach the landlord," Lorne said at dinner, "and see if he's willing to rent the land by the pepper tree. If he agrees, I can park the RV there, put up a fence and get some storage sheds."

Everything was happening too fast…but I was along for the ride whether I liked it or not.

71

A twinge of hope

April 4, 1987

"Nancy, line one," announced the loudspeaker.

"This is Nancy, may I help you?"

"My damn loan was turned down!" Lorne slurred mockingly. "Now what am I suppose to do?"

"Lorne, I'm sorry," I said. "I can't talk right now. I'm in the middle of something. We'll talk when I get home."

"Fine," he said sourly, and hung up.

Why did I feel sorry for him? He was the one causing this mess, not me.

That night I lifted my head off the pillow when I heard his key in the lock. It was after 2 a.m.

April 9, 1987

Apartments were too rich for my pathetic budget, leaving me one choice...I had to find a room to rent. I scanned the newspapers, made a few phone calls and then drove out to see some of the places advertised.

Looking for a room was eye-opening: meeting a stranger I would be expected to live with, going over house rules and viewing a place I would call "home" until God only knew when. Miserable and humiliated, I felt like I was being punished and going to prison...except I had to pay rent.

April 19, 1987

Helena, a chatty real estate agent in her mid-forties with short red hair and chubby cheeks, donned platform shoes and a wide grin. She rented the extra bedrooms in her two-story condo in order to subsidize her alimony. Divorced for two years, she had a steady boyfriend who stayed one or two nights a week. And she had a hyperactive Chihuahua the size of an overgrown rat, whose high-pitched yapping curled my toenails. Margo,

Helena's current housemate, was tall and attractive and also recently separated from her husband. She avoided eye contact when we met.

The condo was in Valencia, a lovely area not far from work. It was modestly furnished, yet tasteful. Outside, a walkway led through the grounds past gardeners who were fussing in flowerbeds, and to a large fenced-in pool dazzling in the sunlight.

"A fringe benefit," Helena smiled openly.

This was icing on the cake; and I could afford it...if I counted my pennies.

For the first time in so long that I couldn't remember, I felt a twinge of hope. That evening I called Helena and sealed the deal.

April 28, 1987

Desperate for a better paying job, I applied for a buyer's position in aerospace although I had no background in aerospace. In Texas, I was a buyer in the wire and cable industry for many years, dealing with chauvinist rednecks in the oil field. Surely aerospace couldn't be any more challenging, but I had stiff competition against someone with experience. Determined, I vowed not to go down without a fight. Destined to be on my own, I needed this job. Everything cost more in California. I mustered up my last drop of tenacity—which surprised even me—calling the purchasing manager every other day about his decision. He hemmed and hawed.

"Dennis, this is Nancy, any good news?" I asked with a contrived lilt in my voice. Dennis knew none of the details for my persistence.

"Actually, Nancy," he replied warily, "I have made a decision, I was going to call you."

I held my breath and braced for disappointment.

"I've decided to hire you both...and give you a shot at it."

Emotions flooded over me. God answered my prayers.

April 29, 1987

Lorne was then able to buy a Winnebago RV with my additional income. Reluctantly I agreed to sign the purchase agreement…too defeated to fight with him.

72

First night alone

May 1, 1987

I started my new job.

That weekend Lorne rented a truck so we could move everything into storage, except for the bedroom furniture and my clothes. These were left for the last trip of the day.

We struggled to squeeze our king-sized mattress up the narrow staircase at the condo. Once through the bedroom door, we pushed it into the corner under the windows, making the room two-thirds bed…now with a dent in the middle from trying to bend it in half.

On my first night alone in a strange place, I lay in the dark wondering what lie ahead. Like a leaf on the ocean I had no direction. Lorne was my husband, why must we live apart? Why had things gone so wrong? Was there an answer? I knew I must survive for my children. Even though they didn't need me, I had to show them courage and teach them God is always near no matter what happens…and He loves us unconditionally. I fought the battle long and hard, now I needed time to rest and regain my strength.

Life moves on. We were still married but once again we lived apart. We continued to do shows every weekend that one was booked as if nothing had changed. That is, until we arrived home. Now we had different addresses. Sometimes I spent the night with Lorne, leaving early in the morning so I could shower and dress at home and still be at work by eight.

And I loved my new job!

May 10, 1987

It was Mother's Day and Lorne took me out for a lovely champagne brunch.

The following weekend the RV developed an attitude. First the battery died, and then the ignition went out, followed by an electrical short that shut down the headlights. That made it scary to drive home after a gem show at night.

Lorne and his problems mixed like oil and water, tossing him into an agitated state. One good thing…when the situation became more than I chose to handle…I could go home and leave him to rant and rave alone.

This became our new way of life: go to work, live separately, do shows, enjoy meals out, pay bills and sleep together on the weekends that Lorne wasn't being a pain. It was a strange way to live, but I refused to give up. The shows allowed us trips to the mountains overlooking the valleys, plus moonlight walks on the beach under a canopy of stars. It was like being on vacation.

June 18, 1987

On my birthday, Lorne surprised me with a tiny white package tied with a silver-blue ribbon. "Happy Birthday Baby," he said, smiling tenderly.

I gingerly peeled off the wrapping to uncover a small black velvet box. I looked at Lorne; his eyes gently met mine. I lifted the lid. Inside was a gold ring set with a pale aquamarine flanked by tiny diamonds. It fit my little finger perfectly.

"Lorne, it's beautiful," I said softly. "Thank you." I got up and walked to his side of the table, then leaned to kiss him. He took me in his arms and soon we were lost in a time from long ago, a time we traveled so seldom.

Once again, I decided it was time for me to get back to the gym. I enjoyed the solitude of working out with my thoughts. This had saved me in the past and I was praying it would again.

July 31, 1987

It was a Friday when Lorne dropped the bomb—he quit his job. What a shock! Lorne had always worked—no matter what was going on in his head—so I had no clue this would happen. It wasn't good. How was he going to pay for his RV and all his bills? I knew I didn't have money to help him; I couldn't say a word. I was no match for his rage. All I could do was sit back and wait.

Lorne then decided to sell used cars and I wondered where in the world he got that idea. He was brilliant; he could have done so much more. But that job didn't last. He quit a few days later only to go with a different dealership. Lorne was floundering like a fish on the sand. I wondered what was next.

Our marriage was straining at the seams; and Lorne gave me no opening to be an active part of his life. I dared not ask—I wasn't brave enough I had no idea what was going on when I wasn't around. Lorne, being the strong silent type, now lived in a world of his own making.

Locked in solitude, I wallowed in self-pity, unwilling to admit my marriage was over. On the outside, I appeared to be a strong, independent woman able to handle whatever came my way. On the inside I was scared to death. The love of my life was living with an untreated illness, one with no name and no cure. And there was nothing I could do about it...other than love him from a distance until he needed me.

But Dr. Jekyll and Mr. Hyde were a tiring twosome.

73

Someone I could talk to

September 11, 1987

It was a Friday night. I was at Lorne's attempting to pay bills while he slammed cupboards and grumbled. Cut and dried, the consequences of his actions had caught up with him. He was overwhelmed. No more fun and games. This was his doing. He's the one who quit a good paying job. He's the one with the outrageous bar bills. We got into an argument and I walked out. This was a first!

The next day we worked a gem show and he acted like nothing had happened. He didn't remember he was mad at me.

It was usually very late at night when Lorne called. I would pick up the phone quickly, so as not to disturb the others. This was my life and now my sickness. I let him vent while lying in the dark with my eyes closed, the receiver resting on my pillow. Some nights his words were gentle and loving; other nights he was a sloppy drunk, blaming everyone else for his problems. I threatened to hang up when he called drunk, but I never did. He knew he had me wrapped around his little finger.

September 14, 1987

Little by little I shared bits of my saga with my housemates.

"I wish I knew someone I could talk to," I mentioned one night after dinner. "There's got to be someone who can offer some guidance. I feel like I'm drowning."

Helena's eyes lit up. "Why not call my doctor and set an appointment? He's on the other side of McBean Highway."

A recommendation's always better than the Yellow Pages.

So I went to see Dr. Levy the next evening after work. At seventy dollars an hour, his only recommendation was Al Anon. Guess I'd been living under a rock. I had never heard of Al Anon, though I had never known an alcoholic before. I found a group and began attending meetings which seemed to be every night. I sat and listened, comparing stories, but no one could tell me how to fix Lorne. He was broken and I wanted him fixed.

I told Lorne about the meetings and he said nothing. His drinking continued and so did his phone calls. We did shows on the weekends and during the week I squeezed Al Anon into my already busy schedule. Maybe I felt a little better but it wasn't helping Lorne.

74

Putting on a facade

October 12, 1987

My next visit with Dr. Levy was strange. After I expressed the latest chain of events, he proceeded to verify the soundness of my mental health.

"Nancy," he said, looking up from his notepad, "you appear to be handling the situation exactly as you should." He paused. "Honestly, I see no further need for counseling unless you run into trouble. You're a strong woman and you've found the best way to deal with this on your own."

I was surprised. I had heard that shrinks kept you coming back for years to fill their bank accounts. At his prices I didn't argue, but I could guess. I had mastered the art of putting on a facade for so long that I even fooled my shrink.

The next day Lorne called me at work. He wanted a thousand dollars I didn't have. There was only our business money that was earmarked to buy inventory. I'd already booked some shows that ran as high as three hundred dollars a weekend. Without inventory, we would be out of business. I explained this to Lorne…but he slammed the receiver in my ear.

Later that night he called…demanding that we split the business.

October 14, 1987

Two days later, I went to see a lawyer to find out my rights. Lorne was my husband and I loved him but I couldn't let him destroy me just because there was no one else to help him.

October 19, 1987

When Lorne heard about the lawyer, he called me at work again. "Baby, so you want to play hardball," he sneered sarcastically. Then he hung up on me.

October 20, 1987

I made another appointment with the lawyer, this time to discuss the possibility of divorce. I had to protect myself. At this point I didn't know what else to do. All we had going for us was my job and our business. I was terrified we were going to lose everything and I'd end up out on the street with Lorne. Or have to move back east to the snow.

October 23, 1987

The next time Lorne called me at work he was sober, but panic stricken. Our dog, Benji, had been hit by a car. At that point, that little dog was the only companion Lorne allowed in his life. Benji loved him unconditionally and asked for nothing more than a bowl of food and water once a day.

October 26, 1987

When Lorne called my office again a few days later, I knew he had been drinking.

"The vet told me she doesn't know if Benji's going to make it." He sobbed. "Without Benji, I have no reason to live." He hung up.

October 27, 1987

But next day he called and meekly asked, "Baby, can we meet at Marie Callender's tonight after work? We need to talk about the business."

I agreed. He wanted to split the inventory.

There was a huge three-day show in San Diego that weekend. I asked to keep the inventory until after the show. He agreed.

I managed the show alone, but it wasn't easy. If I hadn't needed the money to pay bills, I'd have stopped the madness altogether. This whole business was Lorne's idea…not mine.

75

Dreaded his phone calls

November 1987

Lorne's calls continued at all hours...he was getting desperate. Our conversations went in circles. He needed money and I kept telling him I didn't have any. I was barely staying afloat.

All that fall, I did shows on the weekends alone, if one was scheduled. Any profit went back into inventory and to pay bills. I was working myself ragged, yet it tore my heart out to say no to Lorne. He was my husband; I loved him in sickness and in health but he was spiraling out of control. His addiction was consuming him and everything he had. He needed professional help to break the cycle and get a job. But who could help? Who out there could reach him? It surely wasn't me.

November 6, 1987

Lorne called work. The vet wanted five hundred dollars for Benji's surgery. Again I told him I couldn't help. He was highly agitated with my response.

November 10, 1987

It felt like I was splitting in two; I needed to vent. I called Dr. Levy's office and he was able to squeeze me in. He suggested a change of routine—find something that made me happy, or gave me purpose. Easier said than done—I didn't know what the words meant anymore.

It was sometime after midnight when Lorne called.

November 12, 1987

I made a decision to hit the gym three days a week, no matter how hopeless I felt. I was grateful we had signed a three-year non-refundable contract when we first came to California, before the trouble began. Maybe this would ease the panic building inside of me like cancer cells gone wild, and finally help me face the fact that I had no solution for Lorne's problems. Also, I knew he couldn't reach me at the gym. But in the end I had to go home. I dreaded those phone calls.

November 17, 1987
It was a Tuesday when Lorne called to talk. As usual he was short on money…but he expected me to get us out of this mess. I was suffocating. I felt so guilty for not being able to help him.

November 19, 1987
We had already split the business, the inventory and the shows, and the upcoming weekend was his turn to do the GLDA show…alone. It was a three-day show and sales were bound to give him some relief. But only God knew what he would do with the money. He couldn't control his spending when we lived together. I definitely had no say so now.

My heart ached. I loved my husband but he was an alcoholic and a Vietnam vet, a toxic combination. Where was someone to help him? I didn't know how. I lent him my inventory without hope of getting anything in return. His promises were hollow. His heart was willing but he was lost in the past. He couldn't escape.

November 23, 1987
Lorne's answering machine picked up when I called a few days later. "I'm not home, leave a message," his voice told me.

"Hi there, it's me. Just checking in to see how the show went this weekend. Give me a call when you get a chance. I love you," I said hopefully.

He never called back.

November 24, 1987
I made a trip to the suppliers to pick up inventory for my next show. I knew I couldn't count on Lorne to keep his word. I was on my own.

His illness was eating away his mind, his common sense, his rationale. Everything seemed upside down. I didn't know how long I could keep up the pretense. It was horrible. Lorne was in pain but I feared going down with him.

76

Digging a hole

December 1, 1987

The phone jarred me awake before my alarm went off. It was 5:45 a.m. It had to be Lorne, but this was a first. He had never called in the morning, especially not that early.

"Nancy, I don't know what to do," he uttered, his voice riding on panic. "I haven't paid bills in two months,"

"Lorne, I'm sorry, I don't know what to tell you," I said honestly. "If I had any extra I'd give it to you but I don't—maybe twenty or thirty dollars, but that won't help." It broke my heart to hear him this desperate. "Lorne, you need to find a job."

He was digging a hole deeper and deeper. I had no idea how he was going to get out of it. And I had no way to help him—all I could do was pray.

December 6, 1987

It was Lorne's weekend to work the show I booked in Saugus. I knew he could make money if he tried. People were shopping for Christmas. I drove over to see how he was doing. I couldn't find him—he never showed up.

It was futile. How could I help him when he wouldn't help himself?

Where was support for these men and women veterans during these critical times? Who would deal with their demons? Who would show them how to fit back into society? I was just a wife and a mother. I had no idea what to do—I was now fighting to survive myself.

Plans were made for me to fly to Houston on Christmas Day. I would stay with Tiffy but planned to spend time with my dad and Lorne's family as well.

December 25, 1987

Lorne continued to badger me right up until the time of my flight. It was heartbreaking. But there was nothing I could do. Even if I gave him a little cash, he'd continue to drink and put it on plastic with no regard to the consequence. No, I couldn't do it. I had worked too hard to stay afloat. I'd find a way to help the children in an emergency—Lorne was on his own.

77

Stolen moments

January 5, 1988

It was Lorne's first call since my return from Houston on New Year's Day. He was sober. We had a nice talk like old times. He asked about my trip—Tiffy—my dad—and his parents. But money was never mentioned. I was curious but afraid to open Pandora's Box.

"I talked with Cory," I said cautiously, "and he asked if you would sign over the Honda." I didn't wait for an answer. "He wanted me to thank you for cosigning his loan. He's paid it off in full as promised." I held my breath.

"Sure, no problem," he said, surprisingly. "Why not meet me at Marie Callender's tomorrow after work...about five-thirty?"

"Okay, that's good for me," I said, relieved. I had anticipated a battle.

Lorne was settled back in a dimly lit booth smoking a cigarette when I walked in the restaurant. I approached the table, noticing he was still as handsome and charming as ever. He signed over the title without a hitch. We talked over coffee for almost an hour. He was telling me about a project he was working on with a friend. It had something to do with massive security doors, made from a rare metal that they would sell to the government. He seemed upbeat over the idea. This made me happy. I knew he was brilliant and a great salesman—if people didn't mess with his head. Maybe this venture would give him the boost he needed.

He seemed at ease and I had his full attention. It was then I decided.

"Lorne, since you've signed over Cory's Honda," I said gently, "will you sign over the Nissan 280ZX to me?" I held my breath. He knew I was making the car payments.

He searched my eyes quizzically. "Right now I've got another appointment," he said crushing his cigarette in the ashtray. He stood up. "I'll give you a call."

I had no idea what he was thinking. The last time my car was the topic, Lorne wanted to trade it in on a panel truck and I refused. So all I could do was wait for his answer.

Lorne called the next evening and agreed.

January 11, 1988
We met at Marie Callender's again on a Monday. Being near Lorne again was hard. I wanted my husband back. I loved him. What was I supposed to do?

This time he signed over a car title to me and sealed it with a kiss. But it hurt. I had no idea if we would ever be together again.

January 20, 1988
Lorne called work and asked if I'd come over to the RV. He wanted to see me. I vacillated, believing I shouldn't go, but wanting to be with him. After all, we were still husband and wife.

After work, I headed for Canyon Country, drawn to Lorne like a starving person to a banquet. Why was life so hard? We were married and in love, why did we have to live apart?

I drove up the driveway to his fence. Pulling open the gate, I stepped inside and closed it behind me. I walked through the yard to the door of the

RV. I stood a moment then knocked. The door opened and Lorne ushered me in. There was little light except for a candle on the table.

Not a word was spoken. Our hands touched, fingers entwined, and Lorne's heat radiated through me. He took my shoulders and bent to kiss me, my arms reached around his back. His kiss grew hard; his arms pulled me to him. My head was swimming. I wanted this moment to last forever. Time stood still as we floated in and out of a dream, knowing it wasn't real but not wanting to wake up.

When I opened my eyes, I could see a huge moon shining through the blinds on the window. Lorne slept peacefully in my arms. Carefully I untangled myself from him, slipping out of bed. I quietly got dressed and tiptoed out the door not waking him.

It was late, traffic was sparse. How could we go on like this? What was the answer? Only God knew.

January 23, 1988

It was Saturday. Lorne called that morning to invite me to dinner. Still in the afterglow of the other night, I accepted. He cooked fajitas on the grill; the aroma was tantalizing, coupled with a bottle of Merlot.

Once again, we shared stolen moments that were rightfully ours. But our circumstances were too bizarre to discuss. Who would understand? Who could help us straighten out this mess?

78

Sparked my curiosity

February 4, 1988

One day at lunch, Brad Bishop, a coworker, mentioned he had a house in Northridge. "...and rather than rattle around all by myself," he went on, "I rent out the extra bedrooms. It helps pay the mortgage. Besides I work most weekends so I'm gone a lot. At the moment one's vacant, if you're interested?"

The thought of living in a real house sparked my curiosity. Moving in with Helena solved the immediate problem but I felt like an outcast. That evening I went to take a look and met Brad's current housemate, Gwen.

It was a ranch style house with three bedrooms and two baths, located in a quiet neighborhood. Stepping through the front door, it felt like a home. A blazing fireplace rested between two narrow, etched glass windows opposite a long white couch. The walls were a rich azure blue accented by white blinds and trim. Spotlights hit a large framed photograph of a white lily behind the couch.

"You'd have full house privileges plus the washer and dryer," Brad said, leading me to the kitchen. "And you could cook up a storm," he gestured, "if you're ever in the mood."

There in front of me stood an antique gas stove with six burners and a double oven and broiler. Wow! I loved to cook and could see myself in this kitchen—Julia Child, step aside.

"We'd share a bathroom," Gwen interrupted, poking her head into the kitchen.

Settled in the living room to chat, Gwen was all grins at the thought of another woman in the house. Plain and a little plump with short brown hair, she was feisty and funny. I liked her immediately. She was divorced with an older daughter and had lived in the house more than a year with no intention of leaving anytime soon.

The house felt comfortable. I could picture myself living there. Better yet, the rent was what I was paying at the condo.

February 9, 1988

I told Lorne all about the house—the the fireplace—and the stove. He wasn't thrilled that I would be moving to the valley, not that I needed his approval. But codependents don't like to make waves. The next day I told Brad and Helena I would be moving on the first.

"You know," Brad said, standing at my desk, "there's no need to wait until the end of the month. The room is vacant. You can start moving in whenever you want, and start paying rent on the first.

"Great," I replied.

My only concern was what to do with my king sized mattress. It was in excellent condition except for the dent down the middle. My new bedroom had a regular sized bed with a brass head-board, leaving room for my other furniture…my old mattress had to go.

February 20, 1988

I moved on a Saturday. Brad had access to a truck. I was grateful for his help and grateful that I didn't have to ask Lorne, or find movers.

"Gee," Gwen said, "if you really don't want your mattress, can I have it?" She pleaded with puppy dog eyes. "Mine's older and my room is bigger…and I don't care about the dent, I can turn it over."

February 22, 1988

Two days later, I was called into my manager's office. He awarded me my own accounts, plus the use of two junior buyers and a raise. I was speechless. Was I dreaming? I wasn't used to good things happening—and so close together. Prone to doom and gloom, I held my breath waiting for the backlash.

February 26, 1988

Lorne called on Friday. He'd been drinking and wanted to get a motel after my show on Saturday. I said no. The drunken phone calls were getting old. I loved him, but enough was enough. I told him from now on I would hang up if he called in that condition again. I didn't know what else to do.

February 27-28, 1988

I worked the San Fernando Gem and Mineral show alone that weekend. Lorne came by and we had a fight. I was in tears when he left.

March 1, 1988

The sheriff showed up at my office on Monday looking for Lorne who apparently had several outstanding traffic violations. I told the sheriff we were separated and I didn't know where he was. I lied for Lorne and left a message to warn him.

79

Pray for an answer

April 3, 1988

I spent a nice Sunday at Point Dume with Gwen. It was a perfect day relaxing in the sunshine. Lorne called that evening. He was really down.

April 7, 1988

The phone rang at 1:30 a.m. Lorne was drunk and threatening suicide. I didn't know what to do. I barely slept a wink all night.

Lorne continued to call three or four times that week, extremely distraught. Tax time had arrived which was another commitment he wrestled with. He couldn't wrap his mind around the mess he had made, let alone work his way out of it. He turned a deaf ear to anything I had to say, yet there was no where he could turn. I couldn't do my taxes without his paperwork that was strewn helter-skelter in boxes throughout his RV. Lorne was sick and I was codependent. I loved him too much. What was I to do? God knew I didn't want to be arrested for tax evasion.

April 14, 1988

Lorne called to ask me to meet him at Marie Callender's after work. He wanted me to sign an extension on our taxes so I willingly agreed. Maybe, by some miracle, we could get them done before the next deadline. But I had lost faith in Lorne.

April 24, 1988

Upon returning from a peaceful day at the beach, there was a message on my answering machine from Lorne.

I called him back.

"Benji's lost," he blurted out. "I've looked everywhere and I can't find him," he wept.

"I'm so sorry," I said honestly.

"Nancy, it's not your fault. You didn't do anything wrong," he sobbed. "I'm the one responsible for this mess, not you. I never should have let you go."

I sank into the bed, reeling from his words, yanked back into the past.

"You're the best thing that ever happened to me," he sniffled. "And I promise if you'll just come back, I'll buy you another house and be the foundation of our family." His choking sobs broke my heart. "I miss talking with the kids..."

I was speechless and totally caught off guard . . .

"Baby, I want to be a real husband for you; the kind of husband you deserve. I want us to grow old together," he gushed. "I promise to talk to God, and attend AA. Please promise me you'll think about what I said. Please?"

I drew a deep breath. "Of course I'll think about it," I said with care, not wanting to hurt him more. Yet I knew he probably wouldn't remember a word of this in the morning. "I love you Lorne, and always will. You're my husband, but we have issues to work through before we can discuss living together." The sobbing stopped. I could hear him breathing. "Right now, I think we both need sleep. We'll talk tomorrow, okay?"

May 1, 1988

A week later I saw Lorne at Trader Joe's, but he didn't see me. I didn't want a scene where I normally shopped, so I slipped out the door unnoticed.

The calls continued, but were earlier in the evening and Lorne wasn't drunk. He seemed to be doing better, though I never mentioned our earlier conversation. We were both doing shows and I lent him part of my inventory when he asked. I continued to pray for an answer.

80

This is my life

June 8, 1988

I was flying in for Scott's graduation from Ohio State on Friday. Lorne called and offered to drive me to the airport. I accepted.

June 10, 1988

The graduation was everything I envisioned, my first born graduating from college. I was proud of my children, each working part-time jobs to get through school. Peter, the children's father came in from Chicago, Tiffy flew in from Houston and Cory was all smiles. We looked like one happy family. Onlookers would never suspect our shattered existence. Or do most families put on a façade?

Another blistering summer sailed into fall. Nothing much changed except the dates on the calendar. Lorne continued to call on a regular basis— sober or drunk. His calls blended like a smoothie after a while and I gave up trying to figure out why. His words were filled with love when he was sober, but he was an angry drunk—Dr. Jekyll and Mr. Hyde. Still I loved him and excused his behavior because of his illness. He was a Vietnam Vet who became an alcoholic because there was no help for him. He was too proud to seek counseling, and he refused any suggestions I made. I could only continue to pray that help would come in time.

October 14, 1988

"Hello," I said, knowing full well who it was…it was a Friday night.

"I don't want to do any more shows," were the first words out of Lorne's mouth. "It's too much of a hassle."

I couldn't tell if he was drunk or just depressed.

"What happened?" I asked cautiously, not wanting to push any buttons.

"Life sucks, everything is falling apart all around me and I don't know how to stop it."

His words were clear, but sad. I didn't know what to say. We talked for almost an hour, going around in circles—going nowhere. This was my life with Lorne.

A few days later he called again. He had changed his mind. He wanted to borrow my inventory for his regular show. This was my husband, up one day and down the next. I felt like a surfer riding the swells, anticipating the big one, yet wondering if a shark was cruising just below the surface waiting to pull me under.

I was thankful my job was stable because the rest of my life was such a mess.

81

Dragged into a fight

December 15, 1988

Tiffy flew to California over Christmas break; she was staying until the third of January. I was much too excited to sleep. It was heaven having her close, no matter what we were doing, and I could tuck her in and kiss her goodnight.

Each day was crammed. We shopped, trimmed the tree, and cooked Christmas dinner together. We spent a day at the beach climbing rocks and fattening the seagulls. And another day we drove to Frazier Park and played in the snow, until our feet froze. No boots of course. We tackled the Rose Bowl Parade crowd at 4:30 in the morning. It was too early, too crowded and too cold sitting on the sidewalk. Lastly, we even hit Magic Mountain Amusement Park and indulged in piles of junk food and rides. The days were filled with pure happiness, but all good things must end—her visit vaporized like sea mist.

January 3, 1989

I took a vacation day to drive Tiffy to the airport. It was sad and we both cry easily. For me, airports denote sorrow or bliss, someone coming or leaving. This was my life, fifteen hundred miles away from my family and friends. Lorne and I were alone, struggling through our dysfunctional marriage with no real friends. One must be venerable to have close friends; and I had secrets I wasn't willing or strong enough to share.

Lorne called every couple of days. He was usually drunk, nothing new. I met him at Marie Callender's one evening after work to discuss the shows...and stayed for dinner.

"I'm flying to Boston tomorrow for a couple of days," he said matter-of-factly.

"What's in Boston?" My curiosity piqued.

"My partner and I are going to a convention," he replied. "We need to check out our competition. Hear there are a couple other companies making the same type of doors."

"That sounds interesting." I wanted to encourage him in any way I could.

"Yea, if we could land one contract, we'd have cash coming in."

January 31, 1989

It was our fourteenth wedding anniversary. It felt like we were suspended between two worlds without a breeze, going nowhere. I called Lorne, but he wasn't home. I left a message,

"Happy Anniversary—hard to believe its number fourteen . . . I love you."

February 14, 1989

Valentine's Day—I decided to quit smoking again. For sure! I had to stop before lung cancer invaded my body. In that case, exercise at the gym would be futile.

"Nancy, line three," announced the speaker on my phone.

"Hello, this is Nancy."

"Happy Valentine's Day, Baby," Lorne said soberly. "I love you."

"I love you, too," I replied happily.

February 19, 1989

Lorne left word that he was working on our taxes. I was encouraged to hear he was doing it without any prompting from me—and early.

March 2, 1989

I was already asleep when Lorne called. He was drunk—mean drunk. I listened, but kept my distance. I wouldn't be dragged into a fight. I surmised he was frustrated over our tax situation. He knew how serious it was—so I became his sounding board.

March 5, 1989

I started my part of the taxes, so they'd be done, if he asked for them. We were already two years behind.

Lorne called every couple of days drunk and mean.

March 14, 1989

One month without cigarettes. I felt good. Proud of myself for not caving in which would have been easy.

March 21, 1989

I finished my part of our 1987 taxes. Called Lorne's—left a message.

March 27, 1989

I dropped off a package of Lorne's mail that came to my address. He wasn't home.

March 28, 1989

There were two nasty messages on my answering machine. Taxes were messing with Lorne's head, but there was nothing I could do about it.

March 30, 1989

Lorne called drunk and talked a long, long time—but now he was jealous—but of what? I had no idea. He was seething.

82

Not a thing had changed

April 2, 1989

My first day at the beach for the year was like heaven. I was so in need of some peace and solitude. The sun was warm and the breeze lifted a gentle mist from the crashing surf. The seagulls and I basked in the serenity surrounding us.

April 8, 1989

Lorne called at 9 a.m. on Saturday. We had a nice talk. He was working on the RV's generator and he wanted me to know he was going to be out of town all next week.

April 17, 1989

I met Lorne at Marie Callender's after work where we signed our tax extension. Every year was the same hassle. We had a nice talk over a glass of wine.

April 26, 1989

Lorne called. He wanted to meet me, but he was drunk and I said no. We had a huge fight. How much more can I take?

April 28, 1989

Lorne called me at work. He was meek but I couldn't talk.

April 29, 1989

Lorne left a message on my answering machine. He apologized for his behavior the other night. At least this showed he did remember some things.

April 30, 1989

Lorne called. We had a long talk about all of our problems—without resolution, of course.

May 2, 1989

Today marked the two-year anniversary of our separation. Not a thing had changed. Lorne still refused to seek help and I still loved him for better or worse. There was no light at the end of the tunnel. It was like the movie, *Ground Hog Day*, except in the movie each day got better. Ours didn't.

May 10, 1989

Lorne called work and wanted to see me but I was in no mood to deal with him. He left a message on my answering machine.

83

Do not open until Monday

I traveled alone locked in solitude with secrets too horrible to talk about. I clung to the love that was mine yet out of reach. Plagued with self pity and razor sharp memories, I wallowed in a nightmare I could not flee. Yet did I really want to?

May 14, 1989

Mother's Day without my children felt empty, but the day was gorgeous and the ocean beckoned to me like a lover. Barefoot on the cool sand, I walked the shoreline wrapped in the mighty roar of the churning surf. The afternoon sun fused with the curling waves. Their murky hue transformed to a translucent turquoise blue. Nothing else soothed my pain like the sea and salt air. There I found peace.

Late that afternoon, I pulled up at the curb in front of the house embraced in tranquility. I gathered my beach gear and started up the driveway. But something caught my eye that brought me to a standstill. Tears blurred my vision.

There on the porch, blocking the screen door, was a huge vase laden with long stemmed red roses. I knew they were from Lorne. As I approached I noticed a bulging envelope propped against its base. I leaned down and picked it up. It was addressed to me in Lorne's handwriting. On the back was written—"do not open until Monday."

I ran my finger over his words, desperately wanting to touch him.

I unlocked the door, carried the vase and envelope into the house, and set them on the dining room table. Brad's car was gone. I knew he went to visit his mother in San Diego, so I was alone.

Burying my face in the delicate rose petals, I inhaled their sweet scent, knowing Lorne had held them in his hands hours earlier. Tears slipped down my cheeks. He had more important places to spend his money, but the gesture confirmed his love, giving me hope.

I removed the small white envelope stuck in the flowers and opened it— *"Happy Mother's Day. Thank you for sharing your children with me. Lorne."*

A swollen lump lodged painfully in my throat. I still loved him so much.

Then I picked up the bloated envelope, my curiosity stirred. His instructions were to wait until tomorrow but I couldn't—I had to know what it said.

"*Dear Lord,*" I prayed silently, tearing at the end of the envelope, "*Please don't let this be something terrible.*"

Inside were eighteen handwritten pages, which I spread out on the dining room table and then began to read.

Dear Nancy,

As you well know, I'm not much of a letter writer, but its Saturday morning and I feel the need to talk to you. I need to let some of the things I'm thinking and feeling out, and you're the only one that might understand me. Please bear with my disorganization of thoughts, as they don't seem to be very organized anymore. I want you to know that I have admitted to myself that I am an alcoholic and I've started my own program of "not drinking today." I've been totally sober since May seventh and I intend to continue this each day. Physically, I feel a little bit better, but it's hard to tell as I'm smoking a lot more. Mentally, I guess that alcohol was somewhat of a self medication that allowed me to not face any of my problems head-on. In a way, I would love to be at a party right now, drunk, because I would have a few hours of relief from my garble of thoughts, my realization of what tasks I've created for myself to become a whole person again. I won't do that "today" because I know how temporary it would be, and could only add to my liability in life. I am now doing my best to live on a budget, to get enough money to seek outside help for my mental problems. If I can make it that far, I'm going to go to a psychiatrist to determine what can be done, if anything, to get out of my depressed state of mind. Never in my life, did I ever think that I would feel so helpless to do anything at all to go forward with life itself. Please believe me, I am not writing to you for you to feel sympathy or worse yet, pity for me. I would like to think there is still a little man left in me, and I will face my own problems by myself, to the end. As one person loves another, I know you love me, and I hope you realize that I love you. I know that you were the best wife any man could ever ask for, the best friend a husband could ever have. I wish I could give you something to show you how much, but as you know, I've destroyed all of my assets. I've drank them up, let them rust, destroyed them with hits, kicks and hammers of rage, or just thrown them away. If I have anything left, it was obtained with false promises of payment. You know I'm not just talking about material things; I'm talking of all the things in life we feel are good to create or process. I am not prepared for the future, most people are. In my current state of mind, I can't see any future at all. I feel like a computer that has some facts left in its memory, but has lost its entire program. The only sensible thing to do with one of these is unplug it, because it serves no purpose for which it was intended to accomplish. When I remember my old program, so to speak, it was one of self destruction. I am no longer the man you married. You are no longer the woman I married because I have destroyed you. The part of you I didn't destroy, I have rejected. You have the total right to save and build on what you have. I can only apologize and feel remorse, which I do infinitely, but it serves no real purpose. It does no good to either of us. I thank you for your love as a person, I enjoy hearing your voice on my answering machine some mornings, and it encourages me to go through the day. At least I know that someone other than my mother loves me, despite my failings. What I cherish most is that you don't have to, and she does, as that's what mothers must do for life. Enough of my self-pity.

I want you to know that I have decided to do whatever I can to pull myself out of this hole. By myself for now. It's not going to be easy, I feel like I'm carrying too much weight, my gas tank is empty, I am short on horse power, and I have a long, steep mountain to climb. I am not certain I can make it. I am no longer certain of anything. In any case, you, I'm certain, will go on to accomplish your dreams. You have someone who loves you, and that makes all the difference. Although I have no right to consider you my wife, I am very jealous, but I created the situation, and have accepted it the best I could. If this letter seems unclear to you, forgive me. My thoughts are not clear to me either. I don't know how to finish this letter. This afternoon, I'm going to finish going through all this maze of paperwork I've accumulated; I'll separate all the receipts I have from the business each year. Most is self explanatory as to what type of expense it is. I really didn't mean to get us into this tax mess, I'm sorry I did, but we have to handle it the best we can. I don't know of anything else I can say, I guess I've just run out of things to say except that I want you to accept my gift to you on Mother's day as just a gift. I wanted to give you something. I'm sure you will receive cards, gifts, or phone calls from the kids tomorrow, but I feel like giving you something. I hope this letter doesn't mess up your day. I guess it's kind of selfish on my part, but I had to take advantage of my desire to talk about things in writing, as it's the only chance I have left to communicate. Please understand I must do this for me. Each day I go through thousands of thoughts that no longer make any sense. I can't explain to you, or myself, the reason I feel so much pain and loneliness. I once told you that being drunk and lonely was better than just feeling loneliness. It's very true. The worst part is that I am so disgusted with myself that I don't want to talk to anyone for fear they will see me as I am. I am even afraid of going for psychiatric help because I may have to face who and what I really am. If I could avoid that I would. I only want to know that I was capable of changing things for the best. Some things are certainly lost forever. I've burnt a lot of long bridges that weren't really mine to begin with. I think I finished burning our bridge, what little I hadn't already destroyed, at the Scientology meeting when I sped off in a fit of anger. Forgive me, I was feeling selfish. My future will be without it. If I had a chance to begin life again and do anything I wanted, with respect to profession, I think I would be a psychiatrist. I never knew how bad it can be to be mentally ill. Many times during each day, I feel as if I'm in a zombie state, my thoughts are so slow and so confused that I don't know what's happening. I fear it; I wish I could get free. There is no longer any meaning to life as I once thought there was. There probably is, but I've lost my sight, in that respect. I hate to go to sleep at night, I have nightmares. They are my vision of hell. Waking up isn't much better; I know I might die another night. It scares me worse than any enemy I've ever faced. I was in control of my destiny in warfare; I have lost most of my weapons now and don't know where to find any others, worse yet, there is nowhere to hide. There are no soldiers by my side, radio communication has reached no command post, and I've lost my map. I've lost my way. I create the enemy and their weapons. My enemy is suicide and I see him out there more often than ever before. I can only avoid him. I am doing the best I can. I cannot defeat him. If he defeats me, I get to go home. Where ever that is. And I want peace more than anything else, I've fought enough wars. I am so tired.

Please forgive me if I don't make it. I will try my best, I am trying my best to understand it, but my thoughts run crazy. When people ask me how I'm doing, I just say—I'm still here. They don't understand, but I don't want them to. I don't understand either. All I know is that it is up to me to survive all of this, if I can. Believe me; I am doing all that I can right now. Maybe I'll do better tomorrow. I don't want you to call me to talk to me because I have shared this most private feeling with you. I hate being patted on the head, so to speak, with the phrase, everything will be all right. It is not all right. It sucks. But it is not your problem. I hope someday things will be better. I don't know how I would feel if I were you. I'm in no shape to project; I don't know how I feel, except from time to time according to my confused thought. You don't owe me any help. You are fortunate in that you seem to have your immediate and long term future planned. I envy you. The other day, when I asked if you could see me, I listened to your plans of what you needed to do. I wish I had obligations to myself to do, and could enjoy doing them. I sometimes think I avoid calling you because I don't want to be a burden to your plans. I also am afraid of hearing what I wish to hear when you can't or don't have time for me. It is the loneliness that drives me to call you or to wish to see you. I understand why you can't, but I still have a hard time accepting it. You have no idea how much I long to make love to you. There are beautiful memories of how intimate we were at one time. How wonderful and exciting it was. It really hurts deeply to know that someone else now shares that with you. I've tried very hard to remember or understand why I threw you out two years ago. I hope it was a reason understandable to someone. My feelings were that of confusion and frustration with life, my job, our business, the rest I don't understand. I only know that you owe our relationship nothing. It has only been bad for you in the past. I wish you had met someone else instead of me. I'm sure they would have done far better than I. Maybe your new love will be much better. I'm sure it will be, and you deserve it. I am, at present, avoiding all relationships. I can only do harm as I have not enough good for myself, let alone anyone else, if they saw anything to start with. I've been terribly tempted to have a one nighter but that's too much like getting drunk. You have to deal with the hangover. It's too temporary and would do no good to anyone. It's very confusing to be so lonely and also wish to be alone. I go to some social functions and talk with other people, but it's very boring and I'm sick of cokes, water, coffee and juice when I'm there for more than a few hours. However, I guess it's better than sitting in my mess listening to talk shows on the radio.

I don't know what your show schedule is this year, but I am not going to do any at all and if you wish, you can have all my show tables, and what inventory I have left. My heart just isn't in it anymore and I'm not able to book anything. The motorcycle show is the end of this month and there is a booth reserved for me that you are welcome to. I only hope that I continue to get paid by R&H Valves. I'm trying hard to get out and work, but it's very difficult just to call a customer on the phone. I don't know why, but it is. If I'm ever able to get some psychiatric help maybe they can explain it. I know how to talk, what to say, and how to dial the number, but for some reason I just don't want to do it. I leave the motor home early each morning now (no hangover), but I don't know where to go or what to do to further my efforts as a salesman. I am no longer a salesman, as a matter of fact; I don't know what I am. The only thing I do anymore is feed Benji. I'm sometimes tempted to give him to the girl whose house he goes to when he gets out. He's in love with a little black female cocker spaniel whose been spayed. He even climbs the fence at their house to get in the back yard with her and he doesn't try to get back out. He would probably be happiest there, even though I know he loves me and is very content to just go for a car ride now and then. I can't help feeling he should be with the one he loves. Maybe I just wish for him what I have thrown away.

I hope you can make sense of this rambling on. These are some of the thoughts I have each day and I just felt compelled to communicate them to someone. Once again, "you're it." I wish I had been able to talk to you rationally when it might have done some good, but I know that time has ceased to exist. There must be some truth to the fact that sometimes self destructive people try to hurt the ones they love. I wish to hurt you no longer. I really never rationally wished to hurt you, but I always did. I think the words; "in sickness and in health" should be omitted from marriage vows because it is too much to deal with—with people like me. Aside from my *personal selfishness of writing this down-bummer type letter because I feel I had to talk to you about the ways I feel without getting into conversation, because I lose all thought of what I wish to communicate. I guess the other reason is to tell you that I don't want any more reasons to hold on to you for any support. I love to hear your voice, but it only prolongs my loneliness for you. I love to see you in all your health, but I am also torn apart by wanting you, and wishing I could get to a place in my life that I felt worthy enough to be a viable partner. This seems so impossible at this stage of my life that I feel if I were to see you again, I will know it is because you feel sorry for me. I don't want that. I cannot deal with it. You have no idea how badly it hurts when I talked to you and you said you wouldn't see me that Sunday. And yet I know why, and I don't blame you. I sure blame myself. You have to have respect for the man you love. I know that there isn't any left for me because I have destroyed everything that you had. Going through my paper mess today, I once again came across your love coupons. I am returning them because it hurts too much to see them anymore. They don't have my name on them; perhaps there will be someone else you can give them to. I know that was a stupid thought, but I'm returning them anyway. I have been home most of the past two weekends hoping you would call. I now realize there are many more important things in your life other than calling me. You only call my answering machine because you are a nice person and you want me to know you think of me. I don't know how to communicate with you anymore because I've put us in a very difficult type of association.*

We are not friends, even though you love what is left of me. We are not lovers. We are not really married. We are not really divorced. What are we? We are you and I. I must do what I can for me. You must do what you can for you. It is too painful now to mix in any manner. You have asked and written about what I intend for our trying to save what relationship we had. All my half-baked attempts to go on from here have failed. I told you that we are past the critical stand and would certainly require a neutral outside source to become anything resembling a married couple; I now realize that it would be impossible. I am buried in so many problems I can't face alone that I am not eligible as a candidate. People wiser than myself have told me an alcoholic only begins to carry on maturity after gaining sobriety. I have too far to go for anyone to waste their life with. I guess what I am saying is that in my mind I must relinquish all aspects of our relationship, except that we were married in real life, still are on paper, but no longer man and wife. I see those people who are happily married and I am very jealous. Apparently I didn't see the real meaning of lifelong love. Now that it is too late—well, I've always had great timing. I guess I want it all or nothing at all. That's the way it turned out—nothing at all now. Oh how I wish I could go back to when we had first met. My future looked bright in retrospect. Why did I go so wrong? Well it really does no good to think about such things. Anyway I don't really know what I'm trying to say except that I come home and see my answering machine blinking. I sit and listen to my messages hoping to hear your voice. Especially on weekends—but I never hear it. My dreams were that you would offer to see me Saturday night for dinner, Sunday afternoon, anywhere. I realize that if we had, that making love would be a difficult thing to discuss. I can understand your fear—I would have been afraid too—of how much I would miss you that night, tomorrow, next week, etc. I don't know if it would be better to just know that my blinking light would always be from other sources, then I wouldn't listen for your voice. I just don't know where we went. I know why. I accept all the blame; it's hard to realize the penalty. Death would be much easier to cope with. When you talk to me— what is the reason? Is it that I haven't realized that I haven't hit bottom yet. I think I have. Do you only want to find out when I'm going to quit drinking, get the taxes done, what?

I feel an ever-increasing loneliness when I talk to you—after I hang up. I wonder will it ever be better. Could we really ever live as man and wife? How many conversations will we have to have to see you on a date basis? I am void of anything to gain your respect again. I am in a mess that seems too complicated to straighten out. I fear if you somehow ever wanted to try our marriage out again, that it will be far too late to do it with me. I don't know where I'm headed and it's very scary. Maybe it's the time, the years I've wasted in life that frightens me. Maybe it's the years of your life I've wasted that makes me feel so guilty. I can't sort it all out anymore. Maybe I should have written a different kind of letter, the one that has all the good things I dream of in the future. Maybe just a short note. I probably shouldn't have written at all, as you can see, it all makes no sense at all. I wish I could get that drug that therapists told me about that would block these radical feelings of depression, fear, guilt, hopelessness, whatever I feel from time to time because I'm very mixed up. I know you still have some feelings for the person I once was. I know you love me now, but I don't know how or why. Please don't call me because you got this letter and you want to try to help me. It's only temporary bit of help that gives me strength during the day and more loneliness at night. Please accept the roses for what once was, not for what the future may hold. Please try to understand I just had to talk to you without hearing your voice.

Lorne

I sat staring out the window, tears streaming down my face. My heart was in agony for the man I loved more than life itself. And there was no way I could help him. He was drowning and all I could do was standby and watch him flail.

Sliding to my knees beside my chair, I closed my eyes and prayed. *"Dear Lord, please watch over my husband and keep him safe. Only You can help him, his life is in Your hands. In Jesus' name I ask, Amen."*

I crumpled to the floor, my knees drawn to my chest, and I covered my head with my arms; uncontrolled sobs wrenched my body. Reality ripped at my insides as I mourned the love I shared with Lorne, knowing in my soul, we could never put the pieces together—at least, not in this world.

84

Walking on eggshells

May 15, 1989

I called Lorne to thank him for the roses but said nothing of the letter. Our conversation was short and rather awkward. We both knew I had read the letter, but I honored my husband's request not to speak of it.

May 20, 1989

It was my weekend to work the Lilac Festival on Pine Mountain. The day was breathtakingly beautiful sitting under the giant pine trees amidst the colorful array of vendor's tents. Pine Mountain, where Lorne brought me to view Haley's comet, held a special place in my heart.

On Sunday afternoon, I looked up, surprised to see Lorne standing in front of me holding Benji on a leash. He knew I was doing the show and had decided to pop in, even though it was a long ride. He looked good; I smiled when I saw him. I wanted to run and hold him in my arms but I knew I couldn't. It would hurt him as much as it would hurt me. We talked for a while and then he left.

He called a couple of times during the week. Our conversations were light, which was okay by me. Yet, I felt I was walking on egg shells.

May 29, 1989

It was Memorial Day when Lorne called. He seemed in a bad way. He wasn't drunk, maybe just disoriented. It might have been the holiday—honoring our veterans. But Lorne was still in a war—the battle for his life.

May 30, 1989

Lorne called. I met him at Marie Callender's where he handed over the balance of his inventory.

May 31, 1989

Lorne called. I met him at The Backwood's for dinner. He needed to find a lawyer—something to do with the business venture he was involved in, and he asked if I knew anyone. I said I would check around the office.

June 5, 1989

There was a suicide threat on my answering machine when I got home from work. I knelt and prayed for my husband and then called his number. There was no answer. I didn't sleep all night.

June 6, 1989

Lorne called from Poppi's, his local haunt, to say he was there looking for a lawyer.

June 9, 1989

Lorne called. He wanted me to bring a box I was holding for him in storage. He would meet me at Marie Callender's. I think he had a buyer for its contents.

June 19, 1989

I met Lorne at Marie Callender's and paid him for the balance of the inventory he gave me.

June 29, 1989

Lorne called painfully distraught. He had gone to the Veteran's Administration Office on Tuesday, the 27th, and was turned down. He was too upset and disoriented to clearly explain what happened. All I could do was pray.

85

His behavior was odd

July 5, 1989

I called Lorne. I was worried about him. He hadn't tried to reach me since he told me the VA turned him down. He answered on the second ring.

"Hi, Baby," he replied, sounding a little too cheerful.

"Lorne, are you all right?" I questioned. "I haven't heard from you in almost a week and I was concerned.

"Don't worry, I'm doing fine," he replied briskly, "but I can't talk right now."

"Okay…bye." I was somewhat bewildered; something strange was going on.

July 10, 1989

I called Lorne. His spirits were still up, but again, we only talked a few minutes as he had to leave.

"Oh, by the way," he remarked, "I won't be home this weekend. I'm going to Catalina with some friends."

This surprised me.

"Great," I managed to utter. "The trip will be good for you."

His behavior was odd. I wondered if it was drugs …or another woman.

July 18, 1989
Lorne called on Tuesday. I didn't mention the trip, I wasn't going to pry. I feared his answer. He did say he'd been to a psychiatrist at five—and was put on more medication.

July 19, 1989
Lorne called to say his first Alcohol Rehab meeting with his counselor was tonight. I was thrilled and told him so. Maybe now he would finally get the help he needed.

July 25, 1989
Lorne called. He started attending a group session. His medication had been doubled.

August 2, 1989
Lorne called work; he was drunk.

"The shrink told me to stay away from you," he said pathetically. "I called your house, but you weren't there."

That was not a good thing to tell my husband. *Dear Lord, what was happening?*

August 4, 1989
Lorne called work on Friday. He was calm and he told me about the lawsuit he and his partner were filing against SecureTight Doors in Boston who somehow stole their design.

August 8, 1989
Lorne called. He invited me to attend the couples'-only group meeting with him at rehab tomorrow night—I agreed.

August 9, 1989
It was 6 p.m. I met Lorne at rehab in a huge building located on Ventura Boulevard in Woodland Hills. The Wednesday session for couples was from

six-thirty to nine-thirty. There were six couples. Each had a partner dealing with alcohol abuse. That night I learned about Lorne's disease.

August 10, 1989
The next day I called Lorne. He was calm and thankful that I agreed to attend the meetings with him. We had a pleasant conversation.

August 16, 1989
Our second group session went well. Lorne talked about the children and his family. He hugged me as we stood talking in the parking garage. I got in the car to leave when he leaned in and kissed me. A sweet memory.

August 18, 1989
On Friday night Lorne called late. He was plastered. He gave no explanation and only wanted to vent. No job, no money, no wife. My bubble burst.

August 22, 1989
Lorne called. I met him at Marie Callender's to deliver some product he had sold. I didn't mind helping him as long as I knew he was trying.

August 30, 1989
I attended a group session with Lorne. All went well, though I never mentioned the Friday night incident. Afterwards, he asked me to a Jazz Festival, but I gracefully declined, saying I had birthday plans with a girlfriend. I lied. Lorne was still drinking and I refused to go backwards.

86

"Enbloc Blackouts"

September 2, 1989

Lorne left a message on my answering machine on Saturday: "Where are you?"

I had been at the mall but I didn't call him back. His calls were trying.

September 6, 1989

I attended another group meeting with Lorne. It was a good session, but Lorne wasn't sharing like the others. I couldn't say anything at this point; I was there to support him.

September 8, 1989

Friday night, Lorne called drunk again. It didn't seem like anything had changed, other than we saw each other on Wednesdays. I hated this rut we were trapped in, but had no idea how to crawl out.

"I'm not going to counseling tomorrow," were the last words out of his mouth before he hung up.

September 13, 1989

Lorne called work, wanting to see the warehouse where our furniture was stored. Maybe he planned to sell something. We couldn't agree on a day or time to meet. Later that night, he left a message—he was drunk.

September 20, 1989

At the group meeting, the discussion centered on sobriety, with each client stating the length of time since their last drink. When it came to Lorne he told the group three weeks. I didn't want to say anything but I had to…for Lorne's sake. He couldn't get well if I covered up for him.

"I'm sorry to say," I uttered, my voice tiny as a mouse. "Lorne has called me a number of times during that time frame…and he was drunk."

"Well, Lorne," the counselor spoke up, "what's that all about?"

Lorne appeared surprised. "I have not been drinking," he said curtly.

"It appears to me," the counselor went on, "you're having blackouts or alcohol related amnesia. This happens. "En bloc" blackouts are classified by the inability to later recall any memories from the intoxicated period, even when prompted." He looked at Lorne and said, "I think that's what you're dealing with."

September 22, 1989

Friday night Lorne called three different times and left word…he was smashed. I listened to his drunkenness but didn't pick up. Talking to him in this condition was useless. No matter how much I loved him, I couldn't let him pull me down. All I could do is pray.

October 4, 1989

Lorne called me at work to tell me he was going to Boston for a month and we wouldn't be going to our group sessions.

October 11, 1989

Lorne called from Boston. He was drunk.

October 12, 1989

Lorne left word on my answering machine. He was drunk.

October 17, 1989

Lorne called drunk. He asked if I would continue counseling with him when he got back from Boston. I told him I wasn't sure because he hadn't stopped drinking.

October 19, 1989

Lorne called work. He was drunk.

October 20, 1989

Lorne was drunk when he left the message on my machine.

"I can't believe you gave up," he stated angrily, then slammed down the receiver.

I hadn't given up...but my optimism was on the bottom rung. I didn't know where to go from here...and I had no one to talk to who knew what to do.

October 25, 1989

Lorne left word. He was in Boston and he was sober.

87

He threatened me

November 12, 1989

It was Sunday. I worked the San Diego Gem and Mineral Show. It was a big show. I got home late. The red light on my answering machine was flashing. I knew it was Lorne. Another suicide threat, but this time he cussed me out before slamming down the receiver. I felt helpless; what was I to do? This was the man I loved. Should I call the police? He was making me crazy.

November 21, 1989

The message Lorne left today was frightening...he threatened me.

November 22, 1989

In today's message, Lorne threatened damage to my car. I felt like I was shrinking smaller and smaller and would soon vanish. I loved Lorne and I knew his illness was causing this behavior, but I was scared, not knowing what he'd do next, or what I should do about it.

With my last ounce of courage, I called Lorne...he picked up.

"Why are you doing this to me?" I whimpered. "I haven't done anything wrong. I love you and would never hurt you. But Lorne, you're an alcoholic and you need help." I couldn't stop the words from coming. "You're the one who wanted out...not me. Now you're threatening me. Do you want me to call the police? Is that what I have to do to get you to stop?" Now I was getting angry.

"No," he said sadly, "please don't call the police." There was silence. "I know it's my fault and I hate myself for what I've done. I want it like it used to be but I don't know how to get there."

His words broke my heart. "Lorne you have to stop drinking. This is the only way you'll ever be able to move forward," I pleaded. "Please promise me you'll try."

"I'll try...for you," he said softly.

November 26, 1989

I called Lorne to see how he was doing. He was working on the RV.

"I went up into the mountains this weekend," he said lightly. "Benji and I went camping. The wilderness and fresh air helps keep me sober. The hard part is everyday life."

"I'm glad you made the trip," I said, feeling encouraged by his words. "You sound good."

Dear Lord, please help my husband stay strong. Amen.

December 7, 1989

I called Lorne. He'd been sober 11 days but he lost his job—another blow to his fragile mind.

December 15, 1989

Lorne called. He was sober. *Thank you, God.* He asked me to bring him the title to the MG. I agreed to drop it off the next day.

December 16, 1989

I drove up to Lorne's place but he wasn't there. I slipped the MG title under the fence next to the gate. When I returned home, I left a message telling him where it was.

December 23, 1989

I called Lorne. He wasn't there. I left word. He called me back at four. He had just gotten out of jail. This was a shock. He had been picked up in a stolen car. This shocked me even more.

"Baby, it's not what it looks like," he tried to explain. "I fixed this old car for a friend and he was supposed to pay me parts and labor." He continued. "But when he refused, I told him I'd keep the car until he had the money," he sighed. "That's when he called the police."

I believed him and was heartsick over his misfortune.

December 28 1989

I called Lorne. We talked for half an hour, going over the problems and ways to move forward. He felt defeated but he was sober.

88

Broken promise

January 3 1990

Lorne called me at work. Someone had broken in and robbed the RV while he was out. They found the gun that I knew he bought after we separated. He had no job or income. He asked me to buy the rest of the inventory he was holding to sell. I agreed.

January 5, 1990

Lorne called at 8 p.m. He asked if I'd mailed the check. I told him I had.

January 13, 1990

I called Lorne. We talked for an hour. He was very depressed. Joan, Lorne's mom, called me. She said she was sending money for Lorne's medication. I learned she'd been sending money all along. Not a lot but more than she could afford.

January 14, 1990

I called Lorne to see how he was. He wasn't in the mood to talk. Joan called. We tried to console each other, both knowing the situation was grave but our hands were tied.

January 17, 1990

Lorne left a message on my answering machine. He was drunk for the first time since his promise to stop on November 22nd. He asked me to drop off the jewelry he had just sold. I agreed, but I was devastated he was at it again.

January 18, 1990

I stopped at Lorne's after work with the jewelry. He was there, but I was still reeling from his broken promise. It had been our last ray of hope and its impact on our marriage was huge. I couldn't talk to him. There was a message when I returned home. He wanted to know why I was mad. I never called back.

January 19, 1990

Lorne called after work.

"Why wouldn't you talk to me yesterday?" he pleaded.

I told him he had broken his promise. He said he was sorry. But I was teetering on the edge of sanity myself. God knew I tried to be there for Lorne, but Lorne needed professional counseling, and I was afraid he might not get it in time.

January 23, 1990

I stopped at Lorne's and gave him money for groceries. That was all I could do...and pray.

January 27, 1990

I called Lorne in the morning. He was down, depressed because his world had tumbled down around him and he saw no way out. He hated living in the mess in the RV. He went to bars rather than wallow in it. I tried to encourage him. I offered to come by and clean the RV. He hesitated. I insisted. He cautiously relented.

I picked up lunch—then spent the next four hours cleaning and tossing out clutter.

Lorne sat quietly nearby and watched. His medication appeared to make him lethargic.

January 31, 1990

We should be celebrating our fifteenth wedding anniversary, but our marriage was in shambles all due to a war on the other side of the world. Why was this happening? How could we fix it? I had no answer. I only knew my mental state was at risk as well. Where would our marriage be at this time next year? Only God knew the answer.

89

Afraid to open the door

February 1, 1990

Today was an important day at work. The president of my major account, along with his colleagues, had flown in from Japan for an important meeting. This was our first face-to-face encounter.

I was prepping for the meeting when the receptionist called to say there was someone in the lobby to see me. I ran downstairs. It was Lorne. He had never entered my building before. I ushered him outside.

"Lorne, what's going on?" I asked hastily. "I'm getting ready for an important meeting."

"I need four hundred and fifty dollars right away," he barked, challenging me.

"Lorne, I don't have that kind of money on me." I tried to remain calm. "Wait until I get home tonight. I'll check the business funds and see what I can do."

"Yeah, right," he growled, as he turned on his heels and walked away.

I watched him get in his car and leave. This was not good. Now he was jeopardizing my job. This wasn't like Lorne. Bothering me at home was one thing but coming to my office was crossing the line.

I called Joan when I got home from work. It seemed Lorne had called her as well demanding money. She said he was drunk and spoke mean things to her.

I never called him back. Actually, I was afraid to. I didn't have that kind of money lying around. Lorne needed to get a job.

February 6, 1990

Lorne called me at work. It was the first time since he came by the office. He said he was getting a lawyer and would file for a divorce. He said I'd better get a lawyer, too. I was speechless. What did he want, alimony?

February 13, 1990

Lorne called me at work. His tone was arrogant; he asked if I had found a lawyer yet. I hung up on him.

February 14, 1990—Valentine's Day

Home from work, I was changing my clothes when the doorbell rang. People seldom came to the door. It rang again. I peeked out the blinds. It was Lorne. I was alone and afraid to open the door. It rang once more. I held my breath. Then I watched him step off the porch and head towards his car parked a few houses down.

Once his car was out of sight, I peeked out the door. On the porch, a red velvet, heart-shaped box caught my eye. My heart softened. A metallic balloon hovered three feet above the gift. The words *I love you* were scrolled on both sides. When I leaned over and lifted the velvet box, the balloon slipped away. I grabbed for it but missed. I stood transfixed, watching it drift higher and higher, smaller and smaller, until it disappeared. I knew Lorne loved me; I also knew he hated himself for the mess he made of our marriage.

90

Black skull and cross bones

March 9, 1990

Night settled over my silent house steeped in shadows. The phone rang. I stirred, slipping back into my dream or my nightmare. A huge snake its head raised slithered through the rooms searching for me, its beady eyes black as onyx.

"Brrring..."

Startled, I opened my eyes, relieved to be in my own bed. Groping for the phone, I toppled a stack of books onto the floor.

"Hello?" I whispered.

"Hi Baby...what are you doing?" Lorne slurred with the innocence of a child.

Of course...who else would it be? If only I had the strength or courage to hang up on him. But I couldn't help myself. He was my husband and he needed me. And I needed him. I loved him no matter what time it was.

"Lorne, I was sleeping," I scolded. "Why do you call in the middle of the night, when you know I have to get up and go to work?"

"I know," he said. "I just wanted to tell you I love you."

The experts called it codependency. Lorne was my addiction. Caught up in his illness, I needed to hear his words of love, to somehow compensate for the hell he put me through. And in some sick way I settled for this, instead the real thing. I let him touch my heart. In my mind I could see him with his head down, eyeing the tops of his boots, too drunk to understand.

"Lorne, I know you do," I said, conscious of how much he missed me. I lay on my back, the receiver cradled to my ear, staring at the shadowed ceiling.

"I love you, too," I went on, "but haven't I told you a thousand times that I would hang up the next time you called drunk?" I tried to be firm, but what good did it do? He continued to call, even when he knew it upset me.

"Baby, I know you're mad," he stammered, "but I have something really important to tell you." He did sound urgent.

"Okay, so tell me," I said. "I want to go back to sleep. Please?" Propping the pillows against the headboard, I settled into the softness and pulled the blanket up to my chin.

I had listened to a multitude of drunken stories, excuses and promises over the years. Nothing was new, just the same old garbage. I loved the man buried deep within the shell of this drunk, but the drunk wouldn't set him free.

"Can ya' hold on a minute?" he asked. "I need to feed Benji. I just got home and he hasn't eaten all day."

"Go ahead," I said with a sigh. I was wide awake now. Why did I let him do this to me? And why couldn't I just hang up?

When Lorne picked up the receiver, he was purposely gulping something with great gusto like liquid being sucked from the neck of a bottle.

"Are you still there?" he asked, sounding drunker than before.

"I'm still here," I said, "now what's so important you have to wake me at this hour?"

Again, I heard the same distinct sound. It crossed my mind he was behaving unusually strange.

"Nancy, I can't take it anymore," he finally said. "My life has turned to shit and I can't go on like this." He gulped loudly. "I never should have asked you to leave. It was my biggest mistake," he babbled. "I love you and I don't want to live without you."

"Listen to me, Lorne," I said forcefully, turning on the light. "The alcohol is destroying you. You must get help. You can't do it by yourself, you know that!"

Lorne started to laugh—a deep, sickening laugh I would never forget.

"You believed I was out feeding the dog," he mocked. "Actually, I went to the shed and got a bottle of plating solution." His ghastly laugh blended into sobs. "You'll be pleased to know, I've been washing it down with a bottle of Jack Daniel's," he continued, boasting of his cleverness. "All your worries will be over soon...very soon."

A cool breeze slipped into the room through the open window. My eyes widened. I was trying to comprehend what Lorne was saying. In my mind, I saw the yellow label on the bottle of solution he used to make jewelry. On it was a black skull and crossbones!

"Lorne, stop it!" I screamed into the phone. "Why are you doing this to me?"

The shock of reality was staggering. *Dear God, not again.* His torment was merciless; my only crime was that I loved him too much.

His heartbreaking sobs echoed in my ear, ripping out my heart. "I want you with me when I die," he choked. "I don't want to die alone."

I felt disconnected...like I was floating above my body, calmly looking down on myself sitting in bed. Lorne had said "the word" so often that in my mind it was already planned. What I would do, what I would say, what I would wear. My black Liz Claiborne suit would be perfect for a grieving young widow, mother of three. Maybe I was finally going mad after all.

Then I heard the receiver drop. I panicked, straining to hear something on the other end of the line. A low hideous moan began to swell from deep within Lorne's chest and throat, echoing an agony that pierced my soul.

"NANCY!" he called out my name..."OH MY GOD, THE PAIN!"

Horror gripped my mind...this was really happening. I was the only one who knew and I was helpless. He was there and I was here. Suddenly my fear was overwhelming.

"LORNE! LORNE!...CAN YOU HEAR ME?" I screamed into the mouthpiece, my entire body was shaking.

"THE PAIN...NANCY...IT HURTS SO BAD...HELP ME," he sobbed, pleading with me as he tried to talk into the receiver.

Hysteria was taking over. The room was spinning, my eyes would not focus. I prayed I would lose my mind to escape. Could madness happen that quickly? Maybe I was dreaming and this was a nightmare born in my subconscious. NO...IT WAS REAL! Or was it? Was it insanity or hell? Was I in hell? A whirlpool of terror spiraled through my core. I had to do something right now.

"LORNE!...LORNE, LISTEN!..." I screamed in hope he could still hear me. "I love you...remember I love you," I said through scalding tears. "I have to hang up now so I can call the police. Do you understand what I'm saying? They'll come quickly to help you."

I knew there was no way I could reach him in time, even if I knew what to do when I got there. Northridge was almost twenty miles from Canyon Country. How long does it take for poison to kill someone? I had no idea. This was the only way!

Lorne's moaning was constant now, like a siren on a clear night. He had a hard time talking, the pain was bad. "Don't leave me," he begged. "Please don't let me die alone. I'm afraid to die alone," he sobbed, an agonizing moan rose from his throat.

"Lorne, I have to do this. It's the only way I can get help to you." *Dear God, give me strength,* I prayed silently. "You're not going to die...I promise!"

"Nancy, don't go...please don't leave me, please," he pleaded, shredding my heart.

There was no other way. Time was running out. Every word he spoke consumed more of his life.

"Lorne, I'm hanging up now." I took a deep breath. "I love you and everything's going to be all right."

My finger pushed the button to disconnect us. I heard the click. Then the dial tone hummed in my ear like a giant insect. No longer could I hear his pleas. I dialed 911, hot tears blurring my vision. I loved him so much; I could feel his pain. Adrenaline rushed through my veins; animal instinct had taken over.

"Operator," a female voice interrupted.

"Please connect me with the Santa Clarita police department," I stammered, "it's a matter of life and death." It was all like a dream. I was floating in and out of reality. My words sounded far away like they belonged to someone else. "My husband has swallowed poison and needs help. Please hurry!"

"One moment, please," said the voice in my ear.

Terrified, I sat on the edge of my bed and waited. Unspeakable pictures streamed through my mind. Pictures of Lorne, wrenching in agony, sprawled on the floor of his RV, the poison eating away his insides. He was there alone, dying a slow painful death and I was on hold!

"Santa Clarita Police," said a strange voice. "Sergeant Kelly speaking."

I fell to pieces as I tried to explain.

"Where's your husband's RV parked?" inquired the sergeant, dispatching the paramedics on another line.

My body went limp; the burden was no longer mine alone.

There were questions, so many questions. I erupted like a volcano, everything broke loose and someone was listening. Sergeant Kelly assured me the paramedics would reach him in time. They knew what to do. I was not to worry.

Drained, I hung up the phone and slipped to my knees.

"Dear God, please let the paramedics reach my husband in time. Don't let him die. He's not a bad person; he's just sick and needs Your help." My tears fell on folded hands. *"He won't let me help him, you know how many years I've tried, but I believe in miracles. Please find that person, that one person, who can reach him, and release him from his past. In Jesus name I ask. Amen."*

I crawled back into bed and pulled the comforter up over my head like a womb of safety, while the world around me crumbled. The bed felt hard and my body trembled. I closed my eyes trying to escape. But sleep evaded me. My mind was with Lorne. Did they reach him in time? Would he be all right...or was he dead? Vivid scenes played inside my eyelids: sirens and flashing lights of red and blue bouncing off the canyon walls, lighting the treetops. Uniformed police smashing through the screen door on the RV, only to find they were too late. Lorne lay on the floor as though asleep. A young paramedic knelt over him, pressing paddles to his naked chest. His body bucked lifelessly again and again.

Then somehow, Lorne and I were in the woods making love on a blanket of soft pine needles where rays of sunlight slipped through the canopy of treetops. I could feel his strong warm body against mine, his soft lips kissing my mouth, my cheek, my forehead and the smell of pine enveloping us.

I opened my eyes. I must have dozed off. The clock glowed on my nightstand with the minute hand having barely moved. I felt helpless, suspended in time, waiting and not knowing. The stillness was suffocating.

An hour passed. I could bare it no longer. I called the hospital, still no word. No one would tell me anything. Where was my husband? Was he alive or dead? The not knowing was driving me crazy.

I dialed the operator. "I need the number for the Santa Clarita Police," I stated firmly.

Jotting it down on the back of a book, I dialed the number.

"Santa Clarita Police Department," replied a familiar voice. "Sergeant Kelly speaking."

"Sergeant Kelly, this is Nancy MacMillan," I said nervously. Getting out of bed, I started to pace. "I talked to you earlier—my husband swallowed poison and the last thing you said was that "help was on the way." I took a deep breath. "That was over an hour ago. I called the hospital, but no one will tell me anything. I can't stand the waiting! Can you help me find out what happened...please?"

"Ms. MacMillan, calm down," he commanded, but his voice was gentle. "First of all, your husband's going to be all right," he assured me.

"Thank God." I collapsed on the bed.

"At first our team had trouble finding him because the location was secluded. We called the phone number you gave us; your husband picked up the call, thinking it was you. He was upset, but conversed enough to get us there."

My head dropped, I sobbed softly.

"They got him in time," he went on. "They pumped his stomach at the hospital and then gave him something to sleep. He's resting now. You can call in the morning if you like. But right now, there's nothing you can do. I suggest you get some sleep.

"Thank you so much, Sergeant Kelly," I said quietly. "I'll try."

I put the receiver down, got up and walked into the bathroom. Splashing cold water on my swollen eyes, I looked at the image in the mirror. This was all wrong. When would it stop? I loved my husband and I knew he loved me. Why couldn't we just have a normal life like other people?

91

It's time things change

March 10, 1990

Lorne was in the hospital. Should I call him or shouldn't I? Prior to last night's phone call, he wanted me to get a lawyer and file for divorce. I didn't want to make him feel worse by calling. I decided to let him rest without hearing my voice. I hoped the hospital would direct him to a program that would help. I knew I was useless.

March 15, 1990

This morning at work I received a special delivery letter from the Internal Revenue Service. Of course they knew where I worked. It was only a matter of time. I had to call Lorne. He sounded okay but distant, suggesting we meet at Marie Callender's after work. When I arrived he was sitting with his lawyer. The lawyer agreed to contact the IRS which would give us time to get our taxes in order.

March 18, 1990

It was spring break. I drove to LAX to pick up Tiffy and a friend, who were counting on a fun-filled week in paradise. I refused to let them down. Cloaked in pretense, we indulged in every pleasure we could squeeze into seven days. My secret was too horrifying to repeat to a living soul, let alone my daughter.

March 28, 1990

I was changing out of my work clothes when the phone rang. I now screened all calls by letting them go directly to the answering machine. It was Lorne. He sounded sober so I picked up. He was really down. The pain in his words hurt. I loved him more than he'd ever know, but I didn't know how to help him.

"I just don't see any reason for living," he said. "I can't get a job. My unemployment is about to run out and this place looks like a pig sty."

I sat on the edge of the bed, rubbing my temple, letting him talk.

"I worked on a guy's car and now he won't pay me. I can't pay my bills." He was crumbling under the pressure. "And worst of all…I know I've lost you. Why would you want someone like me anyway? I'm nothing but a loser."

It made me mad when Lorne talked like that. I loved my husband. He wasn't a loser, he was sick. If someone has cancer, you don't stop loving them. I told this to Lorne dozens of times but he wouldn't listen.

"Lorne, I love you," I interrupted. "I've never stopped loving you but you're destroying yourself. I can't stand by and let you destroy me, too. I have three children who count on my strength. I have to survive for them."

"You don't love me," he said, "you feel sorry for me. Nancy, you're too good for me. You deserve someone so much better."

Our conversations ran in circles…if only there was someone to help him, someone who knew what to do. Someone he could trust and would listen to. After his first suicide attempt, I was asked to sign papers and have him committed to the Veteran's Administration Hospital for treatment. But I couldn't. I was afraid…afraid he would end up hating me…and worse yet, come after me. If only I had signed those papers, things would be different now. But I no longer had that option.

"Lorne, my strength is in God," I said gently. "You know this. Please turn to Him. He'll help you if you ask...please, Lorne?"

"Nancy, I'm too ashamed. I haven't been a good husband and I don't deserve any help from God," he sobbed. "He doesn't want me either, just like no one else wants me."

Always the same words...over and over and over again. The frailty of my own sanity was faltering.

Lord, please help me say the right words, I prayed silently.

"Lorne, I'll tell you what," I said brightly. "What if I come by on Sunday afternoon, clean up your place a bit...and cook you supper?"

"You don't have to do that, Nancy," he said sadly. "Besides, I don't want your pity; I feel bad enough already."

If I could give him a little hope, maybe something good would happen.

"I know I don't have to. I'm saying this because I want to." And I really did. "I love you, Lorne, and always will...always. But it's time things change. Maybe this will be the turning point."

He was silent, as if the idea were sifting through his jumbled mind.

"I'm not real good company right now," he said softly.

"That's fine," I said reassuringly. "I'm coming to clean, not to be entertained, okay?"

"I guess," he said reluctantly.

"How about two o'clock on Sunday?" I asked hopefully.

"Okay."

92

My 100% isn't very good

April 1, 1990

I pushed my screen door open with the side of my foot, vacuum cleaner in tow. A pail bulging with cleaning supplies and a broom were crammed in my other hand. The roll of paper towels tucked under my arm broke loose and rolled off the porch. As usual, I was running late.

Was I doing the right thing?

I lifted the clumsy vacuum into the back of my car.

Three weeks had passed since Lorne was released from the hospital and the few times we had talked he sounded depressed and despondent. In my opinion, he was released too soon. Wasn't it the hospital's job to care for the sick? Lorne told me he was seeing a counselor who put him on Prozac. This worried me as I had read disturbing articles about Prozac that indicated suicidal tendencies could be a side effect. God knows Lorne didn't need any help in that area. It was always good to hear his voice and I really wanted to encourage him. He usually sounded better by the time we hung up. We could still have a future but we had some major hurdles to get over first.

I merged onto the 405 Freeway heading north. The clock on the dash read one-thirty. I slid over two lanes and punched the accelerator. The turbo kicked into overdrive as the car started its climb through the pass. What a gorgeous day for a drive with the sunroof wide open and the exhilarating fresh air. I was looking forward to seeing Lorne. A strange twinge of happiness tingled through me...a feeling I realized I missed.

It had been two weeks since we last met at Marie Callender's after the IRS reached me at my office. For two years, Lorne had filed extensions but nothing more. And how could I do taxes without his paperwork? Whenever I brought it up all hell broke loose. The day after we met, I finally had the courage to contact an accountant of a friend from work. Once I explained the situation, he recommended I file my half separately to relieve myself of any further liability. I was now praying that my visit would nudge Lorne in a positive direction. The time was here. He had to stop drinking and get his life together. And once he did...we could go from there.

Canyon Country, California

I pulled off the highway onto the road leading to Lorne's RV. He rented a piece of land that included the giant pepper tree down the road from the "House from Hell." Just thinking about that house gave me the creeps. Gravel crunched loudly under my tires as I approached the six foot fence surrounding his property. Bamboo fencing had been lashed to the chain link for privacy. Turning off my ignition, I stepped from the car and noticed Lorne's MG parked off to the side. At the fence I reached up and slid the huge gate open wide enough to enter. A skinny German Shepherd limped to greet me; I reached down to pat his bony head. Lorne loved animals. He was constantly bringing home strays.

Approaching the RV, I noticed the door was open.

"Lorne," I called through the screen.

No answer. I knocked on the doorframe and called out again...still no answer. Cautiously, I turned the handle and the door swung open. Stepping inside, I was captivated by what I saw.

Everything was clean and in order. Rays of sunlight fell on a cluster of pink roses, nestled in a rich blue drinking glass in the middle of the table. I knew they were for me. A blue candle sat nearby. Tears trickled down my cheeks. Maybe the healing had started. Maybe this would be the year of change.

"Lorne," I called out again, but still no answer.

Baffled by his absence, I noticed an overstuffed envelope lying on the couch. I walked over and picked it up. It was addressed to me. I sat down as sunshine streamed over my shoulder onto the envelope. I slowly opened it. In my hands I held pages and pages of yellow lined paper written in pencil...Lorne's thoughts, waiting to be read.

Dear Nancy,

It's 11am Sunday and I'm very confused and actually afraid to see you. I'd love to see you, but I'm always going through an emotional hell when you leave. I always wonder how long it will take to know if there is any hope for the future or will I continue to ride this elevator to hell. Please understand I'm not trying to put any blame on you – you must do what you must do for your own reasons – and I can understand that. My fear is that I won't know how to act this afternoon – I love you and I want so desperately to make love with you and I don't know how anymore. I've never known how to say the right thing the right way, so bear with my trying. I haven't made love with anyone in two years – I don't know if I ever will again. It hurts deeply to see other couples enjoying life – having fun. Loving someone that way is a thousand miles away and I am totally fucked up now. I am so desperate for love – I know I would probably cry and beg you to make love with me and that would only hurt you and me worse...if things could get worse. I can't go on like this. I don't know what will come from hour to hour or day to day. It's just a nightmare. I know I've done it all to us and to me. I don't know why. I feel so much guilt. It's hard to live with. I want out of my prison but I don't know where the door is or where the key is or worse yet – what's outside. I have no more self-esteem – I hate myself and I'm no longer a man – I'm only a living creature that can feel pain. I can't drink forever to dull the pain, so how do I escape it? I haven't any answer. I'm afraid of getting better. I'm afraid of death. Sometimes, I want to walk out to the highway and stick out my thumb. I can survive physically. It's the emotional pain I don't know how to deal with.

I know I've been wrong to ask for help – you have your own problems. Your own life. I put you out there and you have the right to resent me for that. Maybe I'm wrong to wish for a chance with you but I don't want anyone else. I don't even want to meet anyone else. I met your co-worker,

Mary, the other night at the Elks club. She knew me and was nice to me. I was embarrassed and didn't know what to say or what to do. I like strangers because they don't know I'm a total failure. I don't know what to write now. On the positive side, your agreeing to come over inspired me to totally clean up the place and create three more boxes of shit. That's all I have left is lots of shit. I'm sorry you had to drive out here but I just couldn't call. I'll probably regret that but either way I don't have anything together when I'm talking to you or away from you. But I don't know what to do when I'm with you. It's only a brief few minutes of regret and hours and days and weeks of longing for the past. Did we ever have it good or is it just in my mind? When you say – I love you – I don't know you mean it. When you say – I'm your wife – I wonder what that means to you. The papers haven't been undone. If we were divorced you would never consider me for a husband again. I would give anything and everything to live with you as husband and wife as the Bible meant it to be. I guess I never knew who you really were or what you really meant to me – and I'm not saying that because I need so much help. That's my own personal crisis and I have no right to make it your problem. If you think it is – do whatever. I will not ask for your help anymore. I just haven't known where to seek help. I'm bankrupt of true friends who really care – why should anyone? I have only creditors, no debtors. No one owes me anything. Those who know about my stupid stunt two or so weeks ago avoid talking to me. They say, "How are you doing? We're all concerned. Can I buy you a drink? Let me get Mac's. That's on me, bartender." No one really wants to talk about any problems. Never get personal with anyone who is crazy enough to want to die. Maybe that's good advice – I don't know. Hearts are never mended when left unattended. I'm sorry to do this, but I just got cold feet. All I ever say is negative and I don't feel confident that seeing you here would do anything but put me on an emotional downswing – if I could get any lower. Maybe we would argue – or as I said I want you so badly – not just sex – it's hard to explain. I lust for your love. I go crazy every night thinking about it. I don't want to push – I don't want to beg – and most of all I don't want to hurt our relationship – that is if we have one. You've told me you can't and won't make love with me. Yet you let me kiss you or touch you – and it only worsens my confusion. It hurts to see you drive away – time and time again. Like I said, it's driving me crazy. I cry a lot about it. But then I cry about a lot of other things too. If you would be hurt emotionally, if we ever did make love – I guess I would understand. Maybe that's the difference between men and women. I could be thrilled with just dating you, if I had the funds. Not being able to be with the one you love is a terrible hell – maybe not for you but it is for me – Enough rambling on – I hope this letter isn't too selfish on my part. Please try to understand – I don't know what to say or what to do. Maybe the next time we talk I will. I don't know. I can only hope and I don't have much of that left.

Once upon a time – your husband

P.S. Still in Love with You—In Love with you for eternity—no matter what happens. I'm trying 100%. My 100% isn't very good—but it's the best I can do today.

A soft breeze drifted in through the open screen door. I sat quietly clutching Lorne's letter in my lap. I stared into nothingness. I was exhausted from feeling the depth of his raw emotion, his pain, his agony—the personal torture he was enduring. *Dear God, I loved him so very much.* Lorne was my soul mate; I knew in my heart we were one forever. Forever had no beginning and no end. But how would we survive the now? Where would he get the strength to pull himself from the pits of hell?

I gazed at the pages in my hand, my mind lost in his words. Startled, I heard a movement outside. Looking up, I watched Lorne open the screen door and our eyes met. A glint of fear crossed his face. But just as quickly, his beautiful blue eyes filled with love as he stood in the stairwell looking at me.

The look I knew so well and longed for, the look that burned into my very soul.

Stepping into the room, Lorne seemed uneasy. "I thought you'd be gone by now," he said shyly.

"I'm a slow reader," I said, looking up at my husband.

Lorne walked over to the counter and reached for a bottle of wine.

"Can I pour you a glass?" he asked, without looking at me.

"Okay," I said weakly, watching him peel the foil from the bottle's neck.

He must stop drinking, but this was not the time to say anything. It would only hurt him more. And he was in enough pain. It had been such a long time since we were together like this; I didn't want to spoil the moment. Tomorrow would be soon enough to face reality.

Brilliant rays of sunlight slipped through the blinds and reflected through the glasses, turning the wine a translucent ruby red.

"I went over to the Lodge last night," Lorne said uneasily, handing me a glass. "They had a crab leg dinner so I bought some extra. Thought we could have them for lunch. I remember how much you like crab."

I was touched. He was unemployed with little money yet he thought of me.

"Sounds great," I said, trying to sound casual. "And I have all this free time since you left me nothing to clean."

He raised his glass, smiling tenderly. "To the future," he toasted, clinking my glass.

That afternoon we sat sipping wine and eating crab legs like an ordinary couple sharing a quiet Sunday afternoon. I watched him as we ate. He seemed happy. His face was relaxed, no sign of stress. I wanted to guard this moment as long as I could.

Picking up our empty plates, I got up and carried them to the sink. Lorne followed closely behind. Taking me by the shoulders, he turned me around and looked down into my eyes. Then he kissed me softly on the lips. I melted into him. His kiss turned to hunger, which I returned.

The passion of our love spiraled to a peak. Time ceased to exist. Transported to another dimension, we were one again for now and forever.

93

Electric Shock

April 14, 1990

On Saturday afternoon, I came home from grocery shopping to find a bunch of yellow daisies wrapped in paper on the porch. I called and left word thanking Lorne for the flowers.

April 15, 1990

Lorne left word, he was extremely agitated. I didn't know if it was the Prozac or alcohol or both. I started to experience a feeling of fear I never felt before

April 19, 1990

Lorne's message was upsetting. He sounded like someone I didn't know. I didn't know what to do...I barely slept all night.

May 2, 1990

It was three years ago today that Lorne and I began living separately. He hadn't tried to reach me in almost two weeks. It was a relief, yet it was also scary not knowing if he was prowling nearby waiting to get me alone. I had a four-thirty appointment with John Davis, my new tax man, to hand over my taxes for 1989.

May 8, 1990

John Davis stopped at the office with my completed tax return for me to sign.

May 9, 1990

I mailed my 1989 Tax Return. It was a relief not to have this worry anymore. If only Lorne could find someone to help him...but who?

I knew it all started with Vietnam. Our government should be horse whipped for ignoring our soldiers...and their families.

May 17, 1990

Mary, my office manager and friend, called me into her office. Her husband belonged to the Lodge and they attended a lot of the socials. She knew some of my trials, and the Lodge is where she first met Lorne.

"Just to let you know, I heard Lorne was accepted into the Elks last night," she said. "Not a good sign for sobriety."

June 3, 1990

The turbo blew on my 280ZX on the way to the Lilac Festival at Pine Mountain so I had to have it towed home. I needed to find a garage to fix it. Hopefully they wouldn't expect my first born in payment.

June 5, 1990

Left for Ohio for Cory's graduation on Friday.

June 8, 1990

Cory's graduation from Ohio State held the pomp and circumstance of the occasion. He was beaming because his whole family was there. I was so proud of him.

June 9, 1990

There was a big party for Cory with twenty-six people in attendance. I spent time visiting family and friends, until my flight back to California on Tuesday.

June 18, 1990

Lorne called to wish me happy birthday. He sounded strange. His voice was weak and he was having trouble putting a sentence together. It wasn't alcohol…what was it?

"Lorne, your voice sounds different," I said delicately. "Are you on a new medication?"

"No," he said softly. "They gave me an electric shock treatment."

I was stunned. It sounded barbaric. I didn't know they did that anymore.

"It wasn't fun," he went on, "my head still feels weird. Not sure what good it does."

Our conversation was strained. He did say, "I love you" before he hung up.

June 23, 1990

Brad drove me to East Los Angeles to pick up my car. The garage was in a bad neighborhood but their prices were the best. A rebuilt turbo was going to run six hundred and sixty seven dollars. This compared to approximately three thousand dollars anywhere else—a deal I couldn't pass up.

94

Eyes wide in terror

June 27, 1990

It was a hot, smothering night in the San Fernando Valley. Not a wisp of air. I tossed and turned; my damp sheet clung to me. Blankets were kicked to the floor. The ceiling fan strained overhead. The wanton howl of a cat in heat soon pierced the shadows with an unnerving scream.

Exhausted, I got up and shuffled down the dark hall to the spare bedroom. Standing at the window, I pushed a button on the air conditioner and felt the cold air billow my nightgown. The sudden chill was intoxicating.

But enough was enough. Tomorrow was a work day and I had to get some sleep.

At some point, I dozed off.

The sound of shattering glass severed the silence. Eyes wide in terror, I searched the darkness, paralyzed in fear. Streaks of streetlight edged the mini-blinds, no prowling shadows outside the windows. Stillness masked the hum of the air conditioner.

Slipping out of bed, I tiptoed across the bare wood floor. Pounding blood echoed in my ears. I made my way to the doorway and then edged out into the hall. With my back tight to the wall I inched forward, straining to hear any sound or movement.

There...a muffled noise...behind my bedroom door. I went to the door and placed my ear against the wood. There...I heard it again.

"Nancy?" One muffled word...it was Lorne.

I was scared. What did he want? Why was he doing this?

"Nancy...I need to talk to you."

He was close, very close. I didn't move.

"Nancy...where are you?" he pleaded behind the door.

My own bedroom wasn't safe. He was in there somewhere. Unknown terror tingled through my body. He had never gone this far before. I had seen similar stories on the news. Sometimes the estranged wife would end up dead. I had no idea what was next but I knew I had to survive.

The tense silence lingered like bug repellent while I tried to comprehend Lorne's thoughts, and his next move.

"Please answer me," he begged.

I could feel it growing...my need, my addiction, my codependency on Lorne. It was bubbling to the surface and I couldn't stop it. This time his voice told me he was not inside the room. I put one hand on the brass knob, took a deep breath and slowly opened the door.

Dense darkness swallowed me.

Heat enveloped me as the ceiling fan rotated overhead. The only window in the room was dark, held open four inches with security locks.

"Nancy...where are you?" he pleaded, his voice deep with despair.

Lorne was outside the window. Only the closed mini-blinds separated us. Soft carpet cushioned my bare feet. I stepped to the middle of the room. I must remain calm. His muddled words indicated his drunkenness. All these years, I thought I knew him...but not tonight. He appeared desperate. This scared me more.

"Lorne, I'm here," I called out. My mouth was parched. My voice hung suspended in the room. "Why did you do this?" I pleaded. "Why in God's name did you do this?"

Slowly rocking back and forth, my arms wrapped across my breasts to stop the trembling. I couldn't stop.

"I wanted to talk to you. I knocked on your window but you didn't answer." His anguish permeated the darkness. "I knocked harder. The window broke...I'm sorry," he replied naively. His lips were close to the open window. He seemed to whisper, yet I heard every word.

"Lorne, you have to go," I warned, my insides shaking. "I'm sure the neighbors heard the glass breaking and called the police."

It hurt me to know he had gone this far and there was nothing I could do...no matter how much I loved him.

"You need to answer your phone," he accused. "And you don't return my calls." I heard the torment in his voice. "Nancy, I love you. I just wanted to talk to you but I always seem to do everything wrong."

My heart swelled with guilt but I, too, was fighting to survive. I knew Lorne loved me. Yet for years I threatened not to answer the phone if he was drunk. He never listened. His calls continued long after I was asleep. Weekdays, weekends, no matter. I'd lay in the dark listening to his pleas, his pain, and his promises...the words of a drunk. Sometimes I did pick up because I needed him. Then wished I hadn't. The drunkenness, teemed with self hatred at times hurled vile accusations aimed at me. I knew it was his illness, but still it hurt, leaving me to lie awake, my mind churning until the alarm went off. I was in love with Lorne, the man within the drunk. I must break my codependency...no matter how much it hurt...but how?

"Lorne, I love you, too...but, please?" I begged. "You have to go before the police get here."

He was silent. The air was thick and nauseating. If only I could stick my finger down my throat and throw up...I could think more clearly.

He backed away from the window. Crunching leaves echoed between the houses, revealing he was headed for the street. I groped in the dark, found my robe and quickly made my way into the hall. A dim light shone from the doorway of Brad's room at the back of the house. He was talking on the phone, pacing the floor with a baseball bat resting on his shoulder.

The deadbolt!

Had I locked it before going to bed? I couldn't think. Slipping through the shadows, my fear mounted. I believed Lorne still might try to get to me. I reached the door. My fingers traveled the wood like Braille. I touched the lock. It was secure.

Hidden in darkness, I peeked around the edge of the blinds. I could see Lorne get into the MG parked behind my car in the driveway. He started the engine, turned on the lights, put it in reverse and backed into the middle of the street. And then as I watched, he raced the engine to a roar, threw the car into drive and charged back up the driveway, crashing into my car. My stomach clenched at the sound of twisting, crunching metal and exploding glass.

I couldn't believe what I was seeing.

My God! He's smashing my car! It was all like a dream, a bad dream. *I don't believe it. He's smashing my car!*

My hands flew to my mouth in disbelief. Staggering back to the middle of the room, my eyes were fixated on the window. Numb and helpless, I watched his brilliant headlights slip through the blinds as he backed into the street. For a moment there was stillness. I waited. He gunned the engine. The MG jumped forward with gears grinding. Dazzling white light tossed paisley patterns around the room like a mirrored ball at a dance as he barreled up the driveway. The sickening sound of cars colliding filled my head. It was a nightmare. Stunned, I stood in the dark and watched the headlights retreat. Grateful numbness guarded my sanity.

In the distance, I heard the sound of helicopter blades slicing the tense night air, competing with the roar of Lorne's racing engine. Seconds later, clipping rotor blades thundered overhead, vibrating the walls and windows. At that moment Lorne slammed into my car for the last time, propelling it through the fence. Splintered wood and twisted nails screeched across its hood and the tires exploded. The car came to a standstill jammed under the bow of Brad's boat that was parked behind the fence, forcing it through the garage door.

"GET OUT OF THE CAR AND KEEP YOUR HANDS OVER YOUR HEAD," a voice bellowed from a bullhorn high overhead.

Circling tight, the helicopter's intense spotlight enveloped the house and yard like an alien spaceship. Bright light seeped in through every crack in the room, creating an eerie aura. The noise and excitement brought the neighbors to their windows. Some poked their heads out their doors, or wandered outside for a better look. Two police cars with sirens screaming and lights ablaze came to a screeching halt at the end of the driveway. Within seconds three unmarked cars juggled for position on the street.

"GET OUT OF THE CAR NOW," the voice commanded. "AND KEEP YOUR HANDS OVER YOUR HEAD."

Brad stayed on the phone with the police until they arrived. Now he watched through the edge of the blinds while I huddled near the corner of the fireplace. My eyes were shut and my hands covered my ears. I wanted to throw up but I couldn't move. Thoughts tumbled through my mind like rolling rocks out of control. I couldn't help my husband, he was on his own.

Dear God please don't let anything worse happen...don't let them shoot him.

Car doors slammed. Uniformed officers dashing for cover surrounded the yard, their guns drawn and pointed at Lorne who sat in his car. The house rumbled as the helicopter circled tightly overhead, its beam of light fastened on the MG.

The car door opened. Two empty hands appeared first, reaching high above the window. Slowly, Lorne maneuvered his long legs from the tiny car. He bent forward and then stood up with his hands raised above his head, squinting into the bright light like a scared rabbit on the highway.

"GET DOWN ON THE GROUND WITH YOUR HANDS BEHIND YOUR HEAD," the voice ordered. "GET DOWN NOW...MOVE!"

Lorne wasn't quick enough. A streak hurtling through the air tackled him behind the knees. Thrown off balance, he went face first into the grass; a knee came down firmly on the back of his neck. His arms were yanked roughly behind his back as the handcuffs were snapped shut. After being pulled to his feet, two officers led him to a waiting police car. Lorne looked back at the house, at the window, seconds before they slammed him over the fender.

Two uniformed officers stood in the living room questioning Brad and me. Neighbors in nightwear huddled in small groups talking. The spotlight ceased. The rumbling helicopter turned, darting back into the night like a mammoth mosquito. The hollow sound of rotating blades echoed long after it disappeared in the dark. Flashing red and blue lights on the police cars danced in the street.

"How long have you and your husband been separated?" asked the lanky dark-haired officer.

"Over three years," I answered, huddled on the hearth of the fireplace, my arms wrapped tightly around my knees.

"Has he ever done anything like this before?" he asked, jotting in his notebook.

"No sir," I replied.

"We're going to have to take him back and book him. The charge will be burglary," he said to my surprise. He noticed my expression. "When an entrance is broken that's the charge. It's the law."

Retreating into grayness, a part of my mind was shutting down. I knew I was answering questions but I couldn't hear myself nor did I want to. Detaching from the real world, I slipped into that quiet dark place I knew so well. There I was safe.

"NANCY! NANCY!" Lorne shouted from the street, "I LOVE YOU."

The sound of his voice yanked me from my room of quiet. I didn't want to come back, it hurt to remember. The pain was deep. The man I loved needed me. He was calling for help but I couldn't go to him. The endless minutes dragged on.

They finished questioning Brad. He stood by the window looking out into the street.

"NANCY! NANCY!" Lorne screamed for me.

"Get him out of here...NOW!" ordered the arresting officer.

He turned towards me. "You may have to come down and file a police report," he stated. Then he looked at me with concern. "I strongly recommend you file a restraining order against your husband. That way if he comes near you again, we can arrest him. Without this restraining order we can do nothing."

Huddled on the corner of the fireplace with my elbows on my knees, my fingers pressed deep into my temples. The officer's lips were moving but his voice was far away. Lorne had gone too far this time, I had no idea what to expect next. Here I was alone in California. My family lived 1500 miles away and my alcoholic husband, a Vietnam vet, was after me. What now? To feel safe I had to hide but I had to work in order to survive. And what did survive mean anyway? Lorne had survived Vietnam.

Feeling safe was not an option.

95

Don't want to scare you

July 2, 1990

My life was like a bottomless black hole whirling out of control, sucking me deeper and deeper, day by day. How does someone have a nervous breakdown? Many times I wished for one, so I could step out of my nightmare and rest a while.

The phone rang on my desk at work.

"This is Nancy, can I help you?" I asked.

"Nancy, please come into my office," Mary said briskly. "We need to talk right away." Mary Carrol was my immediate supervisor but also a friend. We met when we applied for the same position. Mary had experience I didn't have, but I needed the job. The two of us pursued with ruthless persistence. The Director of Operations finally threw up his hands and hired us both.

"Close the door," she said, looking up from her desk. "We need to talk."

I closed the door and took a seat in the chair in front of her desk.

"What's up?" I asked.

"Nancy, I don't even know where to begin," Mary said, concern in her eyes. "Lorne was released from jail on Friday...."

I wasn't aware of this...but I was never called to press charges either.

"Anyway, he's been hanging around the Elks Lodge and he's talking strange." She paused, leaning forward on her elbows. "I don't want to scare you, I just think you should know."

My backbone went rigid...hearing her words did scare me.

"Mary, please tell me. I have to know," I replied.

"Of course, Lorne's drunk when he starts running off at the mouth," she said. "He's spreading tales and for some reason he believes you're living with a man from India. It had something to do with the name on a car registration." Mary was visibly shaken. "I couldn't get his story straight but he vows to kill him."

I was in shock trying to grasp what I heard. Where did Lorne get the idea I was living with a man from India? It was too bizarre. Lorne knew Brad was the landlord and that he lived at the house. He met Brad when he was in the living room and we were going over inventory. Brad in no way resembled a man from India...so who was he talking about?

Dear God what now? There was no other man. How could he kill a man who didn't exist? His illness was talking not the man I loved. Everything was so mixed up. Lorne was desperate this I knew. Some days I wondered...would I live through it all?

96

The agitated red light

July 3, 1990

At five-thirty in the afternoon, the scorching sun still reigned, yet the neighborhood was deserted, void of another living soul. Propping the screen door open with my knee, I struggled to get my key into the lock; my hand was shaking. I opened the door, glanced over my shoulder, and quickly stepped inside. My heart was pounding against my ribs. I shoved the dead bolt into place and slumped against the solid wood barrier. Stifling heat invaded my lungs.

"Thank you, God," I whispered.

Wide-eyed and barely breathing, I searched the unnerving quiet that saturated the room like a deadly gas. The house was empty—no blaring television and no laid-back landlord slouched in his eyesore of a chair with the remote control embedded in the palm of his hand like some benign growth. Then I remembered. Brad mentioned he was driving up to Big Bear right after work. Fourth of July weekend and fishing with his buddies was the one thing that could pry him away from his new, big screen TV.

I was alone.

I slipped off my shoes and padded down the hall to my bedroom, trying to ignore the helpless feeling of doom pursuing me. Fear was now my constant companion.

At the doorway I stopped. Across the room the agitated red light on my answering machine demanded attention. My throat tightened. I knew who it was and I knew he was drunk.

I wanted to turn and run but the pulsating red eye dragged me in like a riptide, across the carpet and around the bed. I hesitated at the nightstand, then reached out and pushed the playback button.

"Nancy, this is Lorne." His voice was low, barely audible. "If you don't...if you don't really care if I live or die...why in the hell did you call 911 when I tried to commit suicide? I don't understand."

My heart stopped as I sank to the bed.

"Would you please come to my graveside...and tell me...goodbye?"

Tears spilled down my cheeks; Lorne's pain tore through my heart.

'Tell me that you...that you...tell me something! I need to talk to you...or you need to talk to me," he begged, his voice quivering. "I will die for you...if that's what you want...if that's the way I have to get," he paused, "right with you...then I will die for you. I will try tomorrow, July Fourth...to die on the Fourth of July for you. If you will just come to my graveside and tell me it's okay," he pleaded. "Tell me you love me...one...last...time. Just do that for me..."

"BEEP..." The machine cut him off.

Lorne's desperate words exploded around me, ricocheting off the delicate green shamrocks in my wallpaper, crashing against my skull. The love of my life was teetering on the edge and I was powerless to help him.

I buried my face in my hands, tears pooling in my palms. Monkey chatter swarmed the corridors of my mind. If only I could make it go away. I pressed my fingertips deep into my temples, rotating in a circular motion. Some days I felt like I was going mad.

I had no strength left to fight back.

Vivid images consumed me: Lorne wandering aimlessly, lost in his nightmare with alcohol, not knowing where to turn, except to me. I knew it wasn't my fault, but I was drowning in guilt. How much more could I take? And God forbid...would he really go through with it?

I fell to my knees beside the bed and made the sign of the cross. "In the name of the Father and the Son and the Holy Ghost," I begged over folded hands. "Please, dear God, don't give him the courage. In Jesus' name I ask. Amen."

I knew Lorne wanted me back but he couldn't stop drinking. There had been too many years and too many promises. No matter how much I loved him, I couldn't go down with him. Threats of suicide loomed in the shadows, but there was nothing left to do. God knows I tried. Lorne knew me too well; he knew how much I loved him and what buttons to push. In the past, I had always gone back, but this time was different. This time I had to resist. I had to be strong even though I longed to run to him, hold him in my arms and tell him everything would be all right.

But everything was not all right.

I knew I had to leave the house; it wasn't safe to stay alone. Lorne's pattern had changed.

I went to the closet and pulled a suitcase from the top shelf and tossed it onto the bed. Adrenaline tore through my veins. Yanking open my dresser drawers, I grabbed enough clothes for a few days and flung them in the direction of the suitcase. Next I shoved my hair dryer and a handful of bottles and jars from the bathroom counter into the side pockets.

In the kitchen, I riffled through the Yellow Pages sprawled open on the counter. I felt like a hunted animal with no place to hide. I slammed the book shut. I had to get out of the Valley, but I couldn't think. Inside my head, the monkeys shrieked. I closed my eyes and rubbed my temples, trying to make them go away. Then I recalled a little motel tucked off of the highway on my way to Point Dume—*The Malibu Hideaway…that's it.*

I called information and dialed the number given me.

"You're one lucky lady," the young man remarked. "We're usually booked over a holiday weekend, but some guy just called with a cancellation."

"Great, I'll take it," I said. *But one lucky lady I'm not.*

"And how many in your party?" he asked.

"Two," I replied impulsively.

Suddenly the front door flung open.

"It's me," Brad hollered through the house. "I need my bait out of the refrigerator in the garage."

Visibly shaking, I went to tell him what had happened.

"Are you all right?" he asked, concern darkening his eyes. "Do you want me to go with you?"

"No, you made plans to go fishing," I said. But I was grateful that someone else knew what was going on. "I'll be okay as long as I'm far away from this house."

"No, I think it's better if you're not alone," Brad insisted. "Let me make a call, my duffle bag's already in the car."

"Honest, I'll be alright," I reiterated warily.

"He may go looking for you, and there's no need to take that risk," Brad stated. "Besides, there's safety in numbers."

The monkey chatter began to fade.

97

Scared all the time

July 13, 1990

It was Friday the thirteenth.

I wasn't superstitious...yet I had an eerie feeling I couldn't shake. The drive home from work was uneventful. Yet the closer I got to the house...the monkey chatter began tuning up like the New York Philharmonic...waiting for the curtain to rise.

Lorne's suicide threat over the Fourth of July weekend told me he was getting worse. The timing between events had narrowed. Lately, the only safe place for me to hide was a secluded motel—which was no way to live. Besides, I couldn't afford it. On the other hand I was a sitting duck in public.

My nerves were shot. I hadn't had a decent night's sleep since the break in—and I knew it wasn't over. Lorne wanted me back, but he was escalating out of control, unable to cope. And there was no one to help him, or who cared to, except me—and I didn't know how. Lorne wasn't a bad person. Buried beneath the horrors of war was a highly-intelligent, loving, sensitive man who had a family and who believed in God. He was sick from the war but our government looked the other way. Prozac was not the answer.

Vietnam and alcohol were demons standing between us, dancing and prancing like skeletons on a grave. They were out to kill him and he was too weak to fight back. I had no idea what to do—or what to expect next.

Instinctively I pulled to the curb at the end of my street and turned off the engine. Sitting behind the wheel, I lit a cigarette and inhaled deeply. Everything appeared normal. No suspicious-looking cars were parked along the curb. The neighborhood cat slept peacefully under a flaming red bougainvillea bush, and the only sound was the willowy swishing of afternoon sprinklers.

I started the engine but decided to circle the block first.

As I pulled up in front of the house, my whitewalls scraped the curb. I winced. Lorne would have had a fit. But right now I had bigger problems.

I was scared all the time, always looking over my shoulder, never knowing when Lorne would be there. I used to look forward to weekends, but not anymore. Now I went into hiding like one of *America's Most Wanted*; I wanted to find a hole and crawl in someplace where he couldn't find me.

I grabbed my purse, got out of the car and headed up the drive, scooping up the morning *Daily News*. No need to hide the car as I wasn't going to be long. Recently, I had started to park in my neighbor's garage—Cheryal had insisted. That way Lorne would never know when I was home.

But right now, I'd be fine. It wasn't six o'clock yet. All I had to do was throw a few things in a bag and be off. Surely he wouldn't be on the prowl so early.

The house was hot and stuffy. I left the front door open but locked the screen door. The fresh air felt good. Brad called at work to say he was having sushi with friends and wouldn't be back until later. No need to worry—I'd be quick.

I dropped the paper on the table and headed towards the kitchen. The sound of a car door slamming caught my attention. I turned…and froze in my steps. Across the street was an old yellow car I had never seen before…and there was Lorne, crossing the street, his hands buried in the pockets of his good gray pants.

Panic seized me like a shark. I raced to the door. Closing it was tricky. In my mind I knew I must unlock the screen first, or the door wouldn't close. It had something to do with the weather stripping. Could I do it in time? I groped for the latch. Once released, I slammed the door shut, sliding the deadbolt into place. Terror tore through my body.

"God please help me," I begged out loud.

I was in a living nightmare. I slowly backed away from the door...then I heard the screen door open...my blood curdled. And as I watched, the doorknob slowly turned back and forth. But the door didn't budge.

"DING...DONG!"

I nearly jumped out of my skin. The sharp peals vibrated through my skull.

"Nancy, I know you're in there," Lorne called through the door.

Frozen in fear, I pictured Lorne standing on the porch holding the screen door open, waiting for me to unlock the door.

"Nancy, I just want to talk to you," he begged. "I don't need to come in. You come out in the front yard, so we can talk...Please?"

What if he had a gun? Fear screamed in my head. What if he planned to shoot me? That way I wouldn't leave him. Maybe he'd shoot me and then kill himself...right there in the front yard. It could make the 11:00 news..."Vietnam vet kills estranged wife, then shoots himself." Gruesome images crossed my mind.

"Lorne, go away," I pleaded, my voice quivering, "please?"

"Nancy, I promise I won't hurt you, I just want to talk to you," he said calmly...a little too calmly.

Then silence...time ceased to exist.

Suddenly a high-pitched, metallic squeak startled my senses, igniting the fight or flight signals in my brain. I dared to stare. The brass lid covering the mail slot in the door slowly opened. Lorne's blue eyes peered in at me. I couldn't stop the tears. Our eyes locked, and I was drawn to the love I saw. But my trust was gone...I knew he saw my fear.

"Lorne, you have to go," I sobbed. Placing one foot behind the other, I inched my way towards the kitchen. "Lorne, you're really scaring me...and I have to call the police," I warned, wiping my nose with the back of my hand.

"Nancy, all I want to do is talk to you," he said softly. The sadness in his eyes ripped at my heart. I was still in love with him, but I couldn't take a chance...not anymore.

The kitchen door frame poked me in the back. I could go no further. Reaching behind me, I felt for the phone on the counter. My eyes never strayed from his. With the phone in hand I dialed 911.

"911...Can I help you?" a female voice interrupted.

Relieved by the sound of another human voice, I broke down.

"Operator, I need the police. Please help me," I whimpered. Lorne's eyes held me hostage. "My estranged husband is on the porch, watching me through the mail slot. I'm terrified." The trembling in my hand traveled throughout my body. "He broke into my bedroom two weeks ago and smashed my car. The police arrested him," I went on, "and I'm not supposed to talk to him...but he keeps calling...and now he's on the porch...and I don't know what he's going to do."

Lorne didn't budge. I knew he heard every word I said.

"Nancy, I love you," he said softly.

"What's your address?" the operator asked.

I gave her all the information she requested and then listened while she dispatched a police unit to the house.

"Does he have a weapon?"

"I don't know," I wept softly. "I can't see his hands. All I can see are his eyes looking back at me." His eyes filled with tears, and I knew my words hurt him deeply, but I was petrified, afraid he might try to kill me, even though he loved me. I wasn't ready to die.

"Nancy, I love you," was barely a whisper. The tears spilled from Lorne's eyes. "And I always will."

"Lorne, you have to go now," I begged. "The police are coming and they'll arrest you again." This was the only way I could help him; he had to run to save himself.

"Is he still there?" asked the operator.

"Yes," I said. Our eyes locked in the love we shared but could not have. My world was upside down. Voices in my head screamed in rage. I could feel my husband's pain like a wounded animal.

Our gaze was transfixed; the blue in his eyes darkened.

"Nancy, I love you," he whispered one last time, staring deep into my soul. Then he lowered the mail slot lid.

I heard the screen door bump shut but I was too scared to move. Seconds later, I heard the engine start and the car pull away.

"He's gone," I said weakly into the mouthpiece as I slumped against the kitchen counter, realizing what might have happened.

"The police should be there in a few minutes," the operator reassured me. "Are you okay?"

"I'm all right," I said softly. "Thank you for staying with me on the line with me."

I hung up the phone and was jarred by a knock at the door. I crossed the living room and peeked out the blinds. Katy, my next door neighbor, was standing on the porch dressed in shorts and a tee shirt, a baby on one hip and a toddler in tow, twitching like a cat on a hot stove.

"Are you all right?" she asked when the door opened.

"Yes...but he really scared me." I said, still dazed.

She then told me that the new neighbor across the street had been watching Lorne from his front yard. He called her and she decided to check on me when she saw Lorne leave.

A black and white squad car rolled up to the curb, blocking the driveway.

"I'll talk to you later," she said, scampering across the lawn like a mother hen with her chicks.

Two officers ambled up the driveway. I stood with the screen door open, watching one of them jot notes on a small pad. Once inside, they questioned me, and dispatched a description of the car Lorne was driving.

"As you were told the last time," the officer stated, "without a restraining order, we can't do a thing. We can haul him in for scaring you...but we can't keep him."

I promised to think about it this time.

Why in hell was this happening? Why did our government send young boys to Vietnam to be killed or maimed for life and ignore those who survived, brushing them aside like nothing happened? Vietnam was killing Lorne like cancer creeping through his body. His behavior was unstable, but jail was not where he belonged—he needed help. The combination of alcohol and Prozac made him a ticking time bomb set to detonate. Lorne was losing his sense of right and wrong. The bolder his advances, the more I feared death.

As they were leaving, one of the officers handed me a card. "I think you should use this. It's for your own protection."

Ironically, the card contained a list of hotline numbers I could call for help.

98

"Dear God, help me"

A hush fell over the house. Huddled in the corner of the couch, I stared into the cold, charred fireplace, my mind scrambling to understand. The bits and pieces of my life pasted together like some bizarre collage made no sense. What was my purpose if I couldn't help the only man I loved?

One thing was certain, I must live through this.

"Bringg..."

"Bringg..."

The sharp ring ripped through me like a stun gun. I sprang to my feet; my heart banged in my chest, and every muscle in my body reacted. I forced myself to breathe deeply and to focus. Shaken, I made my way down the hall to my room. I stopped outside my bedroom door and listened as the answering machine picked up.

"Nancy, please pick up the phone." It was Lorne. "Nancy, please? I need to talk to you, pick up the phone!"

I stood paralyzed in fear. Here was the man I loved calling to me; I could feel his pain, yet I was too scared to go to him.

"Dear God, help me?" I begged, clasping my hands in front of my face.

"Did you tell the police where I live?" His voice was riding on the edge of panic. "Nancy, pick up the phone, damn it! Are they going to be waiting for me when I go home? Did you tell them where I live? Nancy, I have to know!" he pleaded. His agony filled the room like rising water. "Nancy, I can't go back to jail...I can't go back," he sobbed. "They raped me last time, they raped me and I can't go through that again...I'd rather be dead!" He wept openly, unashamed. "Nancy, please tell me if I can go home again, please?"

Unwilling to envision what he said, I let numbness shadow my mind, protecting my sanity...if only for a moment.

Dazed, I walked to the phone and picked up the receiver. "You can go home, Lorne," I spoke softly. "They don't know where you live...I'm so sorry." Then I set the receiver down.

I sat on the bed staring at the phone. Hideous pictures slipped through the fog. Sickening images, faceless scum brutally violating my husband like filthy animals. Even animals wouldn't go that low. The man I loved outnumbered with no way to escape. I didn't want to see the images burning in my mind.

A short time later, I got up and gradually made my way towards the kitchen, my thoughts laced with fog. Time is pointless on the edge of reality where daydreams hide. If only I could slip away unseen, between the layers of here and there.

As I passed the living room I heard rapping at the window. Fear raced to my defense. I turned. Lorne stood at one of the etched glass windows flanking the fireplace, his nose pressed against the glass, both hands shielding his face to look in.

He saw me.

"Nancy, I love you," he shouted through the glass. "I want you to believe that, and that I would never hurt you."

I grabbed a small can of mace that Cheryal had given me from the banister. She said she had it for years and didn't know if it worked, but it was better than nothing. I clutched it behind my back, making my way into the living room. Terrified tears distorted my vision.

"Lorne, I love you, too...but I'm afraid of you," I sobbed, making a bold stand a few feet from the window. "Go away and leave me alone...please?"

"I'm sorry I made you afraid; I never meant to," he continued, "but I love you so much, Nancy. All I want is to grow old with you in a little house with a white picket fence."

His eyes were red from crying. His words were tearing me up but I knew he had been drinking. After so many years, I could tell by his speech pattern. What would he say when he was sober?

"Lorne, I don't believe you," I screamed through my tears, clutching the mace tightly behind me. "You told me all this before but you lied." I wanted to believe him but I couldn't anymore. "You don't love me, you love alcohol! You had a choice. You chose the booze over me. Now go away and leave me alone!"

For a moment, there was silence. "Nancy, can I ask you one question?" he said calmly. "Then I'll go."

"One question," I agreed, standing my ground.

"If I stop drinking for thirty days, will you talk to me?" he asked earnestly.

I really wanted to believe him...he was the love of my life. "Yes, Lorne, I'll talk to you."

A glimmer of hope crossed his face; he backed away from the window, turned and stepped off the porch. I watched the only man I ever really loved head down the street, back to wherever he parked the car, his hands buried deep in the pockets of his good gray pants.

99

"...take their wives hostage"

Brilliant pink-and orange-bellied clouds hung outside the kitchen window like huge hot-air balloons—the setting sun's final encore, but far from my reality. I stood at the kitchen sink turning the small card over in my hand, one side written in English, the other in Spanish—support numbers—the majority were for battered women. During our fifteen-year marriage and through all of our problems, Lorne never hit me. Only a coward would do such a thing.

My love for Lorne was unyielding, despite the fear I felt. But I finally realized my need to talk to someone—someone who could stop the charted calamity I envisioned. Only God knew the details.

The name Detective Mike Malone popped off the card like green chartreuse, a good Irish Catholic name. As a kid, his parents probably dragged him to Mass every Sunday kicking and screaming. I went to the phone and dialed his number before I chickened out.

"West Valley Precinct," a male voice answered.

I couldn't speak. I wanted to hang up but I had to do this. I was trapped in a nightmare and fighting for my life.

"This is West Valley Precinct," the male voice repeated.

"Detective Mike Malone?" I asked in a small voice.

"Just a minute..."

I was put on hold. I paced the yellowed tile floor, winding and unwinding the phone cord around my finger.

"Malone here." His raspy reply resonated like coarse sandpaper.

I took a deep breath. "My name is Nancy MacMillan," I paused. "I...I don't know if I should be talking to you...but I don't know what else to do."

Tears clung to my lower lashes, an aching lump lodged in my throat.

"Okay…first of all, I don't bite," he said, with the grating voice of a heavy smoker. "Now, why don't you sit down, relax a little, and start from the beginning."

Mike Malone sounded dog tired, pushing sixty, and tough as an old tire, straight out of *Hill Street Blues*. Kindness laced his grizzly bear voice, melting the façade I hid behind, offering an ally I could confide in.

"My estranged husband is stalking me," I said bluntly. I pulled out a chair and sat down.

Then I bared my soul. The events of the last few weeks unraveled like a ball of yarn, rolling downhill in surround-sound and living color…the fear, the love, and the confusion. And how never in my life had I been so scared.

Malone let me talk…get it out like pus from a sore.

"…when Lorne was in Vietnam." I paused. The sound of Malone exhaling smoke gave me comfort, I knew he was listening. "He was discharged in '72 with a fistful of medals, including two bronze stars, yet the war still feeds on him daily like some ravenous vulture. There's nothing I can do to help him," I said tearfully.

My codependency had tiptoed out into the open like an old friend.

"Constant flashbacks and terrifying nightmares leave him hollering and the bed soaked with perspiration. He relives the horrors constantly, ghastly things I can't even imagine. The alcohol seemed to help him cope, not that it was right," I explained, "but then something changed. The alcohol stopped working. He became desperate…desperate enough that he finally agreed to counseling, but in vain. The doctors prescribed Prozac to calm his anxiety. And that mixed with the alcohol makes Lorne a walking grenade."

Exhausted, I slumped into the chair. Pain pounded beneath my right temple. I found the spot and pressed it deeply with my middle finger, my eyes closed.

Malone cleared his throat. "Ms. MacMillan, I know this stuff is hard to tell a total stranger and all, but it's important I know everything. The details may help us predict your husband's next move. Is there anything else I should know?"

"Yes," I said, as my eyes rested on a blue iris in the wallpaper. "Suicide," I paused. "He's attempted it twice; it's a word he uses often. It chills my blood...I'm afraid he'll succeed."

Malone listened as I reluctantly traveled back in time, reliving my terror and helplessness. Feeling naked and vulnerable, I laid my unhappy life at his feet like a burnt offering, begging him to grant my wish.

At last I was empty. The rest was in God's hands.

"You've been through a lot; I'm here to help any way I can," Malone said, genuine concern softening his gruffness. "Ms. MacMillan, I've been on the force too many years, and I've seen a lot of bad stuff. Vietnam vets are a whole 'nother breed. That war did strange things to their heads and to tell the truth...I don't trust 'em," he paused, taking a drag on his cigarette. "Not to scare you more, but I've seen strung out vets take their wives hostage, and a whole lot worse."

Icy chills slithered down the back of my neck.

"Then what am I supposed to do?" I was scared. "I have to go to work every day."

"I'll tell you what I think you should do," Malone said decisively, "but I'll deny ever having said it. Understand?"

"I think so," I said. "Please tell me."

"Get yourself a gun," he stated boldly. "Then go someplace and learn how to shoot the damn thing. You should be carrying it with you at all times."

I was shocked. The thought of shooting Lorne turned my stomach. He was sick—it would be like shooting a wounded animal. Besides, I loved him.

"I could never shoot Lorne," I said with alarm. "He's my husband!"

"Let me tell you something," Malone grumbled. "When he's strung out, he doesn't think like you or I do...and suicide is on his mind anyway. You have to protect yourself. If there was another way, I'd tell you. But there isn't. And one other thing," he said emphatically. "If it does come to that...make sure you aim to stop him. Believe what I say...you'll only get one chance. After that, the gun'll be in his hands. Get the picture?"

Reeling from the truth, I couldn't speak as I tried to comprehend my options. Horrifying pictures crossed my mind. I could never shoot Lorne…yet if I didn't…I may die. It was my choice. Suddenly the faces of my children filtered in, and how my death would affect them. At that moment, I knew I had only one option…I had to survive.

Then I remembered something. "Isn't it illegal to carry a gun?" I questioned, "I don't want to go to prison." My broad education on firearms consisted of watching the evening news and movies.

"It's a misdemeanor, not a felony…and it could save your life!" Malone emphasized, now certain that I understood the danger I was in.

I had to buy a gun but had no idea how to go about it. I pulled the Yellow Pages from the cupboard and settled on the couch. There in the index I found a section entitled *Guns*. I flipped to the page, stunned to see over two-dozen listings. Maybe Brad would go with me.

"Ding…Dong." I bolted from the couch, my heart racing.

I peeked through the blinds. There stood Cheryal, a troubled look masking her pretty face.

I flung the door open. "I'm so glad to see you!" I exclaimed. Yanking my friend into the house, I bolted the door.

Cheryal hugged me tightly. "Are you okay?" she asked. "I saw your car parked out in front. My gut instinct told me something was wrong."

"First, I'm going to pour us a glass of wine," I sighed, walking towards the kitchen. "I really need it…then I'll tell you all about it."

Soon we were curled up on the couch, face to face, sipping wine as I narrated my day, one frightening detail at a time. Finally, I told her about Detective Mike Malone…and his warning.

"You don't need to buy a gun," Cheryal piped in, grabbing my knee. "I have one that I've never used. It's yours!"

I was startled by her offer. "Are you sure?"

"Of course, I'm sure," she declared. "I bought the thing years ago, after I broke up with a guy who was giving me grief. He was a surly SOB and I wasn't taking any chances. Never had to use it, but it sure felt good to know it was in the drawer."

Just then, Brad walked in the front door.

"What are you two up to now?" he asked, one eyebrow raised. "And why is your car in the street, instead of in Cheryal's garage? I thought you were going out of town with Sandy."

"Oh, I forgot to call Sandy!"

Cheryal stood up, setting her wine glass on the end table. "I need to run home and get something," she said with a wink. "I'll be right back."

I called Sandy and apologized, briefly explaining the days encounter and that I still had something important to attend to.

When I came back to the den, I told Brad everything.

"God, Nancy," he said, "that's awful. I should have been here." Brad was a good friend, but his words only made me feel worse.

"It's my problem, not yours," I said shamefully. "I'm sorry it followed me to your house. I had no idea things would turn out like this."

The clear night sky was like any other when the doorbell rang. Brad answered it. Cheryal stood on the porch holding a small dusty box; she stepped inside and passed it to Brad.

"Know anything about guns?" she asked lightly, "'cause we sure don't."

Brad dropped into his chair in the den. Intrigued, he lifted the lid of the box as Cheryal and I hovered over him. A dull black, 38-caliber revolver with a wood grain handle rested inside. Brad gingerly picked it up, gazing into the five empty chambers.

I eyed the gun. It looked so small.

Lorne had an M-16 rifle he smuggled back from Vietnam—it was big and awkward. I remember the day we drove to the country for target practice so that Lorne could teach me how to shoot. He showed me how to stand and to cradle the rifle butt into my shoulder. Gazing through the V-shaped eyepiece, I lined up the tin can he had set on a stump. I pulled the trigger. The impact threw me backwards, sending the bullet far beyond its mark. That evening I noticed a bitter bruise, the size of an orange, forming on my shoulder. The deep purple imprint seemed to last forever.

That was the only time I ever fired a gun.

"Here…you hold it," Brad offered, gingerly placing the revolver in my hand. "See how it feels."

The gun felt cold and very heavy for something so small. I gripped the textured handle in my right hand, then cradled my fist to hold the gun in my left palm. My index finger reached around the trigger; it fit like a glove.

I held it out in front of me like I'd seen in the movies. While focusing down the barrel, a vision flooded my mind. *There was Lorne walking through the front door. He was coming to get me, his sandy blond hair unruly, his blue eyes glazed. Holding the gun at arm's length, I yelled, "Stop!" But he kept coming. I yelled again. He smiled lovingly, reaching out to grab me. I closed my eyes and squeezed the trigger. There was an explosion. When I looked, Lorne was stumbling backwards, a look of shock on his face. "Lorne, I'm sorry. I didn't want to hurt you, I love you," I cried, tears streaming down my face.*

"Nancy…Nancy are you all right?" a voice called from a distance. It was Brad. Cheryal was standing next to him. I looked around. I was standing in the den holding the gun, tears spilling down my cheeks.

Later that night, unable to sleep, I lay in the dark with my sheet tossed aside. The air was hot and lifeless. Too scared to sleep in my room I moved to the spare bedroom, afraid to turn on the air conditioner that might pinpoint my location. Slivers of moonlight slipped through the blinds, casting strange shadows on the walls.

Suddenly the sound of dry leaves crunching outside the window became magnified in the darkness. I held my breath, frozen in time, measuring the shadows. My hand covered the heavy gun resting on my belly. My fingers tightened and the jagged grip cut into my palm. Five bullets waited silently in their chambers.

"Step…step…step…." One after another, I heard the sound of leaves crushing under foot. My ears strained to comprehend. Was Lorne out there?

Was it a cat? Unnerved, I closed my eyes and prayed, *"Our Father which art in heaven, hallowed by Thy name..."*

100

Two hundred bullets

July 14, 1990

The thunder of exploding bullets echoed off the gray cinder-block walls. It was like being trapped inside a box of exploding firecrackers with the lid on. I wanted to cover my ears, but I didn't. I knew being here was something I must do.

"I'd like a box of ammo for this 38," Brad said to a tall, skinny guy behind the counter who was wearing a wrinkled black tee shirt with *"Don't Mess With Texas"* in bold white letters across the front. Brad set the gun down.

After a brief discussion, Brad settled on four boxes of 38 SPECIAL Centerfire Cartridges with fifty per box. He pulled out his wallet. "You can pay me later," he said, matter-of-factly.

Two hundred bullets—I wasn't going to war! That was excessive and I said so.

"First and foremost, I want you to shoot this thing until you're not afraid of it," Brad said firmly. "Till you're confident you know how to use it. Okay?"

"Okay," I repeated meekly, eyeing the menacing black gun on the counter.

An attendant led us to an empty stall. A pair of tall partitions was separated by a wooden counter. The space was only big enough for two people, just like I'd seen on police shows. We were handed safety goggles and ear protection, and then shown how to operate the targets. Three-feet high by two-feet wide sheets of paper were clipped to a long wire and hung in front of us. Each displayed a life-sized black silhouette of a man from the waist up. Pulleys moved them back and forth. A huge bull's eye encircled the silhouette's head. As I put on my headgear—I noticed I was the only woman there.

Brad pointed out the safety latch, then showed me how to load the bullets before he handed me the gun. The loaded gun felt extra heavy. Then Brad took my right fist, which held the gun, and placed it into the palm of my left hand

"Right arm rigid, support the gun with your left hand. This will steady your weapon," he said with authority.

"Now, close one eye and look down the barrel at the target," he said. "Focus on the mark you want to hit, then take a breath, hold it and shoot...plain and simple."

That little gun had a hefty kick. My hand jumped six inches. I missed the target all together, but I got the idea.

After practice shooting for over an hour, and more than a hundred rounds spent, I had the hang of it. I was hitting where I aimed most of the time...and from a fair distance.

All I prayed for now was that I never had to use it.

101

All too horrible

The police warned me not to see my husband or talk to him until the trial, but that was easier said than done. I ached for Lorne. I felt my husband's pain as though it were my own, but now I was afraid of him. His mental and emotional pain and anguish because of Vietnam was relentless. He was falling over the edge and there was no one to catch him...it was all too horrible.

July 18, 1990

I called the City Attorney's office. I was told the city was prosecuting Lorne, not me. Lorne called me at work and at home; he was getting aggressive. I didn't talk to him.

I did talk to Joan, Lorne's mother. She and I leaned on each other. Lorne was calling her as well. We both loved him but neither of us had answers to his problems. I told her I was in hiding, parking my car in Cheryal's garage when I was at home, in case Lorne said something to her.

At night I unplugged my phone, yet lie awake wondering...*Will tonight be the night?*

July 19, 1990

Lorne's trial was set for today, but the attorney called to say it was postponed a week. No idea why.

July 23, 1990

Lorne called me at work. I didn't know he was on the line.

"This is Nancy, can I help you...?"

"Nancy, I love you," was all he could say before I hung up. My heart broke. I was all that he had and I was forced to turn my back on him. My pain was as real as his...only different.

I was scared every day. Concealing a gun in my briefcase and never knowing when Lorne would pop-up out of nowhere was stressful to say the least.

July 26, 1990

At Lorne's trial, he pleaded "not guilty."

July 30, 1990

"I love you," Lorne said softly in my ear. He had reached me at work.

I couldn't take it anymore.

"Lorne, you have to stay away from me," I commanded. "The police told me I can't talk to you until after your trial, now leave me alone." I slammed down the phone in tears.

I talked to the prosecuting attorney about Lorne's hearing. He told me the trial date for sentencing would be at the end of August. He had recommended jail time or rehab. I begged him to push for rehab. We talked a long while. I went into detail, going over the reasons for Lorne's problems.

"I'll do everything I can," the attorney said compassionately. "But we'll have to wait for a bed."

This would be Lorne's last chance.

In the meantime, I had to survive…I felt like I was losing it.

If Lorne ends up killing me and then kills himself…we're both dead. How can I stop this? There's one month before his sentencing. For one month he'll be roaming the streets. How can I keep him away from me, so he can get into rehab? My husband needs help badly!

Dear God, I love my husband and I always will. How do I stop him from harming us both?

102

The shock of a divorce

August 1990

Finally, I knew what I had to do.

The last time I spoke with the counselor at the VA hospital, he told me my next step should be divorce…as nothing else was working.

"The shock of divorce can be a driving force for some vets who have not yet hit bottom," he said. "They finally see that their wife means business, and rather than lose her they go into treatment."

A coworker had given me the name of a lawyer who had handled her divorce. She said he was good, reasonable and a few blocks from the office.

His name was safe in my wallet. But now it was time I made the call and set an appointment.

August 1, 1990

Joan called. Lorne had called her. She said he was hallucinating.

"No one answers my calls. I need to find the General, we need helicopters sent in," is all she could remember.

August 6, 1990

Marcus Klein had an impressive waiting room—black leather chairs, and highly polished tables covered with travel and art magazines, angled just so. I sat with my hands in my lap studying the Picasso lithographs covering the wall. I often wondered if people who lived such grand life styles were happy.

He stood up when I entered his office, motioning me to a richly upholstered chair facing his desk. Klein was all class, graying at the temples, articulate, wearing an expensive suit that draped his body like liquid metal.

"Please sit down, Mrs. MacMillan," he said, his voice easy on the ear.

"Would you like any coffee, or water?"

"No, thank you."

"Now, can you please tell me why you want this divorce?" he asked, pen in hand, fully unprepared for my answer.

When I finished reciting my synopsis of grizzly details, I sat back and waited.

Klein's face was blank; his thoughts were elsewhere.

"I'll take the case," he agreed. "My secretary will bring in papers for you to sign. My fee is fifteen hundred dollars...half up front, the other half when the divorce is final. Are you in agreement?"

"Yes," I said, choking on the cost.

It was expensive, more than I expected, but I had no time to shop around. I had to do this now. And if it worked, it was worth every penny. I wrote out a check in the amount of seven hundred and fifty dollars.

August 8, 1990

Marcus Klein called me at the office and asked me to come by to sign the final papers. After that, the divorce would be filed with the courts, and then Lorne would be served.

I did what I was asked to do, and then I sat back and waited.

I was extremely agitated by the whole experience. I didn't want a divorce at all. I just wanted my husband well…so that we could move forward in our marriage.

It seemed ludicrous that this was the only way. What was wrong with our government and its leaders? They take our healthy young people in the prime of their lives, send them to war, and return them broken. They wash their hands of these men and women who served our country with pride and honor, and fought to keep us a free nation. These soldiers and veterans surely weren't in it for the money.

You may see vets wandering the streets in every city of our country. Lost, homeless, dirty and disheveled, the terror of war still raging in their eyes, struggling to make it through another day. They didn't choose to be like this. Who will help them?

Why wasn't mandatory debriefing and counseling provided before they were tossed back into society like used tires? God only knows the true statistics of those who fit back in, and those who did not, now existing like square pegs trying to fit into a round holes. Lorne spent one year in Vietnam. He was discharged in January 1971. Two days later, he was walking the streets in Houston—a ticking time bomb, primed to go off. How can this go on? Is there no one who cares?

When vets go astray they're handed over to doctors who prescribe drugs that worsen the situation, drugs with suicidal side effects. Lorne was only one veteran. How many thousands of other men and women are out there still suffering the throes of the Vietnam war and the wars that followed? Why? Why did the government allow this to happen? Why must I file for a divorce from the only man I ever loved, the love of my life? My heart ached with remorse.

The lawyer stayed in contact. Lorne was difficult to serve because he was never at home.

August 16, 1990

I received the call from the Process Server at 10:00 p.m. Lorne was finally served the divorce papers in front of his RV at 7:00 p.m.

"Your husband said, "Thank you," like he was expecting it," he said.

I could only imagine what was going through Lorne's mind. I felt I had let him down and deserted him. My emotions were raw. Had I done the right thing, listening to other people? I didn't feel good about it, but what else was I to do? Simply wait for a show down? That would be worse.

103

This was in his favor

August 27, 1990

The day was drawing near for Lorne's trial. He would soon be safe as a babe in arms, in the hands of people who cared and could treat him. I knew the next few weeks would be rough on him, but the results would be worth it.

The trial attorney filled me in on the schedule even though I wasn't to appear in court. Tomorrow was Lorne's final trial for restitution. I presumed he would be told the amount of damages he was expected to pay for damaging my car and Brad's property. I knew he was deep in debt but that could be dealt with once he was back on his feet.

The final trial date was scheduled for September eleventh. There, I was told, he would learn his sentence. I knew the lawyers were working hard to negotiate a recommendation of treatment instead of jail time. Lorne was a veteran and hadn't physically hurt anyone; this was in his favor.

"Nancy, call on line two," a voice announced over the speaker, interrupting my thoughts.

"This is Nancy," I said into the receiver.

"Nancy, I love you," Lorne said softly in my ear. "I don't want to lose you."

"Lorne, I love you, too," I said quickly, then hung up.

I knew I shouldn't talk to him, but this was the first time I had heard his voice since he was served with the divorce papers. I had to let him know I still loved him. I had to give him hope.

104

Where was Lorne?

September 5, 1990—Valencia, California

I was sitting in Mary's office going over an issue with one of my accounts when for some reason I looked out the window and happened to see Lorne drive by towards the parking lot behind the building. He was driving the same yellow car he had the last time I saw him—when I had to call 911.

Mixed emotions grabbed me: fear...love...sadness. What was he doing here? And more than that...should I be afraid? I still carried the gun in my briefcase.

I excused myself and went back to my desk. I never mentioned what I saw to Mary.

I often wondered if Lorne would try to get to me at work. All he had to do was walk in the front door.

September 11, 1990 - Northridge, California

The jitters in my stomach wouldn't let me forget what day it was.

Steam rose from the pot on the stove as I poked the broccoli with a fork. It was done. My lawyer promised to call as soon as Lorne's trial was over, but it was almost 8:00 p.m. and still no word.

Opening the broiler, I lifted a golden chicken breast onto the plate in my hand. The phone rang. I tossed the tongs in the sink and ran down the hall to the phone in my room.

It was my lawyer.

"Nancy, I don't want to alarm you," he said, weighing his words, "but Lorne never showed up for court today. His friend went to pick him up, but he was nowhere to be found. I just thought you should know."

My mind froze.

Stunned, I lowered myself to the bed. "I can't believe he did this," I said, as tears welled in my eyes.

"There's a warrant out for his arrest," he warned. "If you see him or if he tries to contact you, call the police immediately...and be careful!"

Damn it...why did Lorne always make things worse for himself? I pounded the pillow with angry fists, hot tears burning my cheeks. The lawyers had worked hard to negotiate his sentence. There was a bed for him; he was going into rehab. This was our last hope.

Sure, rehab would be hard, but no harder than what he was dealing with daily. I know he feared the unknown and being locked up. But he could be safe there while going through treatment. He could have a clean place to sleep, three meals a day, and people who cared. This is what he should have had when he returned from Vietnam. What did it matter if he lost everything? He had nothing left to lose. And his debts could be dealt with later. I would be there for him.

I didn't blame Lorne. He fought long and hard for his country. I can only blame the government and its shameful lack of concern for our military and for those dealing with this illness caused by wars. Lorne medicated himself with alcohol to keep his demons at bay, while everything else fell through the cracks, including our marriage. My heart ached for him. I loved him so much. There was nothing more I could do.

I was fighting for survival myself. All my hopes and dreams were shattered.

And where was Lorne?

105

No one had a clue

September 13, 1990

Merging into morning traffic on Interstate 405 heading north was like swimming among salmon upstream. I spotted an opening, punched the accelerator and said a prayer while perusing every driver in sight. I never knew when Lorne might be following me. I had to stay alert.

It was strange no one had heard from him...and no one had a clue where he was.

Basically, I hadn't talked to Lorne for two months, not since that Friday the thirteenth when I called 911. I had been instructed not to talk to him until after the trial, but he had continued to call and leave messages on my answering machine. He was usually drunk so I refused to pick up. He never did stop drinking like he promised me that day on the porch.

Then again, I knew he couldn't...without help.

On the day he was handed the divorce papers his calls stopped.

But no—he had called me at work on August twenty-seventh. I remember because it was Tiffy's birthday. He only had time to tell me he loved me and that he didn't want to lose me. I told him I loved him, too—and then I hung up.

That was the last time.

But not hearing from Lorne frightened me just as much.

Keeping my eyes on the traffic, I reached over and patted the lump in the brown leather briefcase on the passenger seat. Hidden inside was the short-nosed .38 Special made in Brazil, the gun I prayed I would never have to use.

"Fear not, for I am with you always," I said out loud, resting my hand on my briefcase.

As a Catholic, I never knew the Bible, but from somewhere this verse became my rock when fear tried to eat me alive. Isaiah 43:5 was my only hope when I felt alone and scared. I would repeat this verse every time fear tried to suffocate me, and I would know that God was with me.

As my mind drifted, I came to realize it had been exactly five years ago that Lorne and I had reached California, traveling this same freeway. Our love was strong and our future was bright. We were filled with hope and promise.

That seemed like a thousand years ago. Something had gone terribly wrong.

Once again, fear raised its hideous head as I pulled into the driveway at my office. I double-checked to be sure both doors were locked as I slowly made my way to the back of the building. I hated parking back there because I was terrified Lorne would be waiting. A cold chill ran through me.

That had been the last place I saw him a week ago—sometime in the late afternoon.

I inched around the corner of the building as I visually checked out every car in the parking lot. Everything looked in order. Still, he could be hiding in a back seat and I'd never know it. I found a vacant spot and pulled in. Taking a deep breath, I grabbed my purse and briefcase and stepped from the car. I was on high alert as I proceeded to speed walk down the driveway to the front of the building. I continued to glance over my shoulder with my briefcase purposely in my left hand for easy access.

"Good morning," I said, attempting to appear cheerful.

Laura, a friend at work who knew my situation, was waiting just inside the front door.

"Good morning," she said, with a forced smile that contorted her face. She reached out and took my elbow...which was strange. "Mary wants to see you."

As she escorted me down the hall to Mary's office, her odd behavior set off an alarm within me. The monkeys were stirring; something was not right.

Laura opened the door and motioned me to sit down. She backed out the door, closing it as she went. Mary sat at her desk with her back to me. She slowly turned around. Her eyes were red and swollen. The look on her face was odd, as if she'd seen a ghost, or something horrible.

.She gazed at me for a moment. "I have some bad news to tell you," she said softly, fiddling with a piece of paper on her desk.

I leaned forward in my chair. The monkeys began to screech loudly, vying for attention, from every corridor in my mind.

"I don't know how to tell you this," she paused, searching my eyes. "Lorne's dead." Her words were a whisper.

The two words I never wanted to hear, yet in my heart I had been waiting for, wondering who would say them...and when.

A dense calm enveloped me like a thick coating of molasses. I couldn't breathe. The numbness spread quickly, deadening any pain before it reached my heart. I felt like a living statue, unable to speak or move. Trapped inside, I could only hear and think.

"They found his body last night," Mary went on, mindlessly smoothing the piece of paper on her desk. "I drove past the lodge on my way home from work, checking to see if Barry's car was there. That's when I noticed the swarm of police cars in front of Lorne's place down the street." She dabbed her nose with a Kleenex. "I didn't stop, of course, but once I got home I called the lodge and talked to George. It seemed they just found him." Tears flooded Mary's eyes. "Oh Nancy, I'm so sorry, so very sorry," she sobbed.

How strange...there were no tears. Numbness consumed me. Was this shock? I had no idea. Somewhere deep inside, I heard someone screaming...and screaming...and screaming.

The screams echoed in the emptiness...the emptiness Lorne left behind.

I had to know what happened.

"How did he die?" I heard a small voice ask in the distance.

Mary looked at me. "They found him hanging in the pepper tree," she sobbed openly.

Who am I now without Lorne? My mind was staggering, I wanted it to stop. I was just told my husband killed himself. What am I supposed to do now? Should I go home? Should I stay at work? If I went home, what would I do there? Really be alone. At work I belonged. I was part of a group, a unit. At home I was nobody. I belonged to no one.

I had thought about this very moment so many times over the past fifteen years. I had it pictured in my mind...but now it's here and nothing like I thought...I'm lost...a widow. I am a widow. What does that mean? I'm alone. I have no one.

Lorne is now just another casualty of the Vietnam War, a statistic, even though it took him eighteen years to die. Nevertheless, it was that damn war that killed him.

I sat staring out the window behind Mary's desk where I last saw Lorne. My hands were folded in my lap when a sudden smile touched my lips.

This was the only way Lorne could slay the demons that haunted him day and night, and find the peace he so desperately sought. Lorne was my husband, the love of my life. I know he loved me, nothing that real ever dies. I would never have to be afraid again. May God have mercy on his soul.

PART FIVE

Southern California

The journey home

106

The journey was hard

Time passed like dreams overlapping one another. I traveled to places I had never been to nor wanted to go to again. The journey was hard.

Life is painless without feelings. My soul was wounded, my heart shattered, the horror of the details was beyond my comprehension. Comatose to the world around me, I simply smiled and nodded without thought, without reason. I still could not cry.

I did what had to be done; my mother raised me that way.

The phone call to Joan was the hardest. I was the one who had to do it. How do you tell a woman you love that her son is dead...and that he killed himself?

September 14, 1990

Tiffy took the first flight out of Houston. I met her at LAX the next afternoon, anxious to have my daughter near.

"Mom, I'm so sorry," she sobbed, running into my arms and burying her face in my shoulder.

I held her close, stroking her hair like I did when she was little. I stared out the window at the airplanes on the runway, knowing that my pain had only begun. How does a person begin such an agonizing journey?

The next morning I headed up Interstate 405, grateful to have Tiffy by my side. I knew I was in no shape to make the trip alone. We rode in silence, wondering what we would find when we got there. Had the police locked up when they were finished, or was the RV standing wide open for any vagrant to wander in and take what he pleased? I wanted to get there as soon as possible to salvage anything of importance left by my husband.

Tiffy and I knew this was something we had to do...but dreaded.

I drove up the gravel driveway I had traveled so many times before. I stopped at the fence. The tall bamboo fencing Lorne had lashed to the chain link made it impossible to see inside. Off to the right, Lorne's red MG sat slightly at an angle, the windows rolled down as if he had just pulled in.

Everything looked normal. I got out of my car and walked up to the fence. Tiffy was at my heels. It wasn't locked. Gingerly, I slid the heavy gate back far enough to step through. Once inside, I stood overwhelmed by what I saw.

The place was in shambles. A sweet foul odor permeated the air. The old yellow car sat off to one side. Two metal sheds, doors wide open, were crammed with boxes. More boxes of car parts were scattered everywhere. Two motorcycles were chained to a trailer parked behind one of the sheds. Bulky rolls of aluminum fencing and pieces of machinery I couldn't identify littered the landscape. It looked like a junkyard.

I turned and walked over to the pepper tree; its lush foliage swept the ground. A redwood Jacuzzi topped with a padded cover sat under the tree. The wooden pallet at my feet was coated in a thick layer of white powder, as well as the area under the tree. It looked like flour...I assumed it was lye.

Slowly I raised my eyes up into the tree branches. A length of steel cable, nearly five-feet long, was tied to a sturdy bough that hung over me. My guarded mind unfolded an image of the police cutting Lorne down from this cable and placing him at my feet.

"Mom, come on," Tiffy interrupted, tugging me by the arm. "Let's go inside and get this over with. I want to get out of here. This place gives me the creeps."

I turned. My mind was in overload, my emotions in lockdown. I followed her to the door of the RV. It was unlocked. We stepped inside, stunned by what we saw.

Dozens of cardboard boxes heaped with papers and junk covered every flat surface. Mounds of soiled clothes lurked in corners like musty animals; dirty dishes littered the sink. How in God's name could Lorne live like this?

"Tiff, please help me try to find anything that might be important." I opened a cupboard door over the sink. "Most likely he sold everything he could for cash. But there may be a few things he couldn't part with."

"I'll do my best," Tiffy whined in frustration, "but I don't even know where to start."

There was some fresh food in the refrigerator—that eased my guilt a little. A package of chicken was missing one piece...*this must have been his last meal.* In a cupboard over the driver's seat, I ran my hand under a heap of papers. There I found a picture of Tiffy and me that I had given Lorne years earlier. And next to the picture...his leopard ring. Smiling tenderly, I picked it up and pressed it to my lips. I turned it over and over in my fingers. I put it on my thumb, but it was too big. I slipped it into my pocket.

The armor of shock guarded my sanity, blinding my emotions from the reality of where I was and what had happen only a few days earlier.

We stayed less than an hour, which was morbid enough.

After locking up the RV, I followed Tiffy out of the gate and secured it. Then I wandered over to the MG on the way to the car. I opened the door, got in and put my hands on the steering wheel, knowing Lorne held it last and wanting to feel his nearness. I had seen programs indicating a presence after death...I wanted it to be true.

Leaning over, I opened the glove box. Inside was a stack of papers. I grabbed a handful and set them in my lap. The Summons for Divorce rested on top. I hadn't seen it before. It looked like a standard form with little boxes marked with an X. I slowly read through the statements my lawyer had filled in, and then flipped to the next page.

To my surprise, it was in Lorne's handwriting. The document, *A Confidential Counseling Statement (Marriage)* was dated 9-7-90. Had this form come with the divorce papers, or had Lorne picked it up at the courthouse? The form showed that he contested my petition and was agreeing to marriage counseling. For an instant my heart leapt...but then I realized it was too late. There were no chances left.

The next paper in the stack was a citation. Lorne was arrested that same night Friday, September seventh, for drunk driving.

My mind scurried back in time, trying to piece together my husband's last days.

Lorne contested the petition on the seventh, which was a Friday. He was arrested that night for drunk driving and thrown in jail. Sunday, the ninth, he was last seen closing the gate on his fence. But his body wasn't discovered by his neighbor until Wednesday, the twelfth, three days later. I learned of his death on the thirteenth.

I sat in the car staring at the pepper tree. My mind was scrambling with the facts.

Everything was falling into place.

In my heart I knew Lorne had made his final decision in jail that weekend. His fragile mind refused to allow another brutal attack. He was released late Sunday afternoon, the ninth. His final trial was on Tuesday, the eleventh. Knowing Lorne, I was certain he believed he was going to serve time. He had already told me he would rather die than go to jail again.

This had to be the answer.

That afternoon and the next day, Tiffy made the phone calls I couldn't deal with. The coroner, the funeral parlor and the police were only a few. All the loose ends had to be tied immediately.

The evening of the second day, Tiffy and I flew to Houston for the Memorial Service on the eighteenth. Scott and Cory were there, plus hundreds of people I didn't know. It was a moving service. The soloist sang "On the Wings of an Eagle," my favorite song.

Lorne's body could not be released for cremation until an autopsy had been performed. And because it was a suicide, his case did not take precedent over homicides.

107

"Testing one, two, three"

Lorne was a pack rat at heart. He salvaged anything he thought he might use someday, contrary to my neatnik tendencies...which drove me nuts.

"Baby," he once said with a twinkle in his eye, "when I die, I'm going to leave all my stuff for you to clean up." And he did.

Brad was a good friend throughout the ordeal. He helped me move big stuff and dispose of the rest. The Jacuzzi landed in his backyard after a nightmare of hauling it down Interstate 405 on a trailer. Brad was a saint to allow me to put what seemed like tons of trash into the studio behind the garage, giving me time to sort through it all, once I could emotionally deal with it.

Spring 1991

The newness of spring filtered in through the open screen door of the studio, whisking away the stale smell of death that had lingered all winter.

I sat cross-legged in the middle of the floor, sipping coffee from one of Lorne's mugs, wearing his gray striped bathrobe. Shadowy mountains of debris encircled me. For months I had been slowly weeding through Lorne's things a little bit at a time. That was all I could handle. But rather than shrinking, the piles seemed to be growing like a plate of Lo Mein.

I set my cup on the floor and reached for a small box I had not noticed before. I lifted the lid and looked inside to find old business receipts, nothing special. As I grabbed a handful I touched something solid underneath, wrapped in tissue paper. I peeled away the layers and uncovered Lorne's Zippo lighter. I flicked it open and shut it again and again and again. The all familiar sound and smell gave me comfort, reaching through time and space as though Lorne were in the room with me. I rubbed my finger over his name engraved on one side.

I ached for him. Would this longing ever go away? Only God knew the answer.

I reached for my now cold cup of coffee and brought it to my lips. A light, throaty chirping drew my eyes to the open screen door. Afternoon sunshine cut through the fragile leaves on the huge Sweet Gum tree outside and a little bird's happiness led my mind to wander.

Lorne was dead. This I knew to be true, yet he still lived in my heart, healthy and whole, filled with life and curiosity. Through him, through his love, his struggles and his pain, I learned compassion, strength and survival. The lessons were hard; the exams were excruciating.

How many other women were being tested right now, this very moment? I knew they were out there hiding like I had. Hiding behind closed doors, afraid to let anyone in, afraid of what they might see or hear. Pretending everything was fine or simply being too busy with work and the children to go to the movies. Denying things would get worse. Hoping the bad stuff would just go away. Pacing the floor late at night unable to sleep, trying to find answers. I knew they were out there, but they were hiding to cover their broken hearts.

Where was a soldier's wife or husband supposed to get help? These women and men love and live with a walking time bomb and have no clue how to disarm it. The Veterans Administration Hospital had suggested I file for divorce because Lorne hadn't reached bottom yet. I was told the shock would lead him into recovery, and I believed them. But it didn't work. My husband was dead.

Our soldiers are sent into wars to safeguard our country's interests and far too many return damaged. Then very little is done to support their reentry. This is wrong...terribly wrong!

The wives and husbands of these men and women also need support groups of their own, places where they can go to vent and cry—someplace where someone will wrap them in their arms because they care and understand, rather than leave them wandering lost in the shadows.

I made myself a promise…a promise to somehow find a way to help all of the women and men who are hiding in the dark find a way to hold up their heads again and be counted. I wanted to do this so that Lorne's death would not be in vain.

Back in the shadows I spotted a shoebox. I got up, brought it to the middle of the room and sat back down on the floor. Inside was an array of Lorne's old audiotapes—The Beatles, Barbara Streisand, Janis Joplin, Fleetwood Mac—along with a handful of blanks. When I looked closer, some appeared used, but not labeled.

I went back into the house and returned with my cassette player and an extension cord. Once I plugged it into an outlet, I inserted two of the unmarked tapes. They were blank. I made a note on a Post-It and stuck it to the tapes. Then I inserted the third blank and pushed play.

Scratchy static reached into the corners of the room ricocheting back to me. Suddenly I heard Lorne's voice…*This can't be happening!*

"Testing…one…two…three."

"Testing…one…two…three."

"Testing…one…two…three." His voice was as loud and clear as if I could reach out and touch him.

I was in shock, sitting cross-legged on the floor, wrestling with the reality of what was happening, floating between here and there.

Then to my astonishment, Lorne began to sing!

The moving words from *"Are You Lonesome Tonight?"*

Tears swarmed my eyes, making the room around me a blur. Was this real, or was it a dream? Was I about to wake up?

I had never heard Lorne sing before. His voice was beautiful.

Each tender word was filled with love and longing as though they had been written just for me. My heart cried out for him. Why did this have to happen? How can I go on without him?

Each verse drew me closer to him and away from my reality.

I knew in my heart Lorne had recorded this for me—knowing some day, some way, I would find it…and I did.

Then he spoke, enunciating each and every word—the words in the song left no hope for a future together—only a final end.

My breath caught...a suffocating knot filled my throat.

As the sun cascaded across the studio floor, it rested on the hollow shell of the woman I once was. Curled in a fetal position, I felt the sensation of my body turning inside out, being sucked into a tight, airless ball, crumpling like a wad of paper. I felt a pain greater than childbirth; I could not breathe. My arms covered my head. I opened my mouth and fought for air, wanting to scream. And as I did, an ocean of tears washed over me, uncontrolled sobs wrenched through me, lashing out with anger and pain.

It seemed to last forever. Finally exhausted, I opened my eyes. It was then I was swept with emptiness...a loneliness and sorrow I had never known. Never again would I feel Lorne's kiss, his touch, his need, nor see his ear-to-ear-grin, or his cross-my-heart promise, or sit at his feet and listen to his tales of the universe. Curled in a ball on the floor of the studio, in the midst of all that was left of my husband, I was finally able to grieve the lost love of my life with a broken heart that would surely never mend.

108

I could not forgive myself

I had toppled off the edge of the world, floating hopelessly alone in space. Lorne was gone. The love of my life, my other half, had vanished into the edge of time without me. Left behind, I limped through the weeks and months, now only half a person, trying to find meaning. I traveled alone, unwilling to share the burden of my secret. A smile covered my shattered heart. I didn't want the pity I saw in the eyes of those who knew. I didn't deserve it. I was too riddled with guilt.

It was strange. I knew Lorne was dead, yet he lived in my mind and heart as whole and as alive as ever. Some nights I would lie awake talking to him in the darkness of my room and catch a wisp of his aftershave resting nearby...Royal Copenhagen. Was it only my imagination?

What was I to do? Lorne had captured my heart from the moment I lain eyes on him standing in the doorway at Jackie's party, handsome and shy, running his fingers through his sandy-blond hair, wearing gray elephant-skin boots. Now he was intrinsically woven into my very being. My heart wept.

The guilt I carried was merciless. At times I felt that a demon or two had lagged behind to daunt me. If only I had signed the papers after Lorne's first suicide attempt, and let the V.A. pick him up for treatment. If only I had not filed for a divorce. I could not escape the condemnation nor could I forgive myself.

Each day was a struggle—some were better, some worse. I came to learn that my codependency on Lorne was still as strong as ever, but I had no idea how to deal with it, nor was I sure I wanted to.

I prayed day and night for an answer. I went to a nearby Catholic church every Sunday, but God couldn't hear me. I felt that He was too high in heaven where only the priests could reach Him. Besides, God was mad at me—I was divorced and had married Lorne outside of the Catholic Church, excommunicated from taking the sacraments. God didn't have time for me.

In the meantime, I was being nudged to write a book—a book about my relationship with Lorne. How crazy was that? I didn't know how to write a book. But I felt I needed to find the meaning and significance of our lives together.

The nudge grew into a push.

One day, as Tiffy and I were having lunch at the food court in the Beverly Center, I began to tell her for the umpteenth time that I felt an urge to write about my life with Lorne—that maybe it would have importance to others who were going through what he and I had been through.

"Mother," she said firmly, "stop talking about it and start writing!"

"But I don't know how to write a book," I said baffled. "Besides, I wouldn't even know where to start."

"Start anywhere!" she insisted, taking a bite of her pizza.

And so I began, sixteen years ago to tell the story, a true love story.

Sifting through all those memories – good and bad – brought back so much pain, that in the beginning I found the only way to cope with the trauma was to write in the third person. So I invented new characters, Mitch and Caroline, who began living the lives that were really Lorne's and mine.

Many years later, as the book neared completion, my daughter diplomatically suggested that it was time that I owned my story. I struggled long and hard, finally finding the courage to step back into the past and claim what was mine. I had to let the pain surface again; but this time it wasn't as brutal.

As I looked back over my diary at words written years before, I realized something: the answers lay between the lines of words on the pages. Our experiences and struggles, when shared, could shine a light on a problem that had become all too common in our society. If just one wife, or husband, could be helped by this one account, then it would have been worthwhile and Lorne's struggles would not have been in vain. Putting this story on paper has given me a sense of closure and acceptance, and hopefully it will enable others to do the same.

EPILOGUE

There was still something missing. A restlessness I could not shake persisted, a piece of the puzzle waited to be found. And as I searched for further meaning to my short life on this earth, and trying to understand the injustice of Lorne's ordeal, I discovered an unexpected source of strength and hope.

One day, while in my car, I stumbled upon a radio station—99.5 KKLA in Los Angeles—and heard some words that sent me reeling.

"God allows us to go through trials for a purpose..."

"God speaks all the time; you have to begin to listen..."

Could those words be true? I had to know more.

Every chance I had, I listened to this station—at home, in my car, whenever I possibly could. I was hearing truths I had never known. While listening to one program called *Somebody Loves You*, I learned that the pastor, Raul Ries, had been a Vietnam veteran, who also suffered post traumatic stress disorder. And he had found what I was looking for...a relationship with Jesus. I actually said a prayer to the radio that God would forgive all my sins, by grace alone, through faith alone, and come into my heart. I prayed the prayer a couple of times, just in case He hadn't heard me the first time. It seemed too simple.

I learned I must get into the Bible, the Word of God. I never remember hearing that before. I found an old Bible on my bookshelf, blew the dust off the cover, opened it randomly and started to read. For me, the words leap from the pages and into my heart and provide a peace I never knew possible. I have found the peace that seemed so elusive in the past through a personal relationship with Jesus.

Losing Lorne, I lost the love of my life, but in the Bible, I found the Lover of my soul. (John 3:16)

Not everyone seeks peace in this way. I only wish someone would have shown me the way long ago, but I've been called to this faith and believe it to be true, and I now know it is the reason I wrote Diary of a Vet's Wife. My diary: a tribute to Lorne, a kinship with others, and a hope for healing.

I have never remarried. Nor do I believe in coincidence. One of my seven grandchildren was born on Lorne's birthday!

SELECT REFERENCES

Almost all service members have reactions after returning from deployment. These behaviors and feelings are normal. Most service members successfully readjust with few problems. However, seeking solutions to problems is a SIGN OF STRENGTH. One should not hesitate to take advantage of the resources that are available. Having knowledge, coping skills and social support may positively influence one's ability and attitude to handle the uncertainties of deployment and better prepare him or her for the future.

Are you in crisis? You have options:
- Call 911
- Call the Suicide Prevention Lifeline **1-800-273-8255**
- 24/7 Veterans Crisis Line **1-800-273-8255** and **Press 1** to talk to someone.

NATIONAL CENTER for PTSD / http://ptsd.va.gov

VA's Veterans Crisis Line meets the needs of Veterans and their families and friends through multiple channels—over the phone, through online chats, and via text free of charge at **83-8255**. This support is confidential, personal and IMMEDIATE. All services are available **24 hours a day**, seven days a week, 365 days a year, and they connect users with specially trained VA professionals—many of whom are Veterans themselves.

http://www.veteranscrisisline.net **1-800-273-8355**

http://www.veteranscrisisline.net/chat

Veterans Helping Veterans / http://www.Vets4Warriors.net

Free Hotline **1-855-838-8255/1-855-VET-TALK**

Military Warriors Support Foundation – offers a variety of programs designed to help our wounded veterans and their families, including individual and family mentoring, recreational activities like fishing and hunting, financial planning and counseling are among the many offerings.

http://www.militarywarriors.org.com

Somebody Loves Me ministry, Calvary Chapel Golden Springs, Diamond Bar, CA. Their military ministry has developed the following DVD's:

Taking the Hill—trailer—http://www.takingthehillthefilm.com/

Quiet Hope –7 Vietnam veterans talk openly about their experience and their discovery.

http://www.calvarygs.org/

BLOG OF A VETS WIFE—A blog about writing this book, My Uncharted Journey into Publishing My First Book, which includes posts about veterans and PTSD, and why I wrote this book. Contact the author at http://www.blogofavetswife.blogspot.com

A portion of the proceeds from Diary of a Vet's Wife will be donated to PETS FOR VETS, a national organization that helps heal the emotional wounds of military veterans by pairing them with shelter dogs specifically selected to match their personalities. The bonds of friendship formed between man and animal have the power to ease the suffering of our troops when they return from overseas.

http://www.pets-for-vets

Contact the author at: diaryofavetswife@hotmail.com

CPSIA information can be obtained at www.ICGtesting.com
Printed in the USA
LVOW08s1120210913

353411LV00001B/202/P